DID IT REALLY HAPPEN?

Did it Really Happen?

*Apologetics and Biblical Interpretation
According to Carl F. H. Henry*

JONATHAN A. WOOD

WIPF & STOCK · Eugene, Oregon

DID IT REALLY HAPPEN?
Apologetics and Biblical Interpretation According to Carl F. H. Henry

Wipf & Stock
An Imprint of Wipf and Stock Publishers
199 W. 8th Ave., Suite 3
Eugene, OR 97401

www.wipfandstock.com

PAPERBACK ISBN: 978-1-5326-7822-6
HARDCOVER ISBN: 978-1-5326-7823-3
EBOOK ISBN: 978-1-5326-7824-0

Manufactured in the U.S.A.   AUGUST 27, 2019

For my wife

Ellen

and my children

Jackson, Olivia, Parker, and Lincoln.

Contents

Introduction

The topic of revelation, history, and the biblical text is no mere exercise in the details of biblical interpretation. Rather, the issues undertaken in the pages ahead strike at the importance of the central claims of the Christian faith. The Christian faith rests on a written testimony of ultimate realities. The claim to Scripture as divine revelation is that the pages of the Bible display what is unavailable by direct sight to the modern eye—whether unrepeated historical event or transcendent spiritual realities. Both the *what* and the *why*, the *event* and the *meaning* are portrayed in the Scriptures.

Did God create? Why is there a physical creation, including humanity? Were Adam and Eve real people? How do those people stand in relationship to the ensuing generations of humanity? Did Israel flee Egypt in a haste under the wrath of Pharaoh? What did that deliverance mean for God's chosen people? Was a marvelous baby born under the nose of Herod? How was that baby to fulfill all that was promised across the previous millennia? Did Jesus really rise from the dead? What is the significance of the resurrection? We could go on with the ways in which Scripture claims God has acted in this world, and how the narrative of the Bible portrays the interpretation of those marvelous acts of God.

Lest we take such questions too lightly, let us be reminded these acts, and the meaning of them, seem to be of great importance to practical realities in life. Without the historical elements of the Bible—not the least of which are Adam and Eve as the first people created in God's image, Christ born of a virgin and identified as the second Adam, and the empty tomb of Christ—the textual depictions leave faith untethered from the world in which deliverance from sin is needed and accomplished. The point from the Apostle Paul with regard to the resurrection is sharp in 1 Corinthians 15.

Yet, Scripture does not appear to focus on the vindication of historical veracity, rather upon imparting the spiritual realities of God and His ways through narrative description. Without the textual revelation of God in Scripture, which provides the meaning of the historical events, humanity would be left without the meaning and personal application of historical events as part of God's outworking of redemption. Where does this leave readers of the Bible today? How can one read the Bible well with respect to historical claims and the narrative shape of the writings? Certainly, followers of Christ want to get the interpretive process correct, knowing the pragmatic ways of Christian living inevitably follow Christian reading. These are the very practical hermeneutical questions in play with revelation, history, and the biblical text.

Carl Henry has provided an approach to revelation, history, and the biblical text that is worthy of attention, because he articulates God's involvement in history and humanity's ability to know this history, all the while focusing the interpreter's hermeneutical efforts on Scripture as the authoritative and truthful accounting of God's historical activity. In the chapters ahead, this book will explore the hermeneutical principles of revelation, history, and the biblical text through the writings of Carl F. H. Henry. Henry wrote in conversation with two contemporaries on the subject. Wolfhart Pannenberg stands at the headwaters of the "revelation as history" approach, and Hans Frei is notable as the genesis of narrative hermeneutics. As an evangelical focused on the doctrine of revelation, Henry articulates an approach different from the two aforementioned theologians. The purpose of this book is to argue that, in contrast to the "revelation as history" and to "post-liberal" approaches to revelation, Henry's doctrine of revelation generates a text-oriented, yet apologetically engaged, scheme of the relationship between revelation, history, and biblical text.

After setting a framework for how to evaluate questions of revelation, history, and biblical interpretation in chapter one, chapter two presents Carl F. H. Henry's assertions concerning the concepts of the revelation of God, text, and history in his systematic writings. Henry's doctrine of divine revelation affirms a broad sense of revelation in historical event as God's genuine activity, yet asserts the meaning and interpretation of the historical event is tied inseparably to divinely inspired writings. This approach to revelation produces a hermeneutic focused on the text, yet theologically and apologetically engaged in history.

Chapter three provides an analysis of a notion of revelation, strictly event-oriented, most clearly typified in the writings of Wolfhart Pannenberg. Pannenberg's revelation-as-history approach produces a thoroughly historical approach to hermeneutics. Henry's evaluation of Pannenberg provides instructive critique for the tendency for evangelical emphasis on discerning revelation through history as the goal of interpretation.

Chapter four provides Henry's analysis of the approach of post-liberal method as exclusively text-oriented, specifically addressed through dialogue with Hans Frei. Post-liberal method has found welcome within evangelical method for the purpose of encouraging text-oriented hermeneutics.

After exploring the different hermeneutical priorities on the subject of history and the biblical text in Henry, Pannenberg, and Frei, chapter five undertakes the task of clarifying the value of Henry's voice for an evangelical approach to revelation, event, and biblical text. Analysis of the contemporary discussion will show, contrary to many contemporary descriptions of neo-evangelical hermeneutics, Henry has provided answers to many of the questions at stake. As a result of properly orienting the apologetic interest of biblical history and the revelation oriented nature of biblical interpretation, may it be that Christians read the Bible as God's faithful communication concerning himself and the true revelation of his magnificent accomplishment of saving sinners for his glory.

1

Revelation, History, and the Biblical Text

The Evangelical scholars who gathered at the International Council on Biblical Inerrancy for Summit II (ICBI Summit II) came together under the idea that the necessity of inerrancy had been established in the first summit.[1] The first summit produced what has become the foundational document for an evangelical description of inerrancy—*The Chicago Statement on Biblical Inerrancy*. With the gains concerning the doctrine of revelation, the second council sought to complete the task of the first by carrying through the doctrine of revelation to its impact on hermeneutics as noted through the comment of James Packer, "[b]iblical authority is an empty notion unless we know how to determine what the Bible means."[2] With this comment, the "hermeneutical problem" for evangelical theology was summarized and the trajectory was set for the ICBI Summit II. The notion that the Bible bears authority because it is communication from an authoritative God carries the implicit consequence that it is then authoritative for those to whom it communicates. Yet, as Packer acknowledges, the authority of Scripture as a function in an interpreter's life is dependent upon the apprehension of God's communication through the process of hermeneutics.

The relationship among revelation, history, and the biblical text is a significant factor for the proper apprehension of biblical meaning. This

---

1. ICBI Summit I, which was focused on the nature and defense of inerrancy, took place October 26–28, 1978. ICBI Summit II, which was focused on hermeneutics, took place November 10–13, 1982.

2. Radmacher, "Introduction," xi.

triad is relevant in constructing hermeneutical approaches and thus bears impact on the breadth of theological method. Craig Bartholomew notes the existence of four broad turns in the history of modern hermeneutics. These turns are the historical, literary, postmodern, and theological turns.[3] The narrative provided by Bartholomew's account of these hermeneutical phases leads one from the initiation of hermeneutics that are historically focused to the questions that evangelicals must now face concerning the relation of history to text.[4] As has been documented by chroniclers of interpretive history, beginning in the eighteenth century, a shift took place toward a preoccupation with historical method.[5] The resulting dominance of the historical-critical method in biblical and theological studies had a serious effect as noted by Edgar Krentz who writes:

> It is difficult to overestimate the significance the nineteenth century has for biblical interpretation. It made historical criticism the approved method of interpretation. The result was a revolution of viewpoint in evaluating the Bible. The Scriptures were, so to speak, secularized. The biblical books became historical documents to be studied and questioned like any other ancient sources. The Bible was no longer the criterion for the writing of history; rather history had become the criterion for understanding the Bible. The variety in the Bible was highlighted; its unity had to be discovered and could no longer be presumed. The history it reported was no longer assumed to be everywhere correct. The Bible stood before criticism as defendant before judge. The criticism was largely positivist in orientation, imminentist in its explanations, and incapable of appreciating the category of revelation.[6]

The net effect was that historical justifiability must be present for taking the biblical text seriously. This development still holds influence, and its mark is evident on the most common hermeneutic of modern evangelicalism, the *historical-grammatical method*.[7] While many historical-*grammat-*

3. Bartholomew, "Introduction," 3.

4. Ibid., 3. Important to note is that Bartholomew observes that the progression through various "turns" is not an oversimplification of interpretive history. He notes: (1) none of the turns are monolithic in their nature, (2) other significant epochs could be included on a more granular level, and (3) the initiation of one era did not do away with the presence of previous approaches.

5. The history of the move toward preoccupation with historical ostensive reference is chronicled in Frei, *The Eclipse of Biblical Narrative*.

6. Krentz, *Historical-Critical Method*, 30.

7. John Sailhamer draws the connection between historical referent-focused

ical interpreters may take exception to being identified with the positivist, imminentist trappings of the historical-*critical* method, evangelical interpretation has maintained a basic historical orientation.[8] The historical shape of evangelical hermeneutics is typified in Gordon Fee's statement:

> From the perspective of the biblical scholar, the first step toward valid interpretation of Scripture is a historical investigation known as *exegesis*, which means the determination of the originally intended meaning of a text. "History as context for interpretation" does not refer to our own history, but to the original setting(s) of the biblical texts themselves.[9]

In the early twentieth century, following the historical turn, literary criticism developed out of concern that historically focused reading neglected the literary shape of the text itself. Alter and Kermode note, "[historical] criticism was of great cultural and doctrinal importance; but, as we have said, it diverted attention from biblical narrative, poetry, and prophecy as literature, treating them instead as more or less distorted historical records."[10] The literary turn is marked by an emphasis on the literary analysis of the Bible that does not always have an accompanying concern with historical issues.[11]

Bartholomew points to a development out of literary emphasis into the so-called postmodern turn in the 1980s. The hallmark feature of the postmodern turn is that it served as a challenge to both the historical and

---

interpretive approaches produced by critical theory and its influence on contemporary evangelical historical-grammatical hermeneutics in chapter two of Sailhamer, *Introduction to Old Testament Theology*.

8. Hays and Ansberry, *Evangelical Faith*; and Hoffmeier and Magary, *Do Historical Matters Matter?*. The discussion concerning the relation of historical criticism and the biblical text continues in evangelical scholarship to date with differing conclusions as to its place and practice in hermeneutics. For example, Hays and Ansberry have edited a work that engages many of the pertinent topics for historical concerns and biblical interpretation. In this work, the general approach is amicable toward the claims of historical criticism and its findings. Conversely, Hoffmeier and Magary have edited a work that engages similar topics with a critical appraisal of historical criticism.

9. Fee, "History as Context," 11.

10. Alter and Kermode, *Literary Guide*, 3.

11. A key work in the literary turn is Auerbach, *Mimesis*. Auerbach's work is particularly significant because of its use by theologians in reference to biblical hermeneutics. Most often referenced is Auerbach's argument in chapter seven that the biblical narrative presents a reality into which the reader is drawn. In particular, the influence of Auerbach's work on Hans Frei will be acknowledged in chapter four.

literary mindset, by asserting notions of pluralism and the indeterminacy of texts. Bartholomew's assertion is that "[postmodernity] questions the very foundations of [literary and historical approaches] and alerts us to the inevitability of a plurality of views in biblical interpretation."[12] Subsequent to the challenge presented by the postmodern turn, the door opened for what Bartholomew identifies as a theological turn. This turn is identified by two marks. First, Scripture is to be read according to its plain sense with a limited role for historical criticism. Second, hermeneutical emphasis is placed on reading under the influence of theology for the church and Christian doctrine.[13]

This cursory summary of approaches to text and history serves to indicate the longstanding tensions between historical interests and theological interests when interpreting Scripture. As Bartholomew argues, as a "theological turn" appears to be afoot, the importance of doctrinal presuppositions concerning Scripture is, in turn, influencing how one reads the Bible.[14] These developments in biblical hermeneutics relate specifically to the issues of revelation, history, and biblical hermeneutics in contemporary evangelicalism. Within the concern of this book on Carl F. H. Henry as a significant theologian of the doctrine of revelation, my hope is that one will find beneficial resources in his writings on these issues.

As Henry's theology is articulated in the context of those with whom he was conversing, the particular approaches that merit analysis as significant influences on contemporary approaches to revelation, history, and the biblical text are that of Wolfhart Pannenberg and Hans Frei. The summary of biblical interpretation provided above finds a parallel in corresponding theological approaches to the doctrine of revelation with the historical turn

12. Bartholomew, *Behind the Text*, 10.

13. The concerns of historical interests and the biblical text are not limited to passages that may be identified as historical narratives. Other genres of literature in the Bible (i.e. poetry, prophecy, epistle, etc.) are impacted by how one approaches the issues outlined here. The point of relevance may be the historical occasion for a passage, or it could be that historical claims are expounded upon through a non-narrative literary form. For example, see Psalm 78 as an example of events historically oriented and their significance mediated through poetry.

14. Plummer, *40 Questions*. This has been manifested in the growth of the field identified as Theological Interpretation. Plummer notes "[i]ndeed, the recent publication of many titles related to [the Theological Interpretation of Scripture] demonstrates that the fascination with this hermeneutical approach is only beginning. In a sentence, TIS is an academic movement that seeks to return reflection on the biblical text to the purview of the confessing Christian church."

represented by the revelation-as-history approach of Wolfhart Pannenberg and the literary turn manifested in the post-liberal approach typified by Hans Frei. As a chief representative of the neo-evangelical movement, the writings of Carl F. H. Henry provide fertile ground for considering these issues from the perspective of the doctrine of revelation.

The Path Ahead

The purpose of this book is to argue that, in contrast to the revelation-as-history and post-liberal approaches to revelation, Henry's doctrine of revelation generates a text-oriented, yet apologetically engaged, scheme of the relationship between revelation, history, and biblical text.

The connection between one's doctrine of revelation and hermeneutical approach is not always transparent.[15] In the pages that follow, I aim to make clear through Henry's example that one's approach to the doctrine of revelation in reality bears influence on the hermeneutical relation of text and history. For example, in the sentence, "God reveals himself to man," the doctrinal ideas contained in the word "revelation" have much influence over how one conceives of man appropriating that revelation. As will be demonstrated through Henry's theological writings, issues such as God's relationship to his revealed Word, the locus of revelation, the truth-value of revelation, and the nature of language and reference in revelation, among others, will bear direct influence on one's approach to history and textuality. Throughout Henry's writings on the subject, he interacts with key theologians who operate from differing revelational models. As such, these theologies provide contextual background to Henry's argument and must be considered. These writers, specifically Wolfhart Pannenberg and Hans Frei, will be considered in turn to evaluate Henry's critique of them.

As a chief representative of the revelation as history view, Wolfhart Pannenberg presents a thorough, historically focused model of revelation.

---

15. Note for example the relatively small amount of discussion in hermeneutics texts concerning the nature of divine revelation in terms of inspiration, authority, and reliability of the biblical text. The focus tends to rest on historical, philosophical, or literary dynamics rather than the relation of the text to God as communicator. A survey of contemporary hermeneutics texts bears this emphasis. For example, see: Osborne, *The Hermeneutical Spiral*; Kaiser and Silva, *An Introduction to Biblical Hermeneutics*; Duvall and Hays, *Grasping God's Word*; Brown, *Scripture as Communication*; and Plummer, *40 Questions*. In contrast, Poythress includes a substantive section on the doctrine of revelation in his hermeneutics survey. See Poythress, *God Centered Biblical Interpretation*.

For Pannenberg, God's revelation takes place within universal history. The implication of this model of revelation is that biblical history, in congruence with all history, is the content of revelation. The attached hermeneutical implication is then that man's appropriation of God's revelation is accomplished through man's appropriation of universal history. In terms of universal history, the biblical text is a record of such history and not possessing unique qualities itself.[16] The significance of Pannenberg's revelation-as-history approach is that the biblical text as God's verbal revelation is undermined as the focus of authority and study. As noted above, the patterns of this view are found in varying degrees in evangelical hermeneutics. Given the influence of exegesis that is historically oriented among those who hold a high view of Scripture, engagement with Pannenberg from the perspective of his model of revelation is significant.[17]

Post-liberal theology marks a departure from approaches that are historically oriented and neo-evangelical notions of revelation in propositional terms. As a corrective against the undermining of the biblical text, Hans Frei argued for a restoration of the place of biblical narrative as self-sufficient for conveying meaning.[18] As such, the biblical text does not refer per se to external events in terms of ostensive reference. Frei's notion is that revelation, whatever its particular model, has produced a literary text that is broadly characterized by history-like narrative. This text contains the necessary history-like material for conveying the content of the biblical faith.[19] No need exists to move behind the text for the appropriation of meaning. As will be demonstrated, Henry's concern is that Scripture itself attests to the historical reality of the events about which it speaks, and theological claims rest on the truth of the textual claims to history. For Henry, abstaining from commitment on the truth value of biblical events amounts to excluding an element essential to the authority of the text as communication from God.

---

16. Pannenberg, *Basic Questions in Theology*, 137. Pannenberg's undermining comments toward the idea that the Bible is a text that possesses "normative character," "authority," serves as "revelation of God," capable of significant "translation" into contemporary situations betrays his view concerning the nature of Scripture.

17. This is not to argue that Pannenberg himself is of primary influence on evangelical theologians who claim a high view of Scripture. Rather, it is an acknowledgement of the "eclipse" of biblical narrative (to use Frei's phrase) in favor of historical referent exegesis within evangelical ranks under the influence of the revelation as a history model.

18. Frei, *Eclipse of Biblical Narrative*, 10.

19. Ibid.

With the bracketing of textual authority by the revelation-as-history approach and the bracketing of commitment to historical reality by the post-liberal approach, the question remains: what approach to the triad of revelation, history, and biblical text is appropriate? The approach advocated by Henry is that the biblical text is the locus of God's revelation. Yet, for Henry, revelation as a broader category includes all aspects of God's disclosure of himself.[20] In a broad sense, revelation then includes, for example, the person of Jesus Christ incarnate, his words spoken (whether recorded in Scripture or not), and the miraculous interventions of God in history, like the Exodus or the birth, life, death, and resurrection of Jesus. With this view of revelation, the historical reality of biblical events becomes important for the attestation of divine revelation in text. As will be demonstrated, Henry argues that, while text interprets and provides meaning to event, text may not exist in a vacuum separated from event. The apologetic value of historical reality is a secondary, yet necessary affirmation for Christian belief in Henry's eyes.

Carl F. H. Henry's Voice

The approach for this study is to access the issues of revelation, history, and the biblical text through the writings of Carl F. H. Henry.[21] Henry holds privilege as an elite evangelical theologian, not only through his theological writings, but also through his position as the theologian-figurehead of the neo-evangelical movement in post-World War II America.[22] Writing about Henry, the narrative theologian Gabriel Fackre has noted, "[i]f the twentieth century 'evangelical renaissance' in North America has produced a Michelangelo, that exemplar is surely Carl Henry."[23] Henry's place as the "Dean of Evangelical Theologians" was acquired through his unrelenting insistence on promoting a theological vision that would produce a personal Christian faith able to speak intelligently to every aspect of culture.[24] In his

20. Henry, *God, Revelation and Authority*, vol. 2, 22.

21. For biographical resources concerning the life and thought of Carl F. H. Henry, see the following works: Henry, *Confessions of a Theologian*; Patterson, *Carl F. H. Henry*; Purdy, "Carl F. H. Henry"; and Mohler, "Carl F. H. Henry".

22. Marsden, *Reforming Fundamentalism*; Marsden, *Understanding Fundamentalism*; and Thornbury, *Recovering Classic Evangelicalism*.

23. Fackre, *Ecumenical Faith*, 171.

24. The title of "Dean of Evangelical Theologians" is a designator attributed to Henry

attempt to create a full orbed movement marked by spiritual and academic potency, Henry published key works that interacted with the fields of biblical studies, theological studies, and apologetics.[25]

In particular, Henry's well-known work, which is considered his magnum opus, *God, Revelation and Authority* (*GRA*), provides his account of the epistemological basis for Christian belief grounded in the revealed Word of God.[26] *God, Revelation and Authority* seeks to provide a biblically faithful explication of the doctrines of God and revelation, all the while taking seriously the impact of modernity on these subjects in contemporary theology. Henry's eminence is resultant of the fact that his six-volume work, as Trueman references, is the "most exhaustive evangelical statement on these issues to have been produced in the twentieth century and, upon its publication, marked the pinnacle of Henry's career as intellectual evangelical leader and spokesperson."[27] The need of the hour in Henry's estimation was to understand from every angle the world the Enlightenment had produced and respond to it on all levels in a competent manner.[28] Henry's concern for the doctrine of revelation and the doctrine of God extended beyond their consideration as heads of doctrine to developing their implications for the broader outworking of theology.[29]

Similar to Packer's sentiment referenced at the beginning of this chapter at ICBI Summit II, Henry calls attention to the importance of hermeneutics when he states that for multiple generations, Western Christianity

---

in Olson, *A-Z of Evangelical Theology*, 41.

25. It is worth noting that in addition to the breadth of Henry's writings, his voice is of value also, because he has become known as the representative theologian of a significant constituency in modern theology. For example, see Dulles, *Models of Revelation*, 37–41.

26. Henry, *God, Revelation and Authority*, 2:267.

27. Trueman, "Admiring the Sistine Chapel," 49.

28. Ibid., 51. Trueman notes further, ". . . Henry's *God, Revelation and Authority* stands as perhaps the major statement of evangelical epistemology which emerged from the new evangelical movement, designed to demonstrate the coherence of evangelical theology despite the criticisms of its enemies—and indeed, the misguided support of some of its friends."

29. Connor, *Revelation and God*. Carl Henry's works on the doctrines of God and revelation as the roots for religious epistemology certainly warrant the esteem they have earned due to the milieu from which he helped evangelicalism rise. It is worth noting that Henry's approach is not entirely original among American theologians. In 1936, Connor expanded upon his previous systematic writings to focus on the idea that to fix the ideas of God, revelation, and man in relation to each other is to fix the main ideas of theology. That is to say God, his revelation, and man's reception of it are the epistemic starting point for all of theology.

has grappled with the so-called "hermeneutical problem," which is formulated in different ways, but is characterized by serious intellectual work to assess correctly the message of Scripture for contemporary readers.[30] Henry comments that "[n]owhere does the crisis of modern theology find a more critical centre than in the controversy over the reality and nature of divine disclosure."[31] This is because, according to Henry, who God is, how he has revealed himself, and how humanity avails himself of God's revelation are three aspects of one central theological issue.

Henry's hermeneutical concerns arose in the midst of his broader interest of establishing evangelicalism in contrast to liberal, neo-orthodox, and post-liberal theological methods. If one attempts to locate his hermeneutical concerns on the arc of Henry's career, he will discover the primary writings concerning hermeneutics developed at the point of Henry's in-depth engagement with the issue of divine revelation. A critical concern for Henry is the relationship of revelation, history, and the biblical text. This topic is taken up with the most depth in thesis seven in *God, Revelation and Authority*.[32]

The historical quality of the biblical text is a recurring topic for Henry, because he views the truth value of Christian theology to be dependent upon the relationship of revelation, history, and the biblical text. Henry states, "[w]hile twentieth-century theologians frequently stress the redemptive faith of the Hebrew Old Testament, they minimize the historical factuality of the miraculous events that so prominently mark the ancient Jewish literature."[33] The fullness of Henry's approach to revelation, history, and text is brought to light through his assessment of two rival theologies of revelation in Pannenberg and Frei.

Recent Discussions of Revelation, History, and the Biblical Text

The historical claims of the biblical text are no new concern for interpreters and theologians. From the early formation of the church, the historical

30. Henry, *God, Revelation and Authority*, 4:296.

31. Ibid., 2:7.

32. Ibid., 2:247. Thesis seven states, "God reveals himself not only universally in the history of the cosmos and of the nations, but also redemptively within this external history in unique saving acts."

33. Ibid., 2:267.

claims of the biblical text have been accompanied by theological significance. For example, the foundational creeds of the Christian faith express grounding for the faith in certain historical facts. The Apostle's Creed describes Christ as the one who was "born of the virgin Mary; suffered under Pontus Pilate, was crucified, dead and buried . . . rose from the dead; he ascended into heaven; and sitteth at the right hand of God the Father almighty."[34] Similarly, historical presuppositions about the Son of God may be seen in the Chalcedonian and Athanasian creeds.[35] The longstanding historically oriented claims of the Christian creeds demonstrate the significance of the modern hermeneutical debate concerning historical event and the biblical text among theologians. Discussion concerning these historical claims has taken shape in modern theology along various lines that will be described below.

Post-liberal Influence on Evangelical Approaches

As a growing trend, a significant contingent of twenty-first century evangelicals began to make use of post-liberal theological method (at least in part), to the end that post-liberal emphasis on text has called evangelicals to question the usefulness of the historical-grammatical method.[36] The hermeneutical concern for evangelicals of this persuasion became the apparent frontloading of attention on the "historical" portion of the historical-grammatical method, which in turn led to an abdication of the text in hermeneutics and theology. In place of this, a literary approach became preferred as giving the text of Scripture its proper place as the center of spiritual life. The emphasis on the text over event has similarly been accompanied by critiques of propositionalism as a theological method because of its influence over hermeneutical approaches.

Critiques of Propositionalism

Just as propositionalism as a theological method has been critiqued for fostering a theology based on the ideas (propositions) behind the biblical text

34. For the text of the creeds mentioned and leading in-depth discussion, see Pelikan, *Credo*.

35. Ibid.

36. Ashford, "Wittgenstein's Theologians?," 357–75; and idem, "Wittgenstein's Impact on Anglo-American Theology."

rather than drawing on the text itself, so also evangelical hermeneutics is critiqued for making the historical reconstruction behind the text primary in interpretation.[37] This critique is to point out the irony of a theology based in revelation and authoritative text dealing dismissively with the text for the sake of historical reconstruction.[38] The critiques of propositionalism from within evangelical ranks as well as those which come from outside bear relevance for understanding Henry as a figurehead of a propositional approach to theology.[39] In order to bring full understanding to Henry's approach to revelation, history, and the biblical text, the critiques of propositionalism, in general, and Henry, in particular, will be discussed.

Much of the critique of propositionalism and Henry flows from postliberal influence in evangelical hermeneutics and theology. In the midst of these critiques and the distinctions they create between propositional and post-liberal approaches, a third vein of interaction has developed, which seeks to mediate the way of debate between Carl Henry and Hans Frei, noting evangelicalism may gain from moving past foundationalist philosophy as the cornerstone of theological method. This perspective, expressed by George Hunsinger as one of Frei's theological descendants, sees within post-liberalism a dose of epistemic humility that foundationalist method lacks.[40] The epistemic differences related to theological method bear impact on the text/history relationship, because of different interests in what kind of knowledge biblical interpretation yields.[41]

Patterns of Historical Hermeneutics in Evangelical Theology

In many ways, emphasis on the historical-grammatical method in interpretation is part and parcel with the post-World War II recovery of Scripture as divine revelation that bears divine authority. The papers of the second summit of the ICBI II, an assembly focused on hermeneutics, gave primary

37. Vanhoozer, "The Semantics of Biblical Literature," 53–104.

38. Chapman, "Reclaiming Inspiration for the Bible."

39. The significance of critiques against propositions may be seen in the way in which George Lindbeck sets the Postliberal method against a "traditional cognitivist" model for doctrine. Lindbeck, *Nature of Doctrine*, 30.

40. Hunsinger, "Evangelicals and Postliberals," 61–82.

41. Jason Springs similarly proposes a via media between Henry and Frei, in which evangelicalism may gain from a notion of neo-orthodox realism rather than a propositional realism. Springs, "But Did It *Really* Happen?," 271–99.

interest to the historical-grammatical method as a hermeneutic most faithful to the notion that the biblical text itself is communication from God, which holds authority for today.[42] In this setting, apologetic and interpretive concerns were conflated in the pursuit of establishing theological orthodoxy on scriptural grounds. The foundation of neo-evangelicalism in refuting liberalism and overcoming anti-intellectualist fundamentalism appears to have created a situation in which historical reality became more important than the conveyance of meaning through the text. This emphasis on ostensive reference was driven by a deep concern for apologetic defensive measures and a desire to present to society a constructive worldview in which a Christian approach is seen as advantageous to secular alternatives.

One Topic, Five Essential Issues

The theology of revelation articulated by Carl F. H. Henry provides the basic means for navigating the constellation of hermeneutical issues related to the biblical text and historical event. In the process of defending the evangelical notion of divine revelation, Henry adjudicates the text/event relationship by giving attention to five essential issues. These five issues will be used as a rubric for evaluating three approaches to revelation and their subsequent hermeneutical strategies. While the fivefold nature of issues related to revelation, history, and the biblical text are found within Henry's writings, he does not himself articulate this rubric or organize his discussion around this fivefold framework.

The fivefold structure is discerned by this writer through the reading of sources relevant to the topic, and is put forward as a beneficial approach for clarifying the issues involved. The fivefold rubric is helpful inasmuch as it faithfully draws to the surface the critical distinctions in any approach to revelation, history, and the biblical text.

1. Locus of Revelation: Text or Event

2. Nature of History: Duality or Unified

3. Role of Historical Inquiry: Apologetic or Interpretive

4. Goal of Hermeneutics: Theological or Historical

5. Test of History: Negative Test or Positive Test

42. Waltke, "Historical Grammatical Problems," 71–129.

Locus of Revelation

The first element of the fivefold rubric to be considered in determining the relationship between revelation, history, and the biblical text is the locus of revelation. In particular, is the locus of revelation in the verbal text or the event to which the text makes reference? This issue is of critical importance, because it influences the hermeneutical process by which an interpreter will pursue biblical understanding. James Barr highlights the issues at stake when he states, "[t]he question is this: is it true that the biblical evidence, and the evidence of the Old Testament in particular, fits with and supports the assertion that 'history' is the absolutely supreme *milieu* of God's revelation?"[43]

As a matter of historical emphasis, Barr further noted, in 1963, that "[h]istorians of theology in a future age will look back on the mid-twentieth century and call it the revelation-in-history period."[44] The view that the locus of revelation is in history is an affirmation that revelation is conveyed by history and is, therefore, the grounds on which to base theological understanding.[45] In contrast to the revelation-as-history view, Barr sees the affirmation of the locus of revelation in the text as acknowledging the text on its own grounds as the narration of historical events. For those who affirm an understanding of revelation as God's verbal communication, the emphasis falls on the text as the locus of that revelation. The nature of biblical narrative lends itself to the view that the locus of revelation is particularly in the text on account that it is tenuous to "attribute to history a revelatory character in a sense having substantial priority over the particular divine spoken communications with particular men, without doing violence to the way in which the biblical traditions in fact speak."[46]

From within evangelical ranks, John Sailhamer has drawn attention to the importance of the issue. In his *Theology of the Old Testament*, Sailhamer provides in-depth hermeneutical discussion as prolegomena for forming a theology of the Old Testament. According to Sailhamer's reasoning, the locus of revelation, whether principally in text or in historical event, will set the interpreter's course for where and how he looks to understand that

---

43. Barr, "Revelation Through History," 4.

44. Ibid., 5.

45. Ibid.

46. Ibid., 7.

revelation.[47] On the question of the locus of revelation, several influential factors have pushed evangelicalism toward an event-oriented approach to interpreting the biblical text. Similar to Barr's accounting, Sailhamer accounts for the event-oriented trend in evangelicalism through the influence of the historical-critical method, which bore influence on historical-grammatical method.[48]

The post-liberal narrative theologian Hans Frei, in *The Eclipse of Biblical Narrative*, narrates the shift in eighteenth and nineteenth-century hermeneutics toward a principally event-oriented approach to interpretation. No longer was the question what meaning the text conveyed, but rather, what the real facts of the event behind the text were (if the event occurred at all) regardless of the narration in the text.[49] Frei's text-based concern is reflective of the idea that the locus of revelation is not to be primarily identified in the history behind the text, but that the text is to be taken on its own terms. The locus of revelation is a significant driver in the approaches outlined by Henry, Frei, and Pannenberg, ultimately with Henry's approach providing a fruitful text-oriented way forward for evangelicals, as he articulates the nature of God's revelation in the Word, history, and nature.

The Nature of History

When considering the relationship between revelation, history, and the biblical text, determining the nature of biblical history is necessary. Stated as a question, the issue is to ask whether biblical history is of the same nature and category as world history, or whether biblical history belongs to a unique or different category?[50] Modern liberal theological influence on biblical studies has fostered the perspective that the "history" of the biblical

---

47. Sailhamer, *Old Testament Theology*, 73.

48. Barr, "Revelation Through History," 5. Barr notes: "But beyond this, most generally and most profoundly, we may say that revelation through history, and the constellation of our theological thinking around it, is our response to the tremendous and shocking apologetic strains of the nineteenth century, imposed primarily by the rise of historical method and historical criticism."

49. Frei, *Eclipse of Biblical Narrative*, 63.

50. For substantive discussion of the issues related to the nature of history and the biblical text, see Brown's discussion on history and revelation in Brown, "History & the Believer," 185–97.

text is primarily the faith perspective of Israel or the believing community, if not Israel as a whole.

Conversely, others have argued that to place biblical events on a different plane than world history is to destabilize biblical knowledge merely to an intuitionist epistemology. Barr provides clarity to the differences in how interpreters approach the nature of history by making no friends on either side. Against those who claim no distinction exists between what many believe the Bible conveys as history and its legitimacy as genuine historical claim in part with other events of history, Barr notes that the "Bible itself has no linguistic bracket corresponding to 'history,' and, as we have seen, its narrative revelatory passages are not constant but variable in their relation to what we can by any definition call "history."[51]

On the other hand, he critiques those who may attempt to make sense of narratives in Scripture by appealing to some schism in the nature of world history and religious history.[52] In light of these disagreements, the following is clear; how one approaches redemptive historical acts in his doctrine of revelation will ultimately bear strong influence over the interpretive process.[53] The question of the nature of history in biblical interpretation not only raises questions concerning the truth of the historical narratives, but "materially affects the reading of Scripture itself by posing the question of interpretation and meaning."[54]

Of related concern is specifically how the written text and historical event relate in light of the fact that written history is selective and provides interpretation of historical events through narration. For some, the written interpretation of events lead them to separate historical referent from the

51. Barr, "Revelation Through History," 8.

52. Ibid., 9. Barr notes, "But even more noticeable to me is the artificiality and implausibility of the distinctions which we are forced to produce in order to make 'history' do the kind of work into which we have impressed it. Consider only the artificiality of the distinctions between *Geschichte* and *Historie*, between *Heilsgeschichte* and *Weltgeschichte*, or the artificiality of *Sage* and *Urgescheichte* as used by Barth of the creation stories."

53. Harvey, *Historian and the Believer*, 5. The connection between one's doctrine of revelation and hermeneutical process is made clear by Harvey when he states, "If the theologian regards the Scriptures as supernaturally inspired, the historian must assume that the Bible is intelligible only in terms of its historical context and is subject to the same principles of interpretation and criticism that are applied to other ancient literature. If the theologian believes that the events of the Bible are the results of the supernatural intervention of God, the historian regards such an explanation as a hindrance to true historical understanding."

54. Ibid., 19–20.

narration of the biblical text. As will be demonstrated in the writings of Frei, such a separation ultimately leads to a scheme of history in which the connection between biblically narrated events and world history is irrelevant.

Conversely, as in the case of Pannenberg, treating history as unified without concern for verbal revelation leaves one to discern biblical meaning exclusively through the tools of historical inquiry. Thus, the three theologians under examination take distinct approaches to these issues. In support of the thesis, I will argue that Henry provides for a unified approach to biblical history and world history, yet also maintains a distinct place for written Scripture as God's unique revelation.

Role of Historical Inquiry

In his lecture on verification of knowledge and religious belief, R. B. Braithwaite claimed: "[a] man is not, I think, a professing Christian unless he both proposes to live according to Christian moral principles and associates his intention with thinking Christian stories; but he need not believe that the empirical propositions presented by these stories correspond to empirical fact."[55] With the concluding claim of this thought, Braithwaite places before the biblical interpreter the issue of historical knowledge in the interpretation and belief of Scripture. In light of positivist thinking like Braithwaite's, inquiry into the historical claims of the biblical text is a seemingly natural process of human thinking about Scripture and also a determinative element for one's hermeneutical approach.

The purposes for historical inquiry may fall into two general categories—apologetic or interpretive. Apologetic inquiry takes inquiry about the historical circumstances and claims of the text to be less so about determining the meaning of the text as reinforcing the truth value of what the text seems to be claiming.[56] Interpretive inquiry takes historical matters of more significant import for understanding the meaning of the biblical text,

---

55. Braithwaite, "An Empiricist's View," 119.

56. McCall, "Religious Epistemology, Theological Interpretation," 53–54. For example, McCall acknowledges the apologetic value of critical inquiry, but does not suspend the legitimacy of biblical understanding and Christian belief on independent critical verification. He states, "For pragmatic and apologetic reasons [the critical scholar's] work may be very valuable. But in the event that he faces a critical argument that he cannot answer, he does not feel pressure to capitulate immediately. If, after all, he has grounds for belief that are independent of [Critical Biblical Scholarship] and that are not undercut by CBS, he has no reason to despair when faced with difficult arguments from CBS."

whether it is in seeking understanding of the direct claims of Scripture or in determining the cultural backgrounds of a certain piece of literature as a key to understanding meaning.[57]

The apologetic emphasis on historical inquiry takes as its occasion doubt concerning the historical validity of the text. In this way, the apologetic role of historical inquiry has an external motivation prompted by doubt against the claims of Scripture. Generally, the apologetic emphasis takes as its starting point a basic understanding that the biblical text has a truth value. The text in its theological purposes makes real claims about what has happened in the past, and the validity of belief in the theological claims of Scripture are dependent upon the veracity of the historical claims.[58] An evangelical apologetic approach to historical inquiry generally takes the historical claims as accounts faithful to actual events of history (even though the text may not be pure ostensive reference) and seeks to understand tensions in light of potential historical evidence to the contrary.[59] Ultimately, the goal of apologetic historical inquiry is to be supportive of confidence in the veracity of Scripture, and in that way a support to the interpretation of Scripture.[60]

Goal of Hermeneutics

It may not be often that a reader stops to ask exactly what their purpose in reading a text may be, but it seems intuitive that people read texts for a desired purpose. In the focus of this study, one may ask, what is the basic purpose for engaging in the reading of Scripture? With our present concern on the biblical text and its historicity, one may read for attaining certain facts about the nation of Israel, or perhaps the person of Jesus Christ depending on the location in Scripture. For evangelicals who affirm a doctrine of revelation that includes a strong notion of inspiration, the text of Scripture

---

57. Stuhlmacher, *Historical Criticism and Theological Interpretation*. For example, Stuhlmacher seeks to provide a way between unfruitful critical scholarship and theological interpretation that incorporates historical inquiry into theological interpretation of Scripture.

58. Brown, *History and the Believer*, 198.

59. Ibid., 199. Brown affirms "If our faith is of the kind that would persist regardless of evidence and regardless of historical models, it is an unanchored faith."

60. Hoffmeier, "These Things Happened," 99–134. For example, Hoffmeier critiques the impact of historical criticism on biblical interpretation, yet provides an extended apologetic for why a historical exodus is essential for a serious biblical theology.

itself is seen to have a purpose beyond merely relaying historical facts or literature associated with historical provenance (though it need not require denying the text conveys world history). The doctrines of revelation and inspiration themselves imply that, in addition to providing information about people, nations, and events, the text of Scripture reveals the person of God himself. In light of this, engaging in reading Scripture is the means by which people know God.[61] If Scripture reveals God himself in a unique and special way, then it seems the basic goal of reading Scripture would be to know and understand God.[62] Knowing and understanding God is an explicitly theological task; therefore, one could claim the goal of reading Scripture is to arrive at theological, rather than purely historical ends.[63]

Conversely a view that emphasizes history as revelation takes the Bible as the collection of record and interpretation concerning past events. The entire media of revelation is contained in historical events or historical presence.[64] As the chief theological influence on the revelation as historical perspective, Pannenberg notes that "understanding of Jahweh is obtained through his historical activity."[65] The influence of this approach has been to foster a reliance on historical inquiry for accessing revelation. In commenting on Pannenberg's contribution to history as revelation, Braaten notes "[t]heologically, if revelation is history happening, and not something above or alongside history, then why should not the historical method be the appropriate way of finding out what happened?"[66]

61. For evangelical theologies of revelation that support this view of Scripture see: Warfield, "The Biblical Idea of Revelation," 3–36; Henry, *The God Who Shows Himself*; Henry, *God, Revelation and Authority*; Jensen, *The Revelation of God*; and Connor, *Revelation and God*.

62. Poythress, *God Centered Interpretation*, 10. The theological goal of hermeneutics leads Poythress to claim: "It is thus worthwhile to reexamine foundational questions. Who is God? What is his relation to the Bible? What sort of things are human languages in which the Bible is written? What is meaning? How does God expect us to respond to the Bible? What interpretive procedures do justice to the character of the Bible and our responsibility? . . . It is equally important that practical [interpretive] skills should operate within a framework and with a controlling direction set by the word of God."

63. Goldsworthy, *Gospel-Centered Hermeneutics*, 33. Goldsworthy states concerning the theological trajectory of biblical interpretation: "God has spoken by his Word, the Word who became a man for us. He knows us and we know his voice so that we follow him. Any hermeneutics that loses this plot has ceased to be evangelical and is out of touch with biblical truth."

64. Braaten, *History and Hermeneutics*, 17.

65. Pannenberg, "Dogmatic Theses," 125.

66. Braaten, *History and Hermeneutics*, 44.

Connecting the historical nature of revelation and the historical mode of accessing that revelation to hermeneutics, one must conclude that the "question of meaning, of understandability, cannot, however, be settled without referral to the historical events from which the statements of faith arise and which they purport to transmit."[67] In other words, the goal of hermeneutics is historical rather than theological when it flows from a revelation-as-history model, because that is where meaning is found.

Pressing the decision between the goal of historical reading versus the goal of theological reading is to request of the reader to orient his hermeneutics according to what he views to be the primary nature and purpose of Scripture. As will be seen in discussions related to Henry and his conversation partners in Pannenberg and Frei, to select one goal or the other does not entirely exclude the converse option. Rather, by virtue of the goal one selects, the interpretive process will focus on a certain set of interests and yield a different answer as to what it means to understand biblical texts.

Test of History

Essential to the discussion concerning revelation, history, and the biblical text is the principle of the test of history. Asking the question of the test of history is to ask, in order to believe the text, must one establish a positive evidence for the historical claim of the text, or is it sufficient to believe in the historical factuality so long as the claim has not been disproven by negative evidence?[68] If the text bears the burden of carrying external positive proof for every historically oriented claim in order to produce reliability and interpretive validity, then the interpretive process will inevitably be oriented primarily toward historical inquiry behind the text. However, if the biblical text is granted an understanding of historicity and factuality where it has not been disproven by independent historical inquiry, then the text is liberated to become the focus of the interpretive process. The decision concerning the test of history is significant, because it affects how one will interpret and practically relate to Scripture.[69] Along these lines, Iain Provan notes:

---

67. Ibid., 49.
68. Brown, *History and the Believer*, 200.
69. Ibid., 200.

> [To] raise questions about the Bible's historicity is, for many
> people, to raise questions about its truthfulness . . . and to invite
> them to turn elsewhere for the truth that fundamentally shapes
> their lives. That is why the matter of history is a crucial matter for
> those interested in presenting the Bible to the culture with a view
> to the culture taking seriously what it has to say about God and
> the world.[70]

Epistemology is not unrelated to navigating matters of revelation, history, and the text. Provan outlines a shift in historical epistemology in the modern era from philosophy to science as "the foundational method for human endeavor."[71] Under the influence of Modernist thinkers like Descartes and Bacon, epistemology impacted historiography to eschew all prior authority and submit all knowledge to scientific verifiability.

The weakness of the modern shift, according to Provan, is that a positive test for historicity cuts off the category of "testimony" as a source of knowledge.[72] While a claim for the validity of "testimony" as a source of knowledge is not a claim for scientific verification, it is to acknowledge that interpreters cannot avoid basing historical knowledge on accounts of testimony. Therefore, belief that is testified to in the past is the foundation for one's understanding of the past, and is unavoidable. To require a positive test for historicity in order to place justified belief in a narrative is to miss the nature of history itself as a non-repeatable event and to subject textual witness to epistemological requirements foreign to its nature.[73]

Further, the aim of texts that are historically oriented in the Bible is not to mediate bare facts, but rather to convey interpretations, ideology, and theology as part of the narrative structure. The aforementioned elements of the narrative structure mean that texts are not best handled by requirements for historical verification that are empirically driven, but rather through an interpreter considering the testimonies available, reflecting on the various interpretations of history conveyed in these testimonies, and deciding to invest belief and faith in those testimonies.[74]

70. Provan, "Knowing and Believing," 230.

71. Ibid., 230.

72. Ibid., 251.

73. Ibid., 245.

74. Ibid., 251. If the testimony of narrative is central to human knowledge of the past and faith in past realities, then reckoning with the appropriate "test" of history is unavoidable. To subject all historical testimony to a positive test of historicity, that is, to require scientifically justifiable historical affirmation as ground for warranted belief

Provan describes historical knowledge in light of testimony when he states *"knowledge of the past* is more accurately described as *faith in the testimony,* in the interpretations of the past, offered by others."[75] Preference for a negative test of history (versus a positive test) as it has been articulated by Provan is not to discount the importance of affirming historical reality and seeking support for the historical claims of Scripture. While an acknowledgement that one is warranted in belief of historical claims so long as they are not otherwise disproven, the negative test is, likewise, an acknowledgement that the biblical text, indeed, has historical truth-value, and faith may be apologetically undergirded by independent historical inquiry.[76]

Worth noting is the significance of requiring a positive test of history for biblical interpretation. In summary, P. R. Davies captures the sentiment of a positive test when he states,

> If we have no positive grounds for thinking that a biblical account is historically useful, we cannot really adopt it as history. True, the result will be that we have less history than we might. But what little we have we can at least claim we know (in whatever sense we "know" the distant past): this, in my opinion, is better than having more history than we might, much of which we do not know at all, since it consists merely of unverifiable stories.[77]

The particular weakness with making biblical interpretation contingent upon a positive test is that it misses the fact that history is the telling and retelling of events unverifiable by an empirical method.[78] In response to the modern milieu of historical criticism and biblical interpretation, it will be demonstrated that Carl Henry exhibits a chastened reliance on the narrative as justifiable insight into historical knowledge, according to a

---

proves very quickly unworkable as a theory for knowledge and faith.

75. Ibid., 245.

76. Ibid., 263. According to Provan, the trapping of committing to a positive test for history is none other than the remaking of history in our own image. He makes this clear when he states, "[t]he fact is that we either respect and appropriate the testimony of the past, allowing it to challenge us even while thinking hard about it; or we are doomed— even while thinking that we alone have 'objectivity' and can start afresh on the historical quest—to create individualistic fantasies about the past out of the desperate poverty of our own very limited experience and imagination."

77. Davies, "Whose History? Whose Israel?," 105.

78. Provan, "Knowing and Believing," 263. Provan goes further than not requiring "positive grounds" for taking the biblical testimony "seriously" in a historical sense. Additionally, he places the burden on the modernist perspective by requiring "positive grounds" for not accepting the biblical text as non-historical.

negative test model, without diminishing the value of historical inquiry. This contributes to Henry's model for biblical interpretation that finds the text sufficient for historical knowledge, while undergirding his hermeneutics with a concern for historicity.

Scope of Study

This study focuses on Carl F. H. Henry's works as a key theologian writing on the nature of Scripture and hermeneutics. As such, this study will primarily engage the conversation partners Henry engaged in his writings on the subjects of revelation, text, and history. The topics related to revelation, biblical text, history, criticism (in its various manifestations), and historiography are all legitimate concerns of Henry as one primarily identified as a theologian rather than a biblical scholar. As one would expect, the literature on these topics from the multiple disciplines which take them as their concern are expansive and may not be fully engaged in a single book. The selective focus on scholars related to Henry's writings is one of the limits of the present study.

Additionally, this study takes its shape out of a strategy to engage in-depth the two most significant conversation partners Henry engages. The influence of Pannenberg and Frei on theology and biblical studies after their time place them front and center for Henry. Likewise, their subsequent influence presents them as worthy of engagement for considering the issues of history and the text in contemporary evangelical hermeneutics. In light of this, our focus will be on making clear the arguments presented by Henry, Pannenberg, and Frei as representatives of various approaches to revelation, history, and the biblical text.

Space will be given to Henry's interlocutors in order to consider the fairness of his explanation and evaluations of the individuals he critiques. Literature, which relates to the related topics of revelation, the biblical text, history, biblical criticism, and historiography, will be engaged as it assists in the pursuit of the thesis of this study. Given the interdisciplinary nature of these topics, the possible contributors are too numerous to incorporate comprehensively, so selectivity is based on how secondary authors assist the engagement of Henry, Pannenberg, and Frei.

A word concerning the limits of engaging Henry himself is helpful at this point as well. As an author, Henry's concerns were wide and varied, ranging from writings that were theologically dense to popular level defenses of the Christian faith. His voluminous writing output, at over forty volumes, coupled with the depth of material represented by articles, lectures, and sermons require significant limitation. The material written by Henry, which addresses specifically the intersection of revelation, history, and the biblical text, has been identified as the first level of primary source material from Henry. Much interest has ensued in Henry's breadth of work, but even his writings on the doctrine of revelation are so broad that their use in this work have been narrowed to those which bear impact on our immediate concerns of historicity and hermeneutics.

2

Revelation as the Foundation for Carl F. H. Henry

Henry's Epistemological Starting Point

Carl Henry's approach to revelation and the biblical text cannot be separated from his grand vision of the epistemological foundation for religious knowledge. In Henry's view, the commitments one makes at the start of his theology to defining God, how he has communicated, and how he has created humanity to apprehend this communication are determinative for all that follow. Taking his queues from Enlightenment categories, Henry explains that the ultimate a-priori commitment for a person is a metaphysical worldview with God at its center.[1] Fixing God as the cornerstone, Henry's larger program is to demonstrate how all of life and knowledge descends from this initial commitment.[2] The God who exists as transcendent creator is also the God who has spoken into his creation in order to reveal himself.[3] The self-disclosure of God is the essential launching

---

1. Henry, *Toward a Recovery*, 49. Henry claims, "[t]he Christian's primary ontological axiom is the one living God, and his primary epistemological axiom is divine revelation."

2. Ibid. On the necessity of Christians to engage issues of epistemology, Henry comments, "[y]et a metaphysical view that professes to make sense of all reality and life and involves a universal truth claim must adduce some epistemological justification if it is to escape dismissal as fideism or sheer faith that derogates reason."

3. Henry, *God, Revelation and Authority*, 2:17. Thesis one of *God, Revelation and Authority* states, "Revelation is a divinely initiated activity, God's free communication by which he alone turns his personal privacy into a deliberate disclosure of his reality."

point for all of Henry's theology, including his remarks concerning history and the biblical text.[4] Fixing God in his knowledge as the Archimedean point of all reality enables Henry to orient the existence of truth, a philosophy of history, the place and nature of revelation, man as a knower, and the correspondence of God's verbal revelation to his role in history as creator and providential sustainer in historical-redemptive acts.[5]

In many ways, Henry's place in modern theology on issues of revelation and history is set in the context of providing an intelligible response to the effect of Modernism on theology. Henry saw in European theology the pulling away from biblically congruent epistemological commitments under the weight of Cartesian and Kantian epistemologies.[6] In Henry's estimation, the division of the noumenal and the phenomenal realms led continental theologians to re-categorize the knowledge of God into something other than rightly held content about who the person of God is and the life-giving role he plays in human endeavors.[7]

From this setting of modern theology, Henry's pervasive concern throughout his works is to demonstrate how the evangelical view of God, revelation, and humanity provide the sole workable alternative for reasonable belief. The reason this epistemological commitment operates as a control for Carl Henry is because it anchors all other claims to knowledge.

---

4. Trueman, "Admiring the Sistine Chapel," 49. Concerning the epistemological scope of Henry's theological writings, Trueman argues, "Henry's entire work—of which *God, Revelation and Authority* is the greatest single example—must be understood as an attempt to restate conservative Protestant theology in a manner which takes seriously the epistemological concerns of the Enlightenment without surrendering the content and truth-claims of orthodox Christianity."

5. Henry, *Remaking the Modern Mind,* 171. Henry wrote early in his career and maintained the same emphasis throughout his life a fixation of epistemological points. He states in an early theological work, "[f]rom a certain vantage point the concept of God is determinative for all other commitments; it is the Archimedean lever with which one can fashion an entire world view."

6. Thornbury, *Recovering Classic Evangelicalism,* 52. Thornbury summarizes Henry's epistemology in contrast to modernist epistemology when he states, "Henry espoused a Reformation-inspired voluntarism in the best sense of the term. He stressed the absolute dependence of human knowledge upon divine disclosure, whether natural or particular. In other words, according to Henry, we know what we know because God wills both the possibility and the content of that knowledge."

7. Grenz and Olson, *20th Century Theology,* 291. Grenz and Olson note that throughout his career, Henry was "driven by a thesis foundational to all his efforts as a Christian theologian, namely, that to its own peril the twentieth-century mindset had forsaken its rootage in the earlier commitment to divine revelation."

As an example, one crisis of the Enlightenment was manifest in a new direction concerning the role of human beings as knowers. The weakness of the Enlightenment in Henry's estimation was that its epistemology was truncated in religious matters.[8] Human beings as knowers could not truly apprehend that which was outside the empirical senses, and this eventually flowered into the strict empiricism of Logical Positivism.[9] The full effect of modernist epistemology was the truncation of humanity's ability to apprehend divine truth. The contrast between Henry and his assessment of the Enlightenment is palpable and what is clear is that, for Henry, revelation is a matter of religious epistemology.[10]

According to Henry, the options are twofold—either the transcendent God has personally disclosed knowledge of himself which serves as the foundation for all truth and reality, or all statements about God are merely human assertions that provide no real knowledge of God. The only cure, by Henry's prescription, for the developments in epistemology described above was to restore the place of God in his role as the communicator who has conveyed intelligible knowledge of himself through his voluntary and personal revelation.

Henry's Doctrine of Revelation

Getting to the core of Henry's thought on revelation, history, and the biblical text is not possible without first reckoning with Henry's overall approach to divine revelation. This is largely true because, for Henry, one cannot consider revelation without first considering God. Henry's claim is that,

---

8. The chief representatives of modern theology, in their various approaches, were Bultmann, Barth, and Brunner. While Henry acknowledged the distinctions in each of the theologies represented by these individuals, the strand which holds them together in Henry's mind, is the intuitionist approach to revelation and the knowledge of God as an effort to jump the gap between the noumenal and the phenomenal.

9. Soames, *The Dawn of Analysis*. In his two-volume work, Soames traces the history of analytical philosophy through its developments into the hard empiricism of Logical Positivism and subsequent developments into Ordinary Language Philosophy. For details concerning the establishment of the strict empiricism against which Henry wrote, see volume one subtitled *The Dawn of Analysis*.

10. A full discussion of Henry's approach to religious epistemology is outside the scope of this book. For resources related to Henry's epistemology see: Carswell, "A Comparative Study"; Johnson, "A Critical Analysis"; Wagner, "The Revelational Epistemology"; and Waita, "Carl F. H. Henry."

> To an historically given divine revelation Judaism and Christianity trace their confidence that a sovereign personal God is the creator of the universe and the absolute source of meaning and value. This revelation, in contrast to finite human speculation and naturally acquired knowledge about reality, they consider a permanently valid divine disclosure reaching back to ancient patriarchal and prophetic times.[11]

Much in this quote will be discussed in what follows, but for the moment it is sufficient to note the things Henry appears to be affirming as normative for Christian theology.

First, God himself is the personal source, according to Henry, for all meaning and value. As will be seen in further discussions related to history and the text, the realism of correspondence between the person of God and his revelation are significant for Henry. Second, the revelation of God occurred in a particular past time and place, yet this revelation holds universal authority over all human life and thought. The fact that revelation is communication from the transcendent authoritative creator-God leads Henry to the principle from which he does not stray in matters of revelation and history—biblical authority.[12] Third, the fact that this revelation comes from the truthful God as its source and that it reaches "back to ancient patriarchal and prophetic times" leads Henry to conclude historical reality is tied to the affirmation of truthfulness for the One who revealed himself in those historical contexts.[13]

In other words, the historical veracity of the biblical text and the reliability of God as communicator are linked.[14] These emphases are likewise heard when Henry states, "[t]he Christian doctrine is that the living personal God directly and objectively manifests himself by intelligible words, commands and acts. God's redemptive revelation is given once for all at definite times and places, but he also is continually disclosed in nature and history and in and to the mind and conscience of man universally."[15]

11. Henry, "Priority of Divine Revelation," 77.

12. Henry, *God Who Shows Himself*. The authority of Scripture in light of God's authority as revealer is a major point Henry provides throughout his writings.

13. Henry, "Priority of Divine Revelation," 77.

14. Ibid., 79. Henry does not make his assertions concerning revelation in isolation from the alternatives. For example, see his list of eight views concerning revelation that differ from his own.

15. Ibid., 78. Note the breadth of the category of revelation for Henry to include not only writings, but also disclosure in nature, history, and human consciousness.

Revelation and History

Henry's assertion is that the transcendent God has of his own accord chosen to reveal himself to humanity as part of his divine plan for redemption.
The connection Henry forges between history and the biblical text begins
with the person of God. As the active agent in revelation, God's unveiling of
himself is the starting point for history. Henry states it thus, "[t]he revealed
names of God connect the knowledge of God in a special way with his creation of the universe and with his redemptive deeds in the history of Israel
and the founding of the Christian Church."[16] The disclosure of God's names
are significant, because in them God discloses himself in "historical revelation, and that the successively revealed names of God signal distinctive
epochs in the progressive manifestation of God's redemptive purpose."[17]
While the revelation of divine names in particular historical events is not
explicitly detailed by Henry, his comments do illuminate his framework of
revelation and history. The fact of divine self-disclosure to humans in time
and space is essential for Henry because of its significance for the establishment of textual truth and correspondence to reality.[18]

The prominence of the relation between revelation, history, and the
text is emphasized by the fact that of his fifteen theses concerning revelation in *God, Revelation and Authority*, Henry devotes a thesis to this
topic. Henry's exposition of this topic in thesis seven comprises six chapters
(volume two) of discussion and further discussions throughout volumes
three and four are relevant to the topic. Thesis seven states, "God reveals
himself not only universally in the history of the cosmos and of the nations, but also redemptively within this external history in unique saving
acts."[19] Henry's language in this thesis provides the grounding for a view of
history that maintains unity between world history and the saving acts of
God. From the beginning of the discussion, Henry laments the twentieth-
century tendency to question whether history is a viable mode of divine

16. Henry, *God, Revelation and Authority*, 2:180.

17. Ibid., 2:181.

18. Ibid., 2:181–84. Henry explains how the revealed names of God in their biblical-
historical setting expound upon the character of God. The personal nature of revelation
as communication from God is reinforced by Henry's treatment of the proper names for
God: Elohim, El Shaddai, Yahweh, and Jesus Christ. According to Henry, the personal
nature of God's revelation involves historical unveiling of himself by these names.

19. Ibid., 2:247.

revelation in light of a modern subjectivist turn.[20] Given Henry's insistence on revelation which has involved divine events in history, the issue arises of the hermeneutical relationship between investigation of historical events and the interpretation of the biblical text.

Hermeneutics and History

Carl Henry took a hermeneutical approach that emphasized interpreting the historical acts of God through the written revelation of God. Henry took such a hermeneutical approach on account of his view that the Bible as revelation provides the access to the meaning of the redemptive purpose of God's work in history. Out of hermeneutical interest, Henry was concerned that a one-sided historical interest had eclipsed the "revelatory relationships between God and man" through the influence of historical criticism.[21] Henry was committed to a hermeneutical approach based on the idea that "[t]he meaning of a text is linguistic and communal . . . can be reproduced in more than one consciousness, and it is normatively identical with what the author meant by the particular linguistic symbols he employed."[22]

In drawing on the work of E. D. Hirsch,[23] Henry insists valid meaning is textual, and this has priority over an interpreter's constructions (contra existential-subjectivist hermeneutics) and historical reconstruction (contra immanentist critical hermeneutics).[24] Henry identifies Hirsch as the most "formidable challenge to the recent hermeneutical trend" and says that Hirsch's text-oriented approach to general hermeneutics will serve biblical hermeneutics well.[25] Henry, therefore, defines the primary task of hermeneutics as "umpiring competitive meaning-possibilities and identifying the author's intention . . . There is no better rule for interpreting the Bible or any other literary work than to find out what the author meant."[26]

Henry's hermeneutical perspective proceeds from his ideas concerning the nature of Scripture. Henry views the biblical texts as "a deposit of

20. Ibid.

21. Henry, "Interpretation of the Scriptures," 198.

22. Ibid., 206.

23. Hirsch, *Validity in Interpretation*. In particular, Henry draws upon Hirsch's most notable work on general hermeneutics and literary theory published early in his career.

24. Henry, "Doomed to Hermeneutical Nihilism," 206.

25. Ibid., 213.

26. Ibid., 209.

literature distinguished by the Holy Spirit's inspiration of chosen writers and their writings, so that special divine revelation is not sporadically on-going and internally experienced but is biblically given."[27] Henry contin-ues by emphasizing the importance of historical and philological exegesis of the verbal form of the text as indispensable for "identifying the con-tent of the scripturally given revelation, and [the reader] must acknowl-edge that authorial cognitive intention is ultimately definitive for textual meaning."[28] Here the focus is on ascertaining the verbal meaning from the text rather than seeking the meaning behind the text through historical reconstruction.[29]

Henry's approach to the nature of the biblical text as explanation and development of the meaning of historical event is reinforced by the limitations he places upon historical inquiry.[30] He notes, "It is true that the historical method cannot cope with the theological and supernatural ele-ments, and hence it cannot be invoked either for or against the miraculous. The question of transcendent miracle is actually decided, pro or con, by considerations to which the historical method is irrelevant."[31] Hence, the goal of hermeneutical inquiry is not to discern as an end the historical real-ity and validity of the biblical text, because the meaning of historical act is provided in the text through the means of textual inquiry.

Henry goes on to argue, "Evangelicals emphasize the inspired charac-ter of Scripture as a divinely authorized interpretation of redemptive his-tory. Apart from their inspired interpretation, the redemptive acts have no sure meaning: since the interpretation conveys the meaning of historical

---

27. Ibid., 215.

28. Henry, *God, Revelation and Authority*, 2:314–15. Henry's apologetic point comes through at this place in his argument as well when he states, "[a]t stake in these alternatives is nothing less than either forfeiting or preserving the truth and Word of the God of biblical revelation."

29. Ashcraft, "Response to Carl F. H. Henry," 219. It should be noted that Henry's article is not without criticism. Ashcraft agrees with much of Henry's criticism of devel-opments in hermeneutics, but disagrees with Henry's solution of relying on a particular definition of revelation. Ashcraft asserts that Henry's insistence on authorial intent is the product of over-reliance on a cognitive-propositional view of revelation. This critique of Henry will be addressed further in a subsequent portion of this chapter.

30. Henry, *God, Revelation and Authority*, 2:320. Henry boldly claims, "Evangelical Christianity in no way presumes to regard historical investigation, now or in the past, as the sufficient method of knowing the truth of revelation."

31. Ibid., 4:338.

acts, it presupposes and requires those acts."[32] Stated differently, while divine events are revelation in the sense that they are genuine acts of God in history for the purpose of making himself known, the interpreter's focus should be on the locus of revelation in the biblical text, because the text is the divinely inspired interpretation and explanation of the meaning of God's activity in history.

The impact of Henry's mindset concerning meaning and historical act bears direct impact on his hermeneutical methods when he cautions against the extent empirically oriented historical inquiry should be deployed by stating, "In this sense the Spirit of revelation, inspiration and illumination does carry a divine testimony that surpasses the fluctuating tentativities of empirical investigations."[33] To make his point further, Henry cites B. B. Warfield in an approving manner to emphasize that the Bible does not depict divine revelation as merely a collection of redemptive historical acts. Warfield states, "[revelation] occupies a far more independent place among [historical events] than this, and as frequently precedes [historical events] to prepare their way as it accompanies or follows them to interpret their meaning."[34] In Henry's estimation, viewing revelation primarily through historical events creates significant hermeneutical problems. [35] For example, the biblical wisdom literature cannot be adequately accounted for hermeneutically with a revelation as history approach.

Henry's hermeneutical goal appears consistently to be discerning the meaning of the text through textually focused methods, because the text bears the quality of inspiration. The limits of the historical-critical method prevent it from providing the hermeneutical fruit required for sound biblical interpretation. Specifically, historical inquiry is not capable, according

32. Ibid., 4:343.

33. Ibid.

34. Warfield, "Biblical Idea of Revelation," 12–13; and Henry, "Divine Revelation and the Bible," 255. Henry similarly affirmed that revelation is a much broader term than simply historical act or biblical text. Henry similarly notes, "[t]he category of revelation is therefore broader than the category of the spoken and written words of Scripture, since it covers special historic events which the Bible normatively interpreted . . . Nothing less may be said than that the category of revelation is identical with the whole unveiling of God, whatever forms that disclosure may assume."

35. It may be stated that Henry viewed revelation as primary rather than exclusive in the biblical text on account that he viewed revelation in a broad-based manner and identified God's historical acts (as well as other forms, such as Jesus Christ as the Word of God) as revelatory. Scripture holds special and primary status as the full revelation of God to which humanity has access that supplies the meaning to God's activity in history.

to Henry, of providing the theological truth specifically necessary for the salvific purposes of God's revelation.[36] With such statements from Henry concerning the limits of historical method, the question arises as to what Henry advocated for in his self-described "grammatico-historical method" for biblical interpretation. In such a self-labeled hermeneutical strategy, it appears that Henry did indeed take into the interpretive process historical inquiry. He favorably cites J. I. Packer's assertion that the evangelical hermeneutic binds one to use a grammatical-historical method.[37]

Is Henry inconsistent in his scheme of revelation, history, and the biblical text? While it may appear so, a look at his argument presents evidence that he has apologetic concerns that impact how he describes the hermeneutical task. Henry is not receptive of the insistence that there is no option but to interpret the Bible historically. Against such a notion, he comments this is an argument foreign to his notion of revelation because,

> [S]ince long before the rise of modern historical criticism, devout believers approached the Scriptures fully confident of their revelational reliability, and they subscribed both to their historical fidelity and to the biblically given meaning of the redemptive acts as divinely authoritative. In short, reliance on the inspired Word of God took priority over reliance on an empirical approach.[38]

Believers of such an era are not condemned in Henry's view for their lack of historical inquiry. Yet, Henry does advocate for the historical competence of evangelical believers on the grounds "it would surely be destructive of evangelical faith were one to hold that the incarnation and resurrection of Jesus Christ are not matters of historical concern."[39]

At his core, Henry seeks to maintain the apologetic value of historical inquiry that results in a blending of hermeneutical and theological

---

36. Henry, *God, Revelation and Authority*, 2:315; and Henry, *Toward a Recovery*, 82. Henry states, "In investigating the articles of the Apostles' Creed, for example, historical criteria are much more serviceable to the confession that Jesus 'suffered under Pontius Pilate' than that 'he descended into hell' or that he is the Father's 'only Son, our Lord.' The impossibility of establishing theological doctrines by historical method is not here disputed. No amount of historical inquiry can prove that Jesus is the Christ, or that the Hebrews rightly believed that Yahweh rescued them from Egypt." Henry makes similar affirmations elsewhere as well.

37. Henry, *God, Revelation and Authority*, 4:394.

38. Ibid.

39. Ibid., 4:395.

apologetic at the connection point of biblical interpretation.[40] The role then of historical criticism is subservient to textually oriented hermeneutics. Henry makes this clear when he states,

> The course whereby Christianity first made its way in the world was charted not by an inerrant Bible but by God's mighty acts and revealed Word. We must avoid any impression that the inspired Scriptures basically create or contribute redemptive history. But that does not of itself mean that historical criticism can in no way be answerable to an inerrant Bible, in line with evangelical confidence in Scripture as the authoritative record and interpretation of divine revelation of whatever form. For it was the *Word*, not the event, that formed the divine truth in the minds of the Hebrews. By this we do not mean that the kerygma created the event, but that mute events cannot be understood. The *event* may indeed have led on to other events, but biblical religion, as an understood set of truths, can be derived only from the Word and not from the event.[41]

The place of historical inquiry then is one of convictional support for the historical importance of the Christian faith. If a reader is careful to liberate historical critical practices from "the arbitrary assumptions of critics who manipulate it in a partisan way," then historical criticism is useful in a limited role for investigating past historical events.[42]

In the final analysis, Henry balances his insistence on the historicity of Scripture that leads him to view historical criticism as viable for some purposes with the insistence that historical criticism may not "deal with questions concerning the supernatural or miraculous," that meaning must be found in the text because "[b]iblical events acquire their meaning from the divinely inspired Scriptures . . . since there could be no meaning of events without the events the inspired records carries its own intrinsic testimony to the factuality of those events."[43]

40. Ibid., 4:398. The inability of historical inquiry to produce absolute confirmation of historical knowledge, whether of earthly event or the spiritual significance of an earthly event, leads Henry to reliance on the biblical text. Concerning the limits of historical knowledge and the place of the text, Henry remarks, "[w]hat Jesus did and taught even with regard to his crucifixion, resurrection and final return is after all set forth in the Gospel records, and the narratives themselves adduce signs intended to validate his claim to a supernatural status and mission."

41. Ibid., 4:401.

42. Ibid.

43. Ibid., 4:403.

Carl Henry signals a clear direction hermeneutically for matters of revelation, history, and the biblical text when he asserts that attempts to understand divine revelation through historical inquiry rather than through the text of Scripture causes confusion. In Henry's words,

> The Bible manifests its unity therefore not simply in this sequence of dramatic divine acts, but also and especially in the meaning and purpose of God's redemptive activity disclosed to the inspired writers. It is not God's deeds alone, but especially God's Word, characterizing those deeds, that constitutes the unity of the Bible. To contemplate any act—the exodus or the exile, the crucifixion or the resurrection—apart from divine interpretation leads only to ambiguity and even confusion.[44]

With these words, Henry appears to draw a distinction between God's revelation through divine events and the textual revelation of those events based on accessibility. Henry thought it of value to describe God's divine historical acts as revelation, but he clearly views these acts of a different revelatory nature than the biblical text in that the textual revelation provides the divine meaning of historical event.

It is fitting with Henry's apologetic interests that he sought to maintain the category of revelation for divine historical act, based on his desire to link divine revelation to the personal God who is both transcendent and imminent. Yet, as real as God's divine interventions in history were, their meaning, and humanity's interaction with their meaning, is contingent on the fullness of revelation in the biblical text. Therefore, interpreting the acts of God through the written revelation of God illuminates and provides access to the redemptive purpose of the work of God in history. Through the work of God in history to redeem the rebellious, he makes clear the meaning of this plan through the revelation of the biblical text.[45]

Revelation and Truth

If one seeks to understand the hermeneutical framework for Carl Henry, he will not progress much if he has not reckoned with the role that the

---

44. Ibid., 4:469.

45. Henry provides several more clarifying paragraphs that consistently point to the simultaneous affirmations of: (1) the limited role of historical inquiry, and (2) the value of historical affirmations for the truth of the biblical text. In particular, see Henry, *God, Revelation and Authority*, 3:315–34.

category of truth holds in Henry's theology of revelation. The importance of this topic goes far deeper than just the assertions one makes regarding Scripture, but strikes at the root of Christianity. Henry states "The most critical question in the history of thought is whether all the convictional frameworks through which different peoples arrive at the meaning and worth of human life are by nature mythical, or whether perhaps at least one of these perspectives stems from divine revelation and has objective cognitive validity."[46]

The difference is immense for Henry, because it boils down to the difference of how one answers the question, "Is Christianity true?" Either individuals project upon the world and its history a spiritual reality that lacks universal application to all or "a transcendent divine reality through intelligible revelation establishes the fact that God is actually at work in the sphere of nature and human affairs."[47] In considering the nature of revelation and, therefore, how one understands Scripture, Henry acknowledges that the agenda is set by what one thinks he is exactly dealing with in terms of the biblical text.[48] Considering the nature of the biblical text leads Henry to draw a distinction between myth and true revelation.[49]

The significant distinction between myth and the biblical text "centers in the fact that the Gospels point to a definite period in time and space and describe real, historical situations."[50] The connection in Henry's scheme between revelation, history, and the biblical text already begins to become transparent with his emphasis on truth. According to Henry, to contend that a separation of the biblical text from historical or metaphysical referent

46. Ibid., 1:44.

47. Ibid., 1:45.

48. Ibid., 1:44. For Henry, it is not sufficient to hold to historical factuality concerning Scripture without attesting to the authority and significance of the Bible as the Word of God. Concerning the nature of truth and Scripture, Henry argues, "Dignifying the Bible as a unique or authoritative source of information about the biblical past . . . is very different from identifying it as a normatively definitive canon of Christian theological and ethical commitments."

49. Ibid., 1:51. Readers of Henry should note he is using the category of myth in a specific manner. Henry's use of the category is not identification of a literary genre per se, but an identification of what the scope of a text seems to intend. For Henry, varieties of genre may be identified as myth based in their intent, which is not expressly factual or intended to represent some category of truth. Conversely, Henry acknowledges varieties of genre in Scripture which are symbolic but non-mythical in that they make claim to truth. Henry makes this clear in his fourfold definition of the literary framework for myth.

50. Ibid., 1:49.

is problematic, because it undermines the text's value for communicating truth and "eclipses the objective truth significance of scriptural representations but also evades a rational critique of modern misrepresentations of the ultimately real world."[51]

The inability to adjudicate truth from falsehood, for Henry, ultimately leaves the interpreter in a wilderness with no navigation out of competing narratives. Henry states,

> If myth lacks objective cognitive validity and historical factuality, no reason can in fact be adduced why one myth should be considered either more or less expressive than others of nonfactual, noncognitive reality. How are we to distinguish between myths in terms of truth or falsity, in whole or in part, if myths are held to be neither cognitively nor historically informative? What valid reason remains for preferring one myth over another, or for not dismissing them all, or for not retaining them all as equally significant? No rational basis then exists for distinguishing between the various mythological representations of reality in respect to truth and adequacy.[52]

The connection to historical interest is strong on account that the stakes are high for Christianity if the truth-value of certain historical acts is not affirmed.[53]

Truth value is at the heart of Henry's approach to revelation, history, and the biblical text, and is why he surmises "[t]he question of literal or symbolical significance is not as decisively important for some religions as it is for Judeo-Christian revelation, which insists on the ultimate significance of certain past events—including the fact of the divine creation of man and the incarnation of God in Jesus Christ."[54] As will become clear through Henry's treatments of genre and truth, his intent is not to flatten literary features into factual reports, but he refuses to avoid the issue of truth in the discussion of revelation and history. On this issue, one hears

---

51. Ibid., 1:55.

52. Ibid., 1:64.

53. Ibid., 2:321. Henry further notes, "Christianity, if true, requires historical reality in its claims about the incarnation, atonement and resurrection of Jesus Christ, and indeed about God's revelation in earlier biblical history." Again, "The evangelists never promote faith in a person at the expense of historical factuality, for they themselves came to know Jesus of Nazareth not independently of historical realities but in and through his historical revelation."

54. Ibid., 1:68.

an ever-present apologetic refrain from Henry to his interlocutors—"But is it true?"[55]

Henry's Engagement with Canonical Theology

Carl Henry's engagement with the thought of Brevard Childs and his canonical theology project provides nuanced insight into Henry's view concerning history and the biblical text. Over thirty-two pages, Henry engages the major points of Childs's approach to the canon and its implications for biblical interpretation. At one point, Henry focuses on historical factuality in Childs's theology.[56] Henry is appreciative of Childs's willingness to qualify his respect for the historical-critical method.[57] For Childs, whatever light historical criticism brings to literary development, it is not "decisive for canonical authority and meaning."[58]

Henry is pleased that Childs puts distance between historical criticism and the biblical text by asserting the biblical text holds its own "implication of the historicity of redemptive acts and does so quite apart from any verdict by historical criticism."[59] This leads Henry to state, "This is an important distinction, one that I [Henry] have made also—although in a somewhat different way—in God, Revelation and Authority (Vol II, 1976, pp 330f.)."[60] The shared ground between Henry and Childs is that "Scripture authoritatively gives the meaning of the divine redemptive acts, which as historical events are not self-interpreting, it implies and presupposes the

---

55. Ibid., 1:69. To this point, Henry simply concludes, "Christianity adduces not simply mythical statements but factual and literal truth about God."

56. Engaging Henry's full appraisal of Childs and canonical theology is not within the scope of this study. However, Henry's comments toward canonical theology on matters of revelation, history, and the biblical text provide insight into his overall hermeneutical priorities.

57. Henry, "Canonical Theology," 104. "The emphasis that redemptive history is not self-interpreting is indeed wholly welcome. Evangelical theology affirms that inspired Scripture gives the meaning of these events. That Jesus died on the cross is historical fact; that Christ died for our sins is the event's revelatory significance as conveyed by Scripture."

58. Ibid., 100.

59. Ibid.

60. Ibid.

authenticity of those acts independently of empirical historical confirmation which as such is but tentative and never absolute."[61]

Yet, Henry's appraisal continues by wondering if Childs has not created too much separation between the biblical text and historical event by focusing on the community of the received canonical text as the locus for meaning. Henry questions, "[i]s Childs, in other words, promoting a canonical hermeneutic that so concentrates on the community of faith's canonical sense that it compromises historical factuality?"[62] Childs himself acknowledged the hesitancy evangelicals like Henry expressed even when they are eager to adopt parts of his canonical theology. Despite adoption, Childs notes concerning evangelical use of his scheme, "However, the caveat is quickly expressed that the historicity of the biblical accounts as the objectively verifiable foundation of the faith has been inadequately defended."[63]

Henry believes it most feasible to combine the emphases that: (1) "divine inspiration vouchsafes the reliability of biblical history," (2) that the "scripturally given meaning of redemptive acts supplies its own track of confidence in the factuality of those events," and (3) that biblical events are fair game for historical investigation "to the extent that they are alleged to be historical."[64] Henry's sticking point with Childs is his apparent unwillingness to embrace the historical reality and reliability of the historical acts on the grounds of biblical evidence. The centrality of the doctrine of revelation for Henry rises again when he claims, "apart from an explicit doctrine of revelation and inspiration, appeals to canonical teaching cannot decide the truth and factuality of the content of Scripture."[65] In this way, Henry's insistence on historical reality underlying the biblical text is not a historical claim as much as it is a theological claim about the doctrines of God and revelation. Such a theological claim to historical reality produces confidence that an interpreter may properly appeal to biblical authority (in texts claiming historical relevance) in support of historical claims just as he would with the Bible's theological and ethical teaching.[66]

61. Ibid., 100-101.

62. Ibid., 101. Thus, Henry worries that Childs has set a paradigm for the church pursuing the theological task in a way divorced from historical grounding.

63. Childs, *New Testament as Canon*, 543.

64. Henry, "Canonical Theology," 102.

65. Ibid., 103.

66. Ibid. Henry notes, "If, as Scripture attests, God reveals himself intelligibly and verbally, then it is credible that the writers of Scripture give us a God-breathed textual content that tells the truth about God and his purposes and actions. Behind the

In mediating the conversation between Henry and Childs, Stephen Chapman views Henry as compromising a text-oriented approach to Scripture by emphasizing the doctrine of inspiration. In Chapman's estimation, Henry's approach to revelation is to attribute the revelatory locus to the history behind the text rather than the text itself. The safer way for Chapman is to emphasize that it is not the "'raw' history that is the bearer of God's revelation," but rather the canonical text that provides the interpreted history as the locus of Divine revelation.[67] Chapman's critique is not as straightforward as it seems in light of the fact that Henry repeatedly affirms the text as the locus of revelation and the bearer of meaning concerning divine acts, including positive remarks toward Childs in this area.[68]

In the final analysis, Henry concludes Canonical Theology has five strengths and five weaknesses. Among the strengths, Childs is commended for text-centered emphasis on Scripture. As it relates to history, Child's strength is his reconnection of redemptive history with the biblical text through biblically given meaning rather than through historical events. The corresponding weakness Henry attempts to shore up is the potential ambiguity by Childs concerning the historical factuality of biblical events. Henry's concern is that Childs is susceptible to missing the importance of the idea that apart from "the historicity of biblical core events the Christian faith collapses."[69] In summary, Henry is affirming of much of Childs's approach and its hermeneutical implications; but at the same time, Henry is uncomfortable with Childs's apparent lack of apologetic concern for historical factuality because of its theological implications.

---

redemptive acts implicit in canonical interpretation stands the rational discourse and communication of God who authoritatively inscripturates his revealed truths and goals."

67. Chapman, "Reclaiming Inspiration," 187.

68. Ibid., 199. Chapman's critique of Henry is best understood in light of his affirmation of the alternatives set forward by Enns and Barth. Chapman states, "The full danger, as Enns and Barth both indicate, is that in reality the now traditional evangelical view of inspiration corrupts crucial knowledge about the Christian faith and life. How so? It communicates that human agency is too flawed for God to use, that God characteristically imposes rather than redeems, and that providence is incurably lame." It is a jump from Henry's caution against giving over historical realism to the conclusions Chapman draws, a jump most likely motivated by preference for an alternative model for revelation rather than chastening of Henry's comments concerning Childs. Further, it is noteworthy the footnotes in Chapman's interaction with Henry's approach to revelation and inspiration are almost exclusively in reference to Henry's article concerning canonical theology without account for Henry's wider body of work.

69. Henry, Canonical Theology, 107–08.

Faith and History as Apologetics

A crucial issue one encounters when delving into the relationship between historical matters and faith is the division in contemporary biblical studies between receptive faith and historical factuality. The issue, present in both Old Testament and New Testament studies, may be illustrated by Gerhard von Rad's methodological assertion that theologians should consider Israel's faith perspective as a community while secular historians may interpret historical factuality without the hypothesis of God.[70] The habit of many following an approach similar to von Rad's has been to focus on the redemptive faith of the biblical writers, while minimizing interest in the historical factuality of the revelatory events. The basic assertion is that the biblical texts are so shaped by faith reflection in their composition, redaction, and final form that they may not be taken at face value as historical record. The texts should remain the provenance of theological inquiry rather than historical inquiry.[71]

By contrast, Carl Henry is clear in his commitment that no distinction should occur between the faith representation of the biblical authors and the genuine historical setting.[72] It will be demonstrated in the following analysis that historical affirmation is not a matter of evidentiary argument for the Christian faith, but is tied to two pillars of Christianity throughout history—objective truth and the reliability of the testimony of Jesus Christ. Henry considers the relationship between faith tradition and factual history in *God, Revelation and Authority*, with a concern for apologetic affirmation of the biblical text. What Henry views as lost in the approach of von Rad is the genuine reliability of the faith representation provided in Scripture. For Henry, the interpretation contained in the biblical narratives is not arbitrarily imposed on the historical events, but "belongs to the history no

70. von Rad, *Old Testament Theology*.

71. The enduring impact of von Rad includes his argument that the various traditions of faith before the texts reached final form are a diversely layered collection of chapters of Israel's theology and the theologian should explore these layers.

72. Henry, *God, Revelation and Authority*, 2:330. Henry notes, "Christian faith requires not simply the redemptive historical act but its meaning or significance as well; historical research alone is impotent either to guarantee any past event or to adduce its meaning or theological import. On the other hand, the theological meaning of a historical act indispensably requires the act if we speak of such an act's significance. Revelation is the act plus its communicated meaning: both historical act and its interpretation belong to the totality of revelation. There would be no biblical meaning of the incarnation, crucifixion and resurrection of Christ apart from these historical redemptive acts."

less than the events themselves."[73] God's superintending over the revelation process means "[t]he act of God is not to be limited simply to isolated historical events as seen by critical historical research or to the confessional account of the meaning of history but includes also the transmission of the redemptive happenings and their meaning."[74]

Henry engages the work of Christopher North concerning the topic of world history versus salvation history. Henry notes that North roots meaning of the biblical events in the internal belief structure of Israel as a faith community rather than the events themselves. North states, "A nation's life and characters can be even more powerfully influenced by what it believes to have been its history than it is by events long past only 'remembered' as they are embodied in national tradition."[75] North's approach is problematic for Henry, because it leaves open the question as to what of the biblical content should qualify as factual history and what should be viewed as salvation history in terms of faith interpretation.

For Henry, it is unacceptable that these faith interpretations be held as true and authoritative when they may not be interpretations of real historical events. In the spirit of confidence in truth, Henry questions if one may believe with genuine conscience the faith representation of Scripture, while also giving over the historicity upon which the faith representation is based.[76] While North articulates comfort with a different kind of belief in faith tradition versus historical factuality, Henry will not follow.[77] Henry articulates his concern for historical truth when he states regarding the split between faith tradition and history, "[w]e are less interested in fundamentalist-nonfundamentalist controversy than in precisely identifying divine redemptive history that is more than simply divine redemptive tradition."[78]

73. Ibid., 2:268.

74. Ibid.

75. North, "History," 608.

76. Henry, *God, Revelation and Authority*, 4:331. Elsewhere Henry notes, "Yet if Moses and Isaiah in fact convey specific information about God's redemptive activity in the history of their times, and announce its meaning by divine inspiration—as Jesus declares them to have done—would not the loss of their trustworthy contemporary historical testimony to divine revelation have costly consequences for Hebrew-Christian faith?"

77. North, "History," 611. North states the dichotomy he perceives between historical fact and salvation history when he states, "[i]f we approach the question from the standpoint of Christian faith . . . our conclusion may be that the biblical interpretation of history is, at least in broad outline, right . . . The Geschichte, which produced the Bible is, take it by and large, only explicable in terms of the biblical *Heilsgeschichte*."

78. Henry, *God, Revelation and Authority*, 2:269.

The congruence of faith representation and historical factuality is an apologetic point for Henry in that it strikes at the claim to an objective foundation of revelation.[79] On the compromise of objective foundations for the truth of revelation, Henry notes "[t]he emphasis on faith-factors in interpretation tends to devalue the importance of external history, eclipse objective historical elements, and shift discussion of divine disclosure to internal considerations."[80] The compromise of historical factual foundation for revelatory events amounts to nothing less than a preference for revelation as internal experience.[81]

While Henry has in view intuitionist models for revelation, the same critique may be extended to preference for communitarian constructions of meaning, which may disregard historical factuality. Emphasis on historical revelation is not to argue that historical events are self-interpreting.[82] Henry is strident in asserting that the revelatory events likewise find their full explanation and meaning through chosen messengers, and this meaning is articulated through the written works of those authors.[83] The apologetic drive for Henry is evident in his insistence on historical genuineness as a key point in his larger assertion that divine disclosure is objectively true as opposed to "non-cognitively life transforming."[84]

Henry points to 1 Corinthians 15 as a place where the Apostle Paul put forward a set of historical truths that are necessary for Christian faith.[85] Henry cites approvingly MacKinnon who states,

79. Fackre, *Ecumenical Faith*, 177. Fackre captures Henry's apologetic drive well when he describes him as a theologian who views his task as clarifying the identity of Christianity and providing defense against the current alternatives.

80. Henry, *God, Revelation and Authority*, 2:271.

81. Ibid., 4:342. Henry further argues the place of historical verification as an apologetic concern when he states, "Since Judeo-Christian religion involves redemptive history, and forfeits credibility if the Bible lacks historical trustworthiness in the events it reports, it is important to show that destructive critical assaults on the reliability of the biblical representations do indeed lack a sound historical basis. Evangelical theologians do not use induction from archaeology to prove inerrancy; they use archaeology to exemplify the liberals' mistakes."

82. In a 1965 lecture, Henry had already offered a nuanced and developed scheme for the historical reality of Christianity, the necessity of biblical revelation to provide meaning to historical events, and that the historical reality of biblical events carries great apologetic weight. This lecture is published as Henry, "What Is Christianity?," 104–14.

83. Henry, *God, Revelation and Authority*, 2:271–75.

84. Ibid., 3:455.

85. The historical truths in view are the death, burial, and resurrection of Christ as

> If this [historical] foundation is ignored, or is treated as of little import, we shall surely find that we have lost precisely that which distinguishes Christianity from every other faith, namely its claiming, among its fundamental truth-conditions, the truth of propositions that might have been otherwise—and this as an aspect of its central affirmation that in human flesh and blood the ultimate secrets of God were disclosed . . . [86]

As an argument for the apologetic value of historicity, Henry points to the claims of Jesus for the historicity of the Old Testament redemptive acts. Since Jesus recognized the validity of historical works of God, to deny the accuracy of said events is to deny the credibility of Jesus. In an apologetic sense, Henry rests his case on the congruence of historical factuality with the teaching of Jesus. Therefore, to undermine historical events according to biblical representation is to compromise Christ as the truthful savior.[87]

The Nature of History

In discussing thesis seven, Henry attempts to reckon with the nature of history, making his case on what he perceives to be biblical grounds. The particular point Henry emphasizes is that biblical history is composed of the acts of God that take place in the very same realm as the history of peoples outside any relationship to God. First and foremost for Henry is that, just as God is the sole initiator of revelation, so he is the initiator of events in history that may be described as revelatory. For Henry, "Yahweh is a personally present guide who makes promises and keeps them, who communicates and 'covenants,' who does what is right and just, and who notably discloses himself in external historical acts and vindicates his promises in the external world."[88]

The relationship between revelation and history, therefore, is one in which revelation may not be isolated to inner-experience or self-referential literature, because to do so would be to exclude the interpersonal relationship of revelation that "involves public decisions and deeds—the promise of progeny and a land, the purchase of a burial place in the promised land for Sarah and other ancients in their time and stipulated relationships with

---

the fulfillment of Old Testament promises.

86. MacKinnon, *The Borderlands of Theology*, 87–88.

87. Henry, *God, Revelation and Authority*, 4:322.

88. Ibid., 2:249.

the Canaanites and Egyptians."[89] The biblical account of religion does not deny the reality of historical revelation, but views history as an indispensable part of Yahweh's revelation. Further, history is the "realm where Yahweh actively operates as a Redeemer and Judge."[90]

In Henry's view, no room exists for a duality between biblical history and world history.[91] Rather, the two are unified as one and the same plane of history and "the realm in which the living God intervenes of his own volition."[92] According to Henry's scheme, the fact that God acts in human history is a weighty presupposition of Scripture in both past revelatory aspects, as well as current faith relationships between God and humanity.[93] Henry claims this historical presupposition is a basic faith affirmation a believer makes by affirming that God is real and active, both past and present.[94]

While Henry does not assert the Bible provides a comprehensive or detailed historiography as it relates to world history and divine redemptive acts, the narrative of Scripture does provide grounding for important convictions concerning historiography. In Henry's view, Scripture sponsors its own historiography of sorts by providing presentations of distinct events as singular events in the governing purposes of God.[95] In contrast to the efforts of historians who attempt to find unifying principles in the isolated details of history, Henry views the Christian as possessing unique resources for historiography. The Bible reader is in an advantageous position because "[t]he Christian . . . derives his philosophy of history not by examining isolated events or from internal impressions, but from the Bible, that is, from divinely inspired writers who convey God's revealed purpose in human affairs."[96]

---

89. Ibid.

90. Ibid.

91. Ibid., 2:250. Henry also states, "The God of the Bible is the God of mighty deeds," and "Christ's death and resurrection are decisively central to historical fortunes."

92. Ibid., 2:251.

93. Ibid., 2:331. Concerning the unified nature of revelation in history and world history, Henry notes, "The Bible sets miraculous redemptive history and the secular world history in which it occurs in the context of two governing facts, namely, God's creation of the world and his final consummation and judgment of human affairs."

94. Ibid., 2:251.

95. Ibid., 2:313.

96. Ibid., 2:320.

Thornbury views Henry's articulation of historiography as privileging evangelicalism "in his contention not only that God reveals himself in history, but also that the very concept of history stems from biblical religion."[97] The role of historical reality for God's actions leads Henry to conclude the following:

> For the New Testament as for the Old, faith in the living God cannot be divorced from historical actualities. The Hebrew canon that records the history of the acts of Yahweh calls into question every rival understanding of ancient history; that record is carried forward by the New Testament. Both Testaments affirm the ongoing significance of the redemptive acts of God and their revealed meaning for man in all ages. The Old Testament, and the New Testament no less so, are at the same time a primary resource of redemptive faith and a historical sourcebook.[98]

For Henry, asserting a unified historiography is essential, because it is part and parcel with his vision of a God who is actively involved in the redemption of humanity in historical time and space.[99] Henry's theocentric construction of the nature of history leads to a reliance on theological convictions for discussing history. For Henry, if one has no center in God, then he has no universal vantage point from which to discuss history.[100] Revelation provides the knowledge of the Center and is, therefore, essential for the existence of history.[101]

97. Thornbury, *Recovering Classic Evangelicalism*, 82.

98. Henry, *God, Revelation and Authority*, 2:256.

99. Ibid., 3:312. The historical nature of Scripture is partially the result of the self-attestation of Scripture for Henry. He notes, "Later Israelites looked back to Moses and the exodus, and the Hebrew people insisted on the details of 1 and 2 Kings and 1 and 2 Chronicles as integral to a proper understanding of their past."

100. Ibid., 2:321. Henry asserts the superiority of biblical historiography when he states ". . . simply by reading the Bible conscientiously anyone can learn the meaning it attaches to crucial historical events; neither the study of archaeology nor of Ugaritic nor of world religions nor of the Vienna School of logical positivism is necessary for knowing the Christian philosophy of history. Alongside descriptive statements about men and nations, the Bible gives a theoretical or theological explanation of the events in its purview, and affirms that all men and nations are alike subject to one and the same sovereignty. Scripture combines testimony to historical acts with divine revelation concerning the meaning of those acts."

101. Fackre, *Ecumenical Faith*, 182. As Fackre notes, Henry's insistence on the historicity of the biblical text does not shade him into a revelation as history mindset. Fackre observes, "Although Henry shares with twentieth-century salvation history theologians this attention to the deeds of God and to the Christological center, he takes pains to

Transcendence and Immanence

On the surface, Henry's affirmations of historicity outlined in the previous section are largely congruent with several affirmations of the revelation as history approach. Given the strong place Henry gives to the divine presence in history as an aspect of revelation, one may perceive Henry to be opening the door to a form of pantheism in which historical manifestations of God, culture, and civilization directly reveal God. While agreeing upon the unified nature of history in concert with Pannenberg, Henry is careful to distinguish himself from Pannenberg's view by stating,

> But Judeo-Christian religion repudiates the theory found both in ancient paganism and in modern Hegelian pantheism that culture and civilization directly reveal the Divine . . . To say that God discloses himself in history, even in universal history, need not mean that human history expressly mirrors the inner life of the Absolute. To say that human history or national history is an aspect of "divine history" objectionably assimilates deity to the historical process and man to the Divine much as does pantheism.[102]

The mechanism by which Henry avoids the notion of pantheism is through returning to the biblical text as a conceptual resource for divine participation in world events. The specific resource Henry draws upon is the category of divine providence. He notes, for example, the Psalms echo that God has a purpose for Israel, and he reveals and brings about this purpose through many other nations. Similarly, Henry finds in the prophetic writings God's rule and intervention in universal history. In particular, "Jewish apocalyptic writing, notably the book of Daniel, prominently sets forth world history in relation to Yahweh's moral will."[103]

In this view of providence, Scripture teaches "[a]ll historical events are subject to his overruling omnipotence and inescapably serve his intended ends; even the untoward actions of wicked men are made

---

distinguish his view from those who would (1) reduce the Bible to the recounting of divine deeds, (2) polarize Jesus Christ with scriptural teaching considered less worthy, (3) understand the prophetic and apostolic interpretation of the deeds of God as only human formulations secondary in significance of the deeds, (4) isolate some deeds and interpretations a trustworthy core with an errant context, or (5) argue for a canon within the canon (II, III, IV). Revelation is the whole cloth of the Bible, not a red thread within it, albeit set forth progressively in the historical flow of the Bible (II, III)."

102. Henry, *God, Revelation and Authority*, 2:248.

103. Ibid., 2:251.

sovereignly instrumental to God's purposes of redemptive grace and triumphant righteousness."[104] Included in the providence of God over history is God's ability to use one who opposes his righteousness to accomplish his purposes, of which Nebuchadnezzar and the Babylonian exile serve as prime examples.[105] The emphasis on divine providence similarly extends to the most significant of historical-redemptive acts for Christianity—the death, burial, and resurrection of Christ. Henry points to the manner in which, through providence, the biblical authors ascribed the spiritual meaning of the Christ-event by attributing the historical death of Christ to the plan and foreknowledge of God in Acts 2:23.[106]

In emphasizing the historical realm and correspondence of Scripture to world history, Henry effectively avoids reducing history to the locus of meaning because the events do not provide the perspective of divine providence. Rather, the literary-theological framing of the events in the biblical narratives supply their divine meaning. Henry states concerning the Bible as a sourcebook of genuine historical fact that provides interpretive framework, "[t]hat sourcebook speaks of history as a moral arena in which the God of creation and redemption and final judgment is even now rewarding righteousness and judging evil in anticipation of an irreversible end-time."[107]

In the midst of asserting that the plane of redemptive-historical acts is level with that of world history, Henry acknowledges the need to justify the distinctive nature of biblical history. It is as if Henry is concerned to answer the question—has he made redemptive historical history too level with world history? This might carry the implications of naturalistic explanations for biblical history or that biblical redemptive history is really no different from other religious claims to the activities of the gods in human affairs. As a representative, one could follow Bertil Albrektson in

104. Ibid., 2:254.

105. Ibid. Henry notes the significance of the connection between biblical history and world history at the nexus of God's providence when he speaks of the Babylonian exile. Henry notes Israel's defeat by pagan powers on the world stage "is declared by Jeremiah to be Yahweh's act. Nebuchadnezzar, in fact, is depicted as Yahweh's servant (Jer. 25:9). To resist the Babylonian armies storming Jerusalem's gates is to resist the very will of God (21:5). Yahweh rewards the king of Babylon with Egypt for his service to Yahweh in punishing Tyre (Ezek. 29:18-19). The words of Amos ring out the theme: 'Shall evil befall a city, and the Lord hast not done it?' (3:6, ASV)."

106. Ibid., 2:255.

107. Ibid., 2:256.

his assertions that the history of Israel is really simply on par with other ancient claims to divine activity and revelation in history.[108] One point of accusation against the Christian historical claim is that the Bible provides little concern for aspects of history outside of its religious concerns. From this perspective, texts which mediate only their closed sets of concern without substantive setting in history outside themselves are much more prone to be viewed as mythical.

In light of his emphasis on the biblical-theological framework for historical events, Henry acknowledges the reality that the Old Testament in particular is not immediately concerned with a full explanation of historical setting. Yet, he argues that to take this perceived lacuna as justification for dismissing the historical quality of the text is misguided on a few counts. First, perspectives such as Albrektson's are operating from a prejudiced view about "the nature, sources, or sequence of the biblical writings," which prevents one from acknowledging the proper weight of historical orientation.[109]

Second, such a perspective is out of step with the nature of the biblical texts as Henry asserts the "Old Testament writers refer repeatedly to God's activity in history, the Gospels speak of God's providential and redemptive involvement in the world. Hence it would be more correct to say that from the Christian standpoint any denial that God is sovereignly active in history reflects a basic departure from the classic texts."[110] In other words, the biblical texts themselves leave no room for an articulation that they are merely mythical writings of a certain time period. It is to go against the nature of the literature itself as a reader to overlook the claim to unique historical interaction by God.

The discussion at-hand has material significance for a view of revelation built upon the insistence of God's initiative in personal disclosure in human affairs. To conclude:

> That the redemptive historical-act form was simply an Israelite way of thinking is then reinforced by the insistence that representations of a worldwide flood or of Noah's ark or of Jonah and the leviathan are really legendary accounts and not to be considered

108. Albrektson, *History and the Gods*. Albrektson has specifically in mind that Hebrew claims to the activity of God are no different than the expected list of ancient Mesopotamian religions and their texts such as the Enuma Elish.

109. Henry, *God, Revelation and Authority*, 2:258.

110. Ibid.

factual. What therefore began as an emphasis on divine saving acts ends in the reduction of biblical religion to a literary rather than historical representation.[111]

In arguing for a unified concept of history and revelation, Henry does not present an immanentist perspective in which the divine is found in culture as some form of pantheism. Moreover, he is not compromising the distinction of redemptive-historical acts attested to in Scripture as particular acts connected to special revelation in their literary representation.[112]

Test of History: Positive or Negative?

In his interest for the historical factuality of Scripture, Henry resists the need to view historical confirmation as a positive test for interpretation. Henry notes, "[a]rchaeology, of course, has not and will not confirm all details of biblical history, and it cannot in any event confirm invisible realities of the spiritual world and revelational truths."[113] Henry continues by observing that, while archaeological discoveries trend toward confirming biblical reliability, historical verification need not become an essential element of interpretive process. Henry's confidence in the biblical text simultaneously does not fall into simple pietistic rejection of critical scholarship. His balance is noteworthy when he states,

> In actuality there need be no objection to historical criticism or to form criticism per se. Various literary forms do exist in the Bible and as such are serviceable to preserving the Word of God; they do not by any inherent necessity either erode or destroy it. What's more, Judeo-Christian religion has nothing to fear from truly scientific historical criticism. What accounts for the adolescent fantasies of

111. Ibid., 2:263.

112. Ibid., 2:265. Against any claim that ancient Israelite religion is simply an ancient Semitic counterpart to other alternatives, Henry provides his criterion for distinction. He states, "One can assuredly parallel bits and pieces of Old Testament religion here and there in the ancient Semitic world. Even in this respect we must be on guard against confusing etymological similarity with theological identity, since conceptual use and intention rather than linguistic form are decisive for meaning. The differences are often more striking than the similarities—the absence of pure monotheism amid the emphasis on the uniqueness of certain divinities, the mechanistic rather than personalistic conceptions of predestination and destiny, the absence of absolute creation in so-called creation accounts, and so on."

113. Ibid., 4:79.

biblical criticism are not its legitimate pursuits but its paramour relationships with questionable philosophical consorts.[114]

Embracing critical scholarship on an apologetic level is not troublesome for hermeneutical engagement with the text to Henry, because the two are capable of operating in their spheres of interest. He notes first concerning the apologetic nature of historicity, "Christian redemption is admittedly suspended on historical factualities. Not only the Chronicler but also Moses and Luke, among others, used extensive sources."[115] Then, in the same flow of thought, Henry supports the historical nature of Christian faith with comment about the state of historical inquiry and biblical authority. In response to the stripe of critical theory that states historical factuality and faith representation are two separate concerns, he states, "according to the indicated theory, must not every historical assertion be considered unsure unless and until it is independently verified? The theory provides no secure basis for discerning where in the revelational history the inspired writings inerrantly report their errant sources and where they inerrantly report the truth."[116]

Moisés Silva illustrates the significance of choosing between a positive or negative test of history for biblical hermeneutics. He observes that, in general, everywhere it seems the historical claims of the book of Acts may be verified it fares well. Yet, most contemporary scholarship maintains the book is not factually true, in large part, based on perspective that much of it may not be proven true.[117] Concerning the impact of the test of history on one's hermeneutics Silva notes, "it should be marked, the impasse arises because of *the scholars' perception as to where the burden of proof lies.*"[118]

114. Ibid., 4:81.

115. Ibid., 4:180.

116. Ibid.

117. Ibid., 4:397. Henry tempers the role of historical inquiry and the possibility of a positive test for historicity when he states, "Whether one believes that Jesus Christ arose bodily from the dead in the first century (or whether one does not so believe) does not decisively depend upon factors empirically accessible to twentieth-century historians, who possess no strategic advantage over critical witnesses contemporaneous with the actual happenings. The verdict of historical criticism as a scientific technique can in no case be final and absolute; its conclusions have at best a hypothetical character, even if many who appeal to it tend to speak in absolute terms of its fruits. Historical investigations in no case leads beyond a very high degree of probability, although this no more disadvantages biblical history than any other."

118. Silva, "The Place of Historical Reconstruction," 132.

Henry's challenge of the legitimacy of a required positive test for biblical interpretation is counterweighted by his insistence that historical inquiry is of value for the believer. Henry notes, "In assessing historical questions, the evangelical scholar introduces biblical data as reliable evidence in the absence of persuasive contrary evidence; he is not called upon to short-circuit historical evaluation by appealing either to the inspiration of the witnesses or to his personal faith."[119]

Critiques of Carl Henry

As a figurehead for a particular theological approach, Carl Henry has not been immune from critique. The critiques of Henry tend to focus in an area highly relevant for his approach to revelation, history, and the biblical text—the interaction of epistemology and revelation in his theological method. The critiques of Henry relevant to this subject may be summarized in two categories: propositional revelation and modernist/rationalist epistemology.

Propositional Revelation

One of Carl Henry's consistent refrains is that the Bible as God's revelation is composed of intelligible propositions that communicate reality about God and the world. For example, see thesis ten in *God, Revelation and Authority*, in which Henry argues the fundamental nature of revelation is missed if the propositional nature is abandoned.[120] The absence of propositions is significant for revelation and history, because Henry's idea is that propositions in written Scripture correspond to reality, whether talking about the person of God in spiritual matters or seemingly mundane references to history. Along these lines, everything claimed in Scripture has a truth-value. Henry notes early in *God, Revelation and Authority*, that "the fundamental issue remains the issue of truth, the truth of theological assertions . . . Durable theology must revive and preserve the distinction between true and false religion."[121]

---

119. Henry, *God, Revelation and Authority*, 4:336.

120. Ibid., 2:12. Thesis ten states "God's revelation is rational communication conveyed in intelligible ideas and meaningful words, that is, in conceptual-verbal form."

121. Ibid., 1:14.

In theological terms, either Jesus is divine and Lord of all creation or he is not. In historical terms, either Jesus lived, died, and was raised or he did not. Each of the propositional claims of Scripture make a demand of the reader to either invest intellectual affirmation or denial, if not at least some provisional decision on the spectrum of these two conclusions. As will be discussed in Henry's interactions with Hans Frei in chapter four, the correspondence of propositional claims to actual historical event is for Henry a measure of truth-value. Henry's insistence on the propositional aspect of revelation has been perhaps the sharpest point of critique brought against him in modern theology, and this critique extends to his insistence on historical correspondence.

One stream of critique surrounding Henry's propositionalism is a product of the postmodernist critique of language, by which some theologians assert an emphasis on the Bible as propositional revelation is problematic.[122] Alistair McGrath offers critique of Henry by stating: "Any means of revelation which regards God's self-disclosure as the mere transmission of facts concerning God is seriously deficient, and risks making God an analogue of a corporate executive who disperses memoranda to underlings."[123]

While perhaps expressing personality alongside critique of Henry's actual theology, this critique captures the spirit of those theologians suspicious of propositional models for revelation. The Bible as a personal book oriented by-and-large around narrative is inadequately handled when it is reduced to a storehouse of facts to be used as the building blocks for theology. McGrath drives this point when he states evangelicals have "laid too much emphasis upon the notion of a purely propositional biblical revelation."[124] In McGrath's estimation, it is healthier to open one's view to the idea that "Revelation concerns the *oracles* of God, the *acts* of God, and the *person and presence* of God."[125]

For McGrath, the critique of propositional revelation is tied closely to his parallel critique of Enlightenment variety rationalism, of which he

122. Ramm, *After Fundamentalism*, 26–27. Ramm critiques Henry on the basis that he reasserts a traditional paradigm for Evangelical theology without dealing sufficiently with the implications of the Enlightenment. Specifically, Ramm views Henry as glossing significant developments in approach to cognitive understanding of language and biblical criticism.

123. McGrath, *Passion for Truth*, 106.

124. Ibid., 108.

125. Ibid., 107.

views Henry to be a participant. McGrath's approach to truth is to eschew the idea that truth is defined in terms of correspondence to reality. He strongly states, "It is a travesty of the biblical idea of 'truth' to equate it with the Enlightenment notion of conceptual or propositional correspondence, or the derived view of evangelicalism as proclamation of the propositional correctness of Christian doctrine."[126] In his appropriation of postmodernism for evangelical theology, McGrath is equating all views which utilize propositions and correspondence with Enlightenment rationalism. As will be demonstrated in a following discussion concerning critique of Henry as a modernist in his epistemology, this monolithic critique may not always be fair and accurate to Henry's actual writings.

Concerning the nature of language and propositional approach to revelation, Kevin Vanhoozer has provided thorough critique and constructive argument. Noting the complexities of language and the perceived simplicity of a propositional approach, he states, "Rightly or wrongly, biblical propositions are often caught between the Scylla and Charybdis of lexical and literary semantics."[127] The difficulty for Vanhoozer, which prevents him from embracing Henry's approach to propositions, lies in the fact that the system presents propositions as distinct from and in the background of words, phrases, and sentences—or in other words, apart from the text. What becomes important to theologians is not the text itself, but the propositions to be mined to the surface from the text.[128]

Vanhoozer picks up on Henry's definition of a proposition "as generally understood, a proposition is a verbal statement that is either true or false."[129] With Henry's assertion that a proposition is defined by an external truth-value, Vanhoozer critiques him on grounds of leading away from the biblical text.[130] In critique of Henry's propositionalism, Vanhoozer offers,

---

126. Ibid., 177.

127. Vanhoozer, "Semantics of Biblical Literature," 55.

128. Vanhoozer, "Lost in Interpretation," 96.

129. Henry, God, Revelation and Authority, 3:456.

130. Vanhoozer, "Lost in Interpretation," 99. Vanhoozer notes, "Evangelicals must not let a particular theory of truth and factuality determine what the author of Genesis 1–11 is proposing for our consideration. It is the text, not some theory of truth, that ought to determine what kind of a claim is being made. To begin with a theory of truth and argue to a particular interpretation is to put the factual cart before the hermeneutical horse. This was Bultmann's mistake: he assumed that the Bible's truth was existential and then set about to demythologizing it. Let us not make a similar mistake and run roughshod over authorial intent in our haste to historicize."

"Only a portion of the Bible seems to qualify as "propositional," understood in its philosophical sense. However, Henry's loose use of "propositional" to refer to rational-verbal communication in general is one way of refuting the serpent's spurious insinuation that God did *not* say."[131] The concern and critique offered here is that this type of propositionalism will lead to, instead of revealing the biblical text, "deriving a set of propositions in a precise discursive language and calling *these* the 'biblical propositions.'"[132] This scheme leads to a type of dogmatism that the truth is "available and within grasp."[133]

A strong theory for correspondence poses a particular problem for Vanhoozer when he states about Henry, "For the biblical record to 'correspond' to historical fact, it must be read as containing assertions about the past. Is there a possibility that 'what is said' has been collapsed into 'what is asserted,' so that every sentence of Scripture is read as fact-stating and proposition-conveying?"[134] Utilizing the *Chicago Statement on Hermeneutics*, Articles VI and XIV, Vanhoozer casts doubt on the correspondence of literary text to historical fact.[135]

Vanhoozer's doubt is built on the ground of questions concerning the nature of language, meaning, and truth put forward by Ludwig Wittgenstein as the father of Ordinary Language Philosophy.[136] In a similar vein as Frei, Vanhoozer finds linguistic philosophy as appropriate grounding for the repudiation of propositionalism as too closely aligned with the positivism of Wittgenstein's earlier career.[137] Wittgenstein's critique of positivism, as Vanhoozer applies it to Henry, is that propositionalism provides a "picture" view of language in which a text merely points to the propositions

131. Vanhoozer, "Semantics of Biblical Literature," 63.

132. Ibid.

133. Ibid.

134. Ibid., 64.

135. Vanhoozer, "Lost in Interpretation," 98. In particular Vanhoozer points to Articles VI, XIV, and XXII as weak points on account of the affirmations to the correspondence of the biblical text to factuality.

136. Ibid., 96. Vanhoozer draws upon Wittgenstein's philosophical development from early in his career as a positivist to later in his career as a language philosopher. Specifically, Vanhoozer draws upon Wittgenstein's later argument that language provides the only access to meaning and, therefore, Vanhoozer concludes the biblical text should not be thought of as inadequate in any of its literary forms.

137. Ibid., 99.

behind it. For Vanhoozer, this leads to a tenuous place for evangelicals when he states,

> This "picture" view of language and meaning would seem to ne-
> cessitate an unpalatable corollary for Evangelicals, namely, that
> there is some imperfection in Scripture, that God could have
> revealed His propositions with greater perspicuity—an idea that
> would have surprised the Reformers. Should theologians *analyze*
> what is said in Scripture and seek the exactness of the proposi-
> tion, or should they *describe* what is said and respect the ordinary
> language?[138]

Vanhoozer takes issue with propositionalism of Henry's stripe again through the ICBI Summit II by critiquing articles X and XIII. For Vanhoozer, even though some statements acknowledge textual features requiring nuance, such as genre variations, these acknowledgements are insufficient, and a strong statement for historicity "is to ride roughshod over the issue of literary genres."[139] While Vanhoozer's critique strikes at an important issue that could find stronger articulation in Henry's theology, he is perhaps not representing all of the substance of Henry's writings.[140]

What Vanhoozer has identified, however, is a concern important to Henry and other neo-evangelical theologians who emphasized proposi-tions—apologetic emphasis. Vanhoozer clearly identifies the apologetic subtext for Henry's theological concern in the setting of modern theology when he states,

> The variety of literary forms is herein smoothed over to ensure
> the unity of historicity. Clearly, some other principle seems to be
> guiding the statement's attitude toward biblical propositions than
> that of recognizing literary genre. It is, we suggest, an apologetic
> rather than hermeneutical interest that dictates that historicity
> take precedence in spite of the variety of literary forms.[141]

Vanhoozer at least acknowledges that Henry attempted to affirm that truth and literary genres are not mutually exclusive. Yet, the friction for

---

138. Vanhoozer, "Semantics of Biblical Literature," 67.

139. Ibid., 68.

140. In particular, Vanhoozer does not note the literary focus Henry takes with refer-ence to meaning when it comes to the nature of revelation, history, and the biblical text. Further, Henry's critics do not engage the role of the Holy Spirit in the interpreter which Henry acknowledges as significant in biblical interpretation.

141. Ibid.

Vanhoozer remains in that he views Henry as still partial to the simple declarative statement when he cites Henry as saying: "[r]egardless of the parables, allegories, emotive phrases and rhetorical questions used by these writers, their literary devices have a logical point which can be propositionally formulated and is objectively true or false."[142]

Even Henry's acknowledgement that "literary forms are not merely ornamental trappings of truth content, but that they have a positive contribution to make in God's revelatory communication" is insufficient for his critics. Henry's critics are likely not appeased, because he believes that all of Scripture communicates about God, so therefore the basic value of literary devices "lies not simply in their capacity to move us but more fundamentally in what they presumably tell us about God."[143] The reliance on Scripture as fundamentally informative is ill-fitting for Vanhoozer, because it "is to invoke the wrath of literary critics who view poetry and other literary forms as other than informative."[144] Vanhoozer holds forward Hans Frei as an exemplar for a theology that relies on literary critical theories rather than the propositional scheme of Henry and the ICBI summits. Rather than claim a descriptive text is true because of its correspondence to an external reference, he holds "a work of literature has another criterion for truth: inner verbal consistency."[145]

For Frei, anything other than an *exclusively* non-referential approach to textual meaning is to undermine the locus of the meaning in the text. The truth value of the text as it relates to history, therefore, is not to ask the question "did this event happen as the text implies?" but is closer to "does this account cohere with the internal features of the text?" Vanhoozer sides with Frei in his insistence that "it is the biblical narrative itself, not its propositional paraphrase, that is the truth-bearer. Whereas for Henry doctrines state the meaning of the narratives, for Frei we only understand the doctrine by understanding the story."[146] The issue with Vanhoozer's description of Henry's approach to hermeneutics is that his description

142. Henry, *God, Revelation and Authority*, 3:453 cited in Vanhoozer, "Semantics of Biblical Literature," 69.

143. Henry, *God, Revelation and Authority*, 4:120.

144. Vanhoozer, "Semantics of Biblical Literature," 69. Notice here that the options are reduced to a binary set in which one must choose either communicative function or affective function of the literary works. The argument may be made that Henry preserves room for both, and it is Vanhoozer who eliminates one of the options.

145. Ibid., 72.

146. Vanhoozer, "Lost in Interpretation," 99.

does not fit much of what has been described by Henry's own words in the previous parts of this chapter where it has been demonstrated Henry's affirmation is that only through textual narration is the meaning of the text given.[147]

Vanhoozer ultimately takes this challenge to the referential nature of literature as a justification for rejecting Henry's approach to history and the biblical text. Vanhoozer views "the challenge to propositional or cognitive revelation, therefore, comes not only from theologians but also from professional literary critics who question whether literature functions to inform."[148] It is peculiar that the informative function of the text is bracketed out on account of literary form. Vanhoozer's scheme leads one to ask why it is the case that literature, whatever its form, may not serve an informative-cognitive function while also producing the ascetic-affective benefits of literature? This view of cognitive-propositional reference for literature accuses Henry as committing to the idea that "literary forms are merely ornamental gilding" rather than thinking that literary shape is essential to meaning.[149] One wonders if a caricature is under critique with this assessment rather than taking Henry at his own words and practice as a biblical interpreter.[150]

---

147. Ibid., 100. Vanhoozer continues the critique of Henry's interpretive approach by stating, "To interpret the Bible truly, then, we must do more than string together individual propositions like beads on a string. This takes us only as far as fortune cookie theology, to a practice of breaking open Scripture in order to find the message contained within. What gets *lost* in propositionalist interpretation are the circumstances of the statement, its poetic and affective elements, and even, then a dimension of truth." While some propositionalist interpreters, either contemporaries of Henry or those who came after, very well may not have represented the neo-evangelical approach to hermeneutics as well as Henry and therefore warrant Vanhoozer's critique; this statement is not a fair assessment of Henry individually.

148. Vanhoozer, "Semantics of Biblical Literature," 72.

149. Ibid.

150. Ibid., 75. Concerning apparent prejudice against genres and the illusory nature of historical veracity, Vanhoozer notes, "The genres that prove most worrisome to Evangelicals include legend, myth, midrash, and saga—genres that appear *prima facie* to vitiate Scripture's truthfulness. But even to read the Bible as history (as many biblical critics do) does not guarantee its truthfulness, for many liberal critics conclude that the Bible presents *false* history. One's reading of Scripture, then, ought not to harbor prejudices against some literary genres out of a concern for what the truth 'must' be. This is the only way to avoid criticisms such as John Barton's that claim that Fundamentalists are seldom students of the humanities and mainly read nonfiction and that *consequently they do not know how to read the Bible*."

Henry argues that meaning and form are indeed inextricably tied (in agreement with Frei). The distinction for Henry comes in that there is always a "something" communicated by the text because the biblical text is communication from God. According to Henry, poetic texts are intended to move the reader in affective ways, but this movement is not void of genuine knowledge of God. Often the cognitive element is considered to be one and the same with the non-cognitive effect the piece of biblical literature aims to produce. For Henry, the problem with their view arises when one seeks to have one without the other, affective movement without cognitive content.

The criticism that Henry's referential interest in history and the biblical text fails because all of Scripture may not be reduced to texts intended to inform is not a defeater for Henry's approach. He makes significant room in the nature of Scripture as divine revelation for the Bible to contain theological and personal reflection on historical events that convey the divine meaning of these events and aim to produce a response on the part of the reader. To assume that all of Scripture is reduced to a historical reference work is to mischaracterize Henry's approach to reference.[151] Yet at the same time, Henry maintains that without affirmation that the text speaks of things objectively true in the history of the world (where it does claim to refer), the theological and devotional reflections of the biblical authors is all for naught. The emptiness of a totally non-referential approach to Scripture is that the Christian faith does not leave room for faith and devotion to God, based on his self-cohering works within a narrative structure. One must believe Christ lived, died, was buried, and raised in a real sense, not just as a legend of special status.

Historicity and Authority

Moisés Silva observes that for "some conservative Christians, certainty about historical details appears to be inseparable from a high view of Scripture."[152] This approach could tempt one into viewing all of Scripture through the lens of historical referent, and requiring a positive test of history for valid belief and utilizing the biblical text itself as the criterion for

151. Trueman, "Admiring the Sistine Chapel," 56. Trueman argues that Henry's arguments do not truly represent a reduction of the Bible to a set of propositions, but that Henry's point is more nuanced than conveyed by much criticism of Henry.

152. Silva, "Place of Historical Reconstruction," 111.

the positive test. Though Henry would agree that historical affirmation is important for faith, he would likewise share in Silva's observation that, hardly anything is more significant to the Christian faith than the "historicity of Jesus' life, death, and resurrection, yet no one knows for sure the date of Jesus' birth nor the year of His death and resurrection."[153]

This observation raises the question as to what kind of historicity is being affirmed and what impact the scope of the biblical text has on affirming historicity. Stated simply, to affirm the historical reality of the biblical text in terms of referent is not to collapse all literary features into encyclopedic report and to treat all texts as such hermeneutically. Rather, the historical emphasis of Scripture is valid in those places "where Scripture speaks directly and unambiguously on the historical question involved."[154] In other words, the interwoven nature of literature (whether prose, poetry, narrative, etc. . . .) and the theological purposes of the text leave the reader with the responsibility to handle the text wisely on matters of history.[155] To do so, according to Henry, is to acknowledge Scripture's intent to do much more than convey intellectual content about history, yet the theological and affective features of the text must rest on a historically real referent.[156]

Vanhoozer leverages the likes of Abraham Kuyper and C. S. Lewis against Henry. Citing Kuyper as in opposition to propositionalism, he points to Kuyper's statement, "The rationale for the diverse literary forms in Scripture is that revelation strikes all the chords of the soul, and not just one, e.g., the rational one. This makes it clear that the historical doctrine of revelation is not the barren propositional one it is often charged with being."[157] Similarly, after several paragraphs of interacting with C. S.

153. Ibid.

154. Ibid.

155. Thornbury, *Recovering Classic Evangelicalism*, 114; and Trueman, "Admiring the Sistine Chapel," 58. Thornbury acknowledges at least some ground for the validity of Vanhoozer's critique when he acknowledges, "Henry was so focused on maintaining evangelical affirmations that he downplayed the richness of language and its setting in canonical linguistic form. Vanhoozer is also correct that language does more theologically than Henry allows." Similarly, while mostly an apologist for Henry against his critics, Trueman acknowledges that developments in hermeneutics do indeed leave Henry inadequate on some points.

156. Henry, "Priority of Divine Revelation," 83. Henry states himself that not all biblical content is propositional when he states, "[w]hile the evangelical view insists on the inerrancy of the whole, it does not conceive every declarative sentence as necessarily conveying revealed information."

157. Vanhoozer, "Semantics of Biblical Literature," 78.

Lewis' ideas Vanhoozer concludes, "Lewis the Christian reader had an appreciation for both the propositional, or rational, truth-bearing function and the non-propositional, or imaginative, reality bearing function of good literature."[158] It is encouraging at this point that Vanhoozer seems to be holding both functions of the biblical text in balance rather than as binary opposite, but how this serves as a critique of Henry is unclear.[159]

Henry indeed sounds consistent with Lewis and Kuyper when he discusses the nature of literary features in textual revelation.[160] For example, one must consider the following, which comes as part of substantive discussion in *God, Revelation and Authority*, thesis twelve, *The Spirit as Communicator*. Concerning the variety and unity of the Bible as literature, Henry states,

> To be sure, when we turn to the canon to find the unity of the Bible, we are met at once by a variety of literary content unlike any ever gathered within any single book claiming to be a literary unity: historical books, prophetic writings, psalms, wisdom literature, Gospels, Epistles, and so on. These writings came moreover from authors living centuries and even millennia apart. The unity of the Bible is not to be found in its literary genres nor in its human writers. It is found in the message and meaning of the book, namely, that the living sovereign God stands at the beginning of the universe. . . .[161]

The takeaway of Vanhoozer's critique of concern for historical referent may be summarized in four implications for exegesis and theology:

1. God reveals himself in the Bible through inscribed discourse acts.

158. Ibid.

159. Ibid., 79. Vanhoozer rightly supports what he views to be Lewis's suggestion that "two biblical passages may not be inerrant in exactly the same way; that is, not every biblical statement must state historical truth. Inerrancy must be construed broadly enough to encompass the truth expressed in Scripture's poetry, romances, proverbs, parables—as well as histories."

160. Henry, "Priority of Divine Revelation," 83. Henry's statements in some ways are not as distinct as Vanhoozer would seem to convey. For example, in response to similar critique from Avery Dulles, Henry states, "The propositional view does indeed regard the whole body of Scripture as grounded in revelation, as verbally inspired, and as conveying divine truths in the form of revelatory sentences. But that does not necessarily imply that every declarative sentence in the Bible, unless contrary can be shown from the context, is to be taken as expressing a revealed truth."

161. Henry, *God, Revelation and Authority*, 4:468.

2. Exegetes should not make a priori decisions about biblical genres.

3. Scripture does many things with words and hence its authority is multifaceted.

4. Infallibility means that Scripture's diverse illocutionary forces will invariably achieve their respective purposes.[162]

In these affirmations, though vocabulary certainly varies based on differing philosophical influence, Vanhoozer is not far from Henry's affirmations outlined earlier in this chapter.[163] Vanhoozer's attempt has been, as an evangelical, to rescue the evangelical agenda from extra-biblical philosophical influences of modernism. This desire is noble, and it has been demonstrated that, even though some of the critique is amiss, the end product is similar to what Henry desired. The interesting piece about Vanhoozer's critique and proposed solution is that he proposes replacing one extra-biblical modernist philosophical influence (propositional realism) with another extra-biblical post-modernist philosophy (Ordinary Language Philosophy and Speech-Act Theory).[164] While Vanhoozer views this as a surer foundation for biblical exegesis, one wonders if the thoroughly non-referential nature

---

162. This list is provided in condensed form by the author from Vanhoozer, "Semantics of Biblical Literature," 93–94.

163. Thornbury, *Recovering Classic Evangelicalism*, 108. In light of Vanhoozer's critiques, Thornbury sees Henry's assertion of propositionalism to be more modest than it is made out to be by Vanhoozer. Thornbury comments, "Although Vanhoozer wants to move theology away from a 'cognitive-propositional' method and toward a genre-informed approach, it is still hard to see how one escapes the inevitable return to the sentences that describe a state of affairs in which some thing or attribute is predicated of a subject, linked by the verbal form 'to be.' This is, I think, all that Carl Henry was really trying to say . . ."

164. Vanhoozer, "Semantics of Biblical Literature," 103. Vanhoozer writes, "Our proposed rejuvenation of the concept of infallibility set forth here preserves the substance of the above-mentioned definition of 'inerrancy' and at the same time puts the semantics of biblical literature on the surer ground of a speech act philosophy of language and literature that does fullest justice to the notion of 'not liable to fail.' Our understanding of infallibility is thus in profound agreement with earlier statements of inerrancy (i.e., the Ligonier statement and the Chicago statement) even while moving beyond them. Our proposed view of infallibility assumes the concept of inerrancy and expands to cover (in a secondary sense) all God's speech acts and all Scripture's literary forms, rather than having application only to direct affirmations or the 'philosophical propositions' extracted from Scripture."

of Speech Act Theory does not leave him open for the same critiques Henry makes of Hans Frei.[165]

Modernist Epistemology

As a general critique, Henry is sometimes perceived as a modernist in his epistemology in the sense that he is a rationalist. This high-level criticism is the product of combined criticism related to his use of propositional categories, his insistence that revelation contains cognitive rational content, and that he appeals to certain laws of logic as necessary for reasonable discourse.[166] With a bit of irony, Chad Owen Brand notes that Henry has become "the candidate of choice for critics seeking to implicate evangelical theology in this new modernism."[167]

One of the earliest critiques in print of Henry along these lines comes from none other than Hans Frei.[168] Frei cites in a critical manner Henry as representative of an entire method of theology that clings to "the basic affirmation that theology must have a foundation that is articulated in terms of basic philosophical principles."[169] In other words, since Henry makes use of principles like rational discourse, he is categorized in such a way

165. Thornbury, *Recovering Classic Evangelicalism*, 114. On balance, Thornbury does acknowledge some legitimacy for Vanhoozer's critiques when he states, "Vanhoozer makes a good point that Henry was so focused on maintaining evangelical affirmations that he downplayed the richness of language and its setting in canonical linguistic form. Vanhoozer is also correct that language does more theologically than Henry allows."

166. Henry, *God, Revelation and Authority*, 1:215; and ibid., 1:233. Henry appeals consistently in his writings to the law of contradiction and logical coherence among other principles of logic. For example, in regard to theological method, Henry notes the laws of logic hold in a way that "[d]ivine revelation is the source of all truth, the truth of Christianity included; reason is the instrument for recognizing it; Scripture is the verifying principle; logical consistency is a negative test for truth and coherence a subordinate test. The task of Christian theology is to exhibit the content of biblical revelation as an orderly whole." Again Henry notes, "Consistency is a negative test of truth; what is logically contradictory cannot be true. A denial of the law of contradiction would make truth and error equivalent; hence in effect it destroys truth."

167. Brand, "Is Carl Henry a Modernist?," 5.

168. Springs, "But Did It *Really* Happen," 271–99. Springs has attempted to reconcile the debate between Carl Henry and Hans Frei concerning historical referent by asserting that, while Frei did not accomplish it himself, the resources lie within his theology to assert a form of historical realism. An alternative proposal has been provided by George Hunsinger in "What Can Evangelicals and Postliberals Learn from Each Other," 161–82.

169. Frei, *Types of Christian Theology*, 24.

his method must be controlled by modernist foundationalism with at least some resemblance to Cartesian methods.[170]

Critique from self-identifying evangelicals has likewise come against Henry's epistemology. Donald Bloesch has leveled critique against evangelical theology in general for possessing too much of a rationalist bent. His particular concern is over-reliance on logical deduction, evidential confirmations, and philosophical methodology.[171] While Bloesch has praise for Carl Henry in many regards, he finds his epistemology to be enduring in weakness. The fault line in Henry's theology lies in that he remains locked into an immanentalist epistemology. Bloesch's account of this is based on his assessment that Henry's focus on epistemology forces him into viewing Scripture as nothing more than a "logical system of shared beliefs," effectively reducing Henry's approach to revelation to a Christian form of rationalism.[172]

Another theologian who thinks Henry has committed himself to a rationalist agenda is James McClendon. McClendon claims "it is helpful to compare Henry with Descartes: though their thought is not identical, whether it be rationalism, dualism, the philosophical role of God, or the role of ideas that correspond to reality by divine guarantee, Henry will be ranked as a twentieth century *Cartesian*."[173] The claims against Henry, whether as bold as McClendon or subtler as Bloesch, are significant in that they imply anthropocentrism, universalizing epistemology as a controlling principle, and foundationalism in terms of knowledge and justified belief. These hallmarks of Modernist epistemology are significant charges against Henry and his evangelical cohorts.

In response to accusations that modern evangelical theology (including Henry) is tainted by rationalist impulses, Gregory Thornbury argues just the opposite. According to Thornbury, the fruit of the Reformation

170. Ibid. Frei provides evidence for this in that he sees Henry's critique of Barth to be based on his failure to appropriately deploy "the law contradiction, the so-called congruity postulate, and the criterion that all propositions must be arrangeable in the form of axioms and theorems, the criterion that coherence obeys the same rules everywhere, and so on."

171. Bloesch, *The Battle for the Trinity*, 70.

172. Bloesch, *A Theology of Word & Spirit*, 4. Henry is not alone as a subject of the rationalist critique. Other evangelical theologians are identified as participants in this weakness. Likewise, Bloesch includes R. C. Sproul, E. J. Carnell, J. Oliver Buswell, Millard Erickson, and John Warwick Montgomery. Ibid., 252–53.

173. Cited by Brand in multiple articles such as: McClendon, "Christian Knowledge in the Sunset of Modernity," 8.

was an epistemology rooted in revelation, yet accountable to and consistent with the canons of reason. The heartbeat of *sola scriptura* for the reformers grounded their epistemology distinctly in the Word of God, yet their discourse was not limited to the cul-de-sac of fideism. For Thornbury, many have misunderstood (or failed to read as he boldly claims at one point) Henry on this matter.[174] In Thornbury's view, Henry actually presents the way forward for evangelicals to remain Word centric in their epistemology.[175] According to Thornbury, Henry may hardly be accused of Cartesian rationalism in light of his espousal of "absolute dependence of human knowledge upon divine disclosure whether natural or particular."[176]

In other words, according to Henry, human knowledge is not anthropocentric but theocentric in its origin and in humanity's ability to apprehend knowledge. Early in his career, Henry made clear the epistemological foundations upon which he would build his theology. Reaching back prior to Cartesian principles, Henry roots his epistemology in an Augustinian model when he states,

> Human knowledge is not a source of knowledge to be contrasted with revelation, but is a means to comprehending revelation . . . Thus God, by his immanence, sustains the human knower, even in his moral and cognitive revolt, and without that divine preservation, ironically enough, man could not even rebel against God, for he would not exist. Augustine, early in the Christian centuries, detected what was implied in this conviction that human reason is not the creator of its own object; neither the external world of sensation nor the internal world of ideas is rooted in subjectivistic factors alone.[177]

In light of Henry's claim that knowledge and the ability to know may not exist without God's active providence as an intelligent Deity, human autonomy is lost. The role of God's providence in human epistemology leads Thornbury to conclude concerning Henry, "Contrary to the trajectory of

---

174. Thornbury, *Recovering Classic Evangelicalism*, 59.

175. Thornbury, "Carl F. H. Henry," 68. Thornbury notes, "Evangelicals should turn once more to the model set forth by Carl F. H. Henry, a man who inherited the epistemology of the Reformers, and faithfully applied it to the challenges of modernity."

176. Ibid.

177. Henry, *The Drift of Western Thought*, 104.

rationalism, no autonomous standard for reason can be offered, since reason itself loses meaning apart from the divine character."[178]

Lest one be tempted to juxtapose an earlier Henry and a later Henry on these points, he held true to a revelational epistemology distinct from rationalism throughout his career. Henry states concerning the major epistemological beliefs of Christianity,

> The Christian ontological axiom is the living, self-revealed God. The Christian epistemological axiom is the intelligible divine revelation. All the essential doctrines of the Christian world-life view flow from these axioms: creation, sin, and the fall; redemption, by promise and fulfillment; the incarnation, substitutionary death and resurrection of the Logos; the church as the new society; the approaching divine consummation of history; the eschatological verities.[179]

Further, in thesis five of *God, Revelation and Authority*, Henry asserts,

> Not only the occurrence of divine revelation, but also its very nature, content, and variety are exclusively of God's determination. God determines not only the *if* and *why* of divine disclosures but also the *when, where, what, how, and who*. If there is to be a general revelation—a revelation universally given in nature, in history, and in the reason and conscience of every man—then that is God's decision. If there is to be a special or particular revelation, that, too, is God's decision and his alone. Only because God so wills is there a cosmic-anthropological revelation.[180]

Finally, Henry emphasizes that the rational nature of revelation and man's ability to understand revelation through reason does not establish human reason as superior over the revelation of God. Henry argues the transcendence of God is not eliminated by the reasonable nature of language and man's rational capacities when he states, "Divine revelation does not completely erase God's transcendent mystery, inasmuch as God the revealer transcends his own revelation."[181] Thus, Thornbury observes Henry's claims that what we know, "we know because God wants us to know it. In this sense, then Henry defies the sort of foundationalist label with which some have recently attempted to place upon him, a trend which began

178. Thornbury, "Heir of Reformation Epistemology," 69.
179. Henry, *Gods of this Age*, 209.
180. Henry, *God, Revelation and Authority*, 2:9–10.
181. Henry, *God, Revelation and Authority*, 2:47.

with Hans Frei's response to Henry's critique of narrative theology."[182] With words such as those above, Henry defies the Cartesian/foundationalist/rationalist character, which Frei, Bloesch, and McClendon have placed upon him.[183] Quite contrary to consistency with rationalism, Henry has maintained "there was no neutral, antiseptic path to knowledge."[184]

The catalog of Henry's statements that place him as distinct from rationalist Modernism could continue. He claims, by his scheme, that revelation "gives no quarter to the idealistic illusion that human reason is intrinsically capable of fashioning eternal truth."[185] Again, "Christian doctrines are not derived from experimental observation or from rationalism, but from God in his revelation."[186] What appears to create the stumbling block for Henry's critics is his insistence that a cognitive-rational component exists to revelation, his insistence that axioms exist, and his insistence that humanity may apprehend this revelation due to unique creation in the image of God.[187] If this is to be defined as rationalism, then it is to run past the fact that both the source of knowledge and the ability to know are fundamentally different between the assertions of the Enlightenment and those of Henry.[188] Since Henry's assertion is that God is intelligent and rational, and therefore his revelation and image-bearers possess a rational quality his epistemology is far from descending to immanentist rationalism.[189]

182. Thornbury, "Heir of Reformation Epistemology," 69.

183. Further evidence of Henry's chastened epistemology comes in his approach to hermeneutics and "The Fallibility of the Exegete" in God, Revelation and Authority, vol. 4, ch. 14.

184. Thornbury, "Heir of Reformation Epistemology," 70.

185. Henry, God, Revelation and Authority, 1:225–26.

186. Ibid., 2:223.

187. Thornbury, Recovering Classical Evangelicalism, 69. Thornbury elsewhere notes, "Defying those who caricature Henry as a trenchant modernist, he posits that scientific credibility, historical continuity, and linguistic peculiarities are second-order considerations when one is engaging the texts of Scripture. Contrary to accusations from contemporary evangelical theologians . . . Henry concedes that these factors are crucial for accurately understanding God's Word, but he is resolute that these methods should not be employed in an a priori or determinative fashion."

188. Fackre, Ecumenical Faith, 187. Fackre articulates the position that Henry is not a rationalist when he states, "In all these matters, a discursive interpretation of Christian faith is to the fore, but it would be wrong to identify Henry simply as a rationalist. He contests evangelical positions that seek to validate Christian faith in total by reason, and also argues with others who think one can come to faith by reason."

189. Brand, "Is Carl Henry a Modernist," 12. Brand notes in Kantian terms of rationalism, "[Henry] skirts the Kantian epistemological bifurcation, which claims knowledge

The question remains and must be answered: was Carl F. H. Henry a rationalist? The answer may depend on one's definition of rationalism. Is Henry a Cartesian or Kantian rationalist who supports the autonomy of the human knower as the producer and arbiter of knowledge? The record has shown this is not the case. While affirming a revelational epistemology, does Henry insist that divine communication necessarily involves cognitive-rational content and that God's authority fixes certain epistemological principles? Henry himself has affirmed this.[190] However, as Brand observes, "Henry then affirms that revelation is rational, but he denies that one can construct theology on positivist or rationalist grounds. Henry's rationalism is more in line with the Anglo-American tradition, in which reason functions as a means of coming to truth, but does not itself provide the content of truth."[191] As has been shown through Kevin Vanhoozer's assessment of Henry, and will be shown further through Henry's interactions with Frei and other post-liberal sources, the charge for rationalism arises because Henry's insistence on a rational component sets him as distinct from most modern philosophical sensibilities.[192]

Conclusion

In conclusion, Carl Henry's theology of revelation has been demonstrated to emphasize a textually oriented hermeneutic that likewise maintains the importance of historical affirmations. On one hand, Henry insists on historical referent for the apologetic establishment of the Christianity as the ultimate steward of truth and human salvation. Likewise, Henry demonstrates a textually-oriented hermeneutic in his articulation that the biblical

---

only for that which is phenomenal and posits faith alone as the means of encountering the realm of noumena, by asserting that God, in his divine condescension, has done what would otherwise be impossible—he has made true theological knowledge and true knowledge of himself available to humanity through Scripture."

190. Ibid., 17. Brand argues that accusing Henry of rationalism and saying that his sole concern is none more than cognitive content is in the end a misreading of Henry. Henry has not said revelation is *exclusively* cognitive-propositional in nature, but that it is not less than cognitive.

191. Ibid., 12.

192. Doyle, *Carl Henry, Theologian for All Seasons*, 108. Doyle attributes the critiques of rationalism against Henry to a failure to identify the distinction Henry draws between rationalism and a commitment to being rational in the sense of accepting standard laws of reason (e.g. the law of contradiction).

text is the only source of true knowledge about the divine acts of God in history. The emphases of Henry operate in balance and, as will be demonstrated in the next two chapters, distinct from the approaches taken by two of his contemporaries in Wolfhart Pannenberg and Hans Frei.

3

Revelation as History for Pannenberg

Background on Pannenberg's Theology of Revelation

Carl Henry gives significant attention to Wolfhart Pannenberg (1928-2014) as an alternative approach to revelation, history, and the biblical text. Pannenberg stands as the source of a significant, broad theological approach, as well as a figurehead in the specific area of revelation and history. Pannenberg rose to theological prominence through his articulation that the eschaton is the point of transcendence, and this transcendent presence of God proleptically broke into history in the Christ-event.[1] Due to its impact on Pannenberg's doctrine of revelation and hermeneutics, the role of the eschaton in Pannenberg will be discussed throughout this chapter. Pannenberg's experience with Nazi Germany and Stalinist Eastern Europe are factors that led him to conclude a perfect social structure would someday come in contrast to the current brokenness of the world.[2] Pannenberg's eschatological focus for his system bears significant influence on his approach to revelation, history, and the biblical text.[3]

1. For biographical resources on the life of Wolfhart Pannenberg see Olive, *Wolfhart Pannenberg*; Tupper, *The Theology of Wolfhart Pannenberg*; Grenz and Olson, *20th Century Theology*, 186–99; and Pannenberg, "An Autobiographical Sketch," 11–18.

2. Grenz and Olson, *20th Century Theology*, 186.

3. Pannenberg, *Basic Questions in Theology*, 15. Pannenberg draws the connection himself in his statements, "History is the most comprehensive horizon of Christian theology. All theological questions and answers are meaningful only within the framework of the history which God has with humanity and through humanity with his whole

A parallel influence in Pannenberg's approach to revelation and religious knowledge is his view of the Enlightenment and its effects on modern theology.[4] Through a period of study under Karl Barth, Pannenberg grew discontent with the notion of a split between natural knowledge and divine revelation.[5] Natural knowledge, accessible through universal and secular means, for Pannenberg, must not be of a separate category as revealed knowledge through the categories of Christ, the Word of God, or Scripture.[6] In contrast to a dichotomy, Pannenberg sought to demonstrate that "God's revelatory work does not come as a stark contradiction to the world, but is the completion of creation."[7] Further, Grenz and Olson note how "Pannenberg seeks to draw out the religious implications found in all secular experience, claiming a continuity between redemption and creation, a continuity he came to find in the historical process."[8]

Pannenberg's refusal to accept the epistemic split between revealed knowledge and natural knowledge marks a break from the existentially oriented mindset of his mentors and surrounding environment in German theology.[9] A reason for Pannenberg's development is that he viewed it as necessary to adjust theology to the implications of the Enlightenment.[10] Maintaining a split between natural and revelational knowledge is to maintain an unacceptable pietistic emphasis on a decision of faith rather than

---

creation—the history moving toward a future still hidden from the world but already revealed in Jesus Christ. This presupposition of Christian theology must be defended today within theology . . ."

4. Pannenberg, "Response to the Discussion," 226. One significant factor of the Enlightenment was the requirement that authoritarian claims on principle are suspicious. Therefore, authoritarian claims as to the nature and meaning of Scripture are to be considered suspect. To this end Pannenberg states, "But for men who live in the sphere in which the Enlightenment has become effective, authoritarian claims are no longer acceptable, in intellectual as little as political life. All authoritarian claims are on principle subject to the suspicion that they clothe human thoughts and institutions with the splendor of divine majesty."

5. Grenz and Olson, *20th Century Theology*, 187. Additionally, concerning the influence and development past Barth in Pannenberg, see Jim S. Halsey, "History, Language and Hermeneutics: The Synthesis of Wolfhart Pannenberg," *Westminster Theological Journal* 41 (Spring 1979): 284–89.

6. Grenz and Olson, *20th Century Theology*, 187.

7. Ibid.

8. Ibid.

9. Pannenberg, *Basic Questions in Theology*, 86.

10. Ibid., 145–46.

on a universal and intellectually justified basis for the Christian faith.[11] Likewise, Pannenberg thinks the Reformation view of Scripture as the authoritative Word of God is no longer a viable approach because of a twofold crisis. On one hand, historical criticism has opened a chasm between the meaning of the biblical writings and the historical events to which they refer. On the other hand, the historical chasm "between primitive Christianity and our age" creates a hermeneutical gap that cannot be spanned by appeal to biblical authority.[12] In processing the Enlightenment, Pannenberg views existential and bibliocentric approaches to theology as partners in ignoring the Enlightenment's demand for proper epistemic grounding.[13]

The dual fault lines modern shifts created in the Scripture-based approach of early Protestantism fostered a corresponding hermeneutical problem. The shift Pannenberg describes is one of moving from a text-oriented hermeneutic to a historical hermeneutic. In Pannenberg's view, the actual history of the Bible "was separated from the biblical texts as something to be sought out behind them."[14] Therefore, the product of the Enlightenment is that it became necessary to distinguish between the events reported in the Bible and the perspectives of the biblical authors as they reported those events.

Pannenberg casts his approach to hermeneutics in the framework of the question the Enlightenment unavoidably raises for biblical interpreters.[15] Specifically, what is "to be considered theologically normative, the biblical texts themselves or the history to be discovered behind them"?[16] The quest of unifying natural and revealed knowledge in an attempt to satisfy congruence with the Enlightenment on the nature of history and revelation leads Pannenberg to assert history is the field in which knowledge and faith is to be based. Along these lines, Grenz and Olson note,

11. Ibid., 18, 141.

12. Ibid., 96.

13. Ibid., 14.

14. Ibid., 97.

15. Ibid., 12. Pannenberg notes the result of the Enlightenment undermining of Reformation approach to Scripture is that "theology cannot continue as a special science of divine revelation on the basis of Holy Scripture. Precisely in endeavoring to understand the biblical writings it will be led back to the question of the events they report about, and of the meaning that belongs to them. Theology, however, can understand the meaning of these events as deeds of God only in relation to universal history, because statements about the origin of all events can be defended only with a view to the totality of all events."

16. Ibid., 7.

[Pannenberg] criticizes any attempt to divide truth into autonomous spheres or to shield the truth content of the Christian tradition from rational inquiry. Theological affirmations must be subject to the rigor of critical inquiry concerning the historical reality on which they are based. Theology, in other words, must be evaluated on the basis of critical canons, just as the other sciences, for it also deals with truth. And the truth of the Christian faith must be measured according to the coherence criterion, that is, insofar as it fits together—even illumines—all human knowledge.[17]

The place of theology in context of all human knowledge is accomplished through justifying an acceptable universal starting point for talk of God.[18] In Pannenberg's view, the Enlightenment left a situation in which theology may not immediately articulate the foundations of theology in the doctrines of God or revelation.[19] In search of a universal foundation for religion, Pannenberg argues that the proper foundation for theology is anthropology.[20] The universal grounding for theology is found in the history of world religions, because here Pannenberg sees that man is universally religious.[21] Pannenberg's descriptive approach to anthropology is paired with his confidence in the eschaton as the as the point where all truth and knowledge is revealed beyond its current provisional state.[22]

In the end, the Christian faith will stand alone, but this is the product of the "entire history of divine-human interaction."[23] Pannenberg's anthropological foundation provides the universal basis on which he may link natural and revealed knowledge.[24] It should be noted that this grounding

17. Grenz and Olson, *20th Century Theology*, 189.

18. Pannenberg, "God's Presence in History," 260–63.

19. Grenz and Olson, *20th Century Theology*, 191.

20. Pannenberg, *Basic Questions in Theology*, 76–77; and idem, *Anthropology in Theological Perspective*, 21. Pannenberg elsewhere describes his approach as a "fundamental-theological anthropology."

21. Pannenberg, *Theology and the Philosophy of Science*, 151–52. Additionally, see in particular chapters one and two in Pannenberg, *The Historicity of Nature*. Pannenberg's claim that a universal, non-revelatory basis be articulated for theology is likewise consistent with his insistence that truth remains partial and truth claims debatable until the eschaton.

22. Pannenberg, "A Response to My American Friends," 314.

23. Ibid.

24. Ibid., 315. In response to concerns about universalism, Pannenberg states, until the finality of the eschaton, a clear claim may not be made for exclusive salvation, because "[t]he Christian faith aims at the *finality* of revelation as well as of salvation, and as

in anthropological world religions likewise provides the starting point for interpreting the Bible historically.[25] Concerning the nature of religious history as the context for a historical approach to the Bible, Pannenberg states, "Theology as a science of God is therefore possible only as a science of religion, and not as the science of religion in general but of the historic religions."[26]

On the hermeneutical front, Gerhard von Rad served as an influence on Pannenberg's thought concerning revelation, history, and the biblical text during a season of study at Heidelberg. The influence of von Rad and the theological course that was set during this season may be heard in Pannenberg's own words:

> After attending a few lectures of Gerhard von Rad, however, the dime dropped. I discovered a new world, the traditions and history of ancient Israel, because von Rad was unique in communicating to his audience its exotic charm: the mind of ancient Israel was presented as exotic, but at the same time as more real than the world of our modern experience. In this way the Old Testament, through the aesthetic skill of von Rad's exegesis, came alive in the hearts of innumerable students. On the basis of this experience, finally the New Testament also began to make sense to me. *History* was the code word of biblical exegesis at Heidelberg in those years, and to my ears it was echoed by the lectures of Karl Lowith on philosophy of history. It was a pity, or so it appeared to us students, that systematic theology at Heidelberg was not yet quite up to that new agenda. Thus a group of students tried to find out for themselves what a systematic theology would look like on the basis of von Rad's exegetical vision. This was how the so-called Heidelberg Circle started to work. But it took 10 years of discussions before our new approach to theology in terms of "Revelation as History" was published in 1961.[27]

---

such it also includes a tendency towards 'universal salvation.' But the historical process is still open in human experience, the controversy about the Christian (and other) truth claims is still continuing, and certainly there will be no salvation for anyone without going through divine judgment."

25. Dulles, "The Place of Christianity Among the World Religions," 295. On history of religions as the basis for theology in Pannenberg's method, Dulles comments, "In Pannenberg's futuristic vision a scientifically based theology of religion and religions would become the essence of a fundamental theology on which could be built a special theology of Christianity as well as each of the other religions."

26. Pannenberg, *Theology and the Philosophy of Science*, 31.

27. Pannenberg, "Autobiographical Sketch," 14.

From the project started in Heidelberg, Pannenberg would go on to argue the focal point of revelation is the history of religions. Describing Pannenberg's interest in the history of religions, Grenz and Olson note, "On the world historical stage conflicting truth claims, which are at their core religious and are ultimately attempts to express the unity of the world, are struggling for supremacy. The religious orientation that best illumines the experience of all reality will in the end prevail and thereby demonstrate its truth value."[28]

According to Pannenberg, the Christian faith is the system which is most coherent and will ultimately prevail. On the privileging of Christianity, Henry, in fact, presses Pannenberg as to why Christianity should be privileged over any other world religions on the anthropological basis from which Pannenberg operates.[29] For Pannenberg, the religious history of Israel (which ultimately resulted in Christianity) is privileged because through "Israel came the breakthrough to monotheism which allowed for an understanding of the world as a unity, and the breakthrough to the future orientation of God's activity in history."[30] The Bible serves as the sourcebook for the unique developments in the history of Israel, and inquiry into Scripture is historically oriented in that the interpreter seeks to understand the history of Israel as distinct from other world religions.[31] Therefore, the authority of the Bible is not the starting point for theological reflection, but rather universal history of religions provides the justification and terms for the use of the Bible in theology.[32]

While this sketch of Pannenberg's thought concerning religious epistemology and the Bible is brief, the implications for hermeneutics are clear. Stanley Grenz notes, "Since the reopening of the discussion in the 19th century, the question of hermeneutic(s) has gained increasing importance in theology . . . Pannenberg has shown himself to be an important party to the more recent debate. In fact, one important aspect of his overall program is the historical hermeneutic he advocates."[33] From the background and brief

---

28. Grenz and Olson, *20th Century Theology*, 192.

29. Henry, *God, Revelation and Authority*, 2:300.

30. Grenz and Olson, *20th Century Theology*, 192.

31. To take the unique place of Christianity to its end on historical terms, Pannenberg argues the history of Israel formed the context for the life of Jesus Christ as the focus of God's revelation. In historical terms, Jesus is the historical preview of God's true revelation that will happen at the end of history.

32. Grenz and Olson, *20th Century Theology*, 196.

33. Grenz, "The Appraisal of Pannenberg," 26–27.

sketch of Pannenberg's approach to revelation, history, and the biblical text, this chapter now turns to the details of Pannenberg's argument and Henry's appraisal.

Pannenberg's Approach to Revelation as History

Before encountering Carl Henry's interaction with Wolfhart Pannenberg's revelation as history hermeneutic, it is appropriate to survey Pannenberg's approach to revelation, history, and the biblical text. As outlined previously in this chapter, Pannenberg formulated his approach to revelation, history, and the biblical text early in his career as part of the formation of his theological method. Pannenberg is not unlike Henry in that the theological convictions he developed early in his career set the trajectory in many ways for his further hermeneutical development on issues related to revelation, history, and the biblical text.[34]

Revelation as Indirect

Pannenberg maintains that revelation as the self-disclosure of God is not direct as if God has personally mediated knowledge of himself to human beings, but rather, the revelation of God is indirect and manifested through the historical acts of God.[35] For Pannenberg, surveying the biblical narrative will demonstrate that earlier notions of God revealing himself directly were supplanted by the ideas that God is revealed in the acts of history.[36] The emphasis on historical acts begins in the narrative of Scripture with the

---

34. Pannenberg, *Basic Questions in Theology*, xv. Henry and Pannenberg are likewise similar in that they both maintained their approach throughout their careers, while continuing to develop and deepen the application of their revelational models. Pannenberg notes, "To say that the revelation of God is not a supernatural event which breaks into history perpendicularly from above but rather that it is the theme of history itself, the power that moves it in its deepest dimension, is to say something about God and his relation to the world."

35. Pannenberg, "Dogmatic Theses," 125. Thesis one in Pannenberg's systematic presentation of the doctrine of revelation as history states, "The self-revelation of God in the biblical witnesses is not of a direct type in the sense of a theophany, but is indirect and brought about by means of the historical acts of God."

36. Ibid.

Exodus and the collection of divine interventions recorded in connection with "Jahweh's primal acts of salvation."[37]

According to the narration of God's historical acts in the plagues, crossing the Red Sea, and so forth, Pannenberg concludes "faithful trust was effected by the evidence of historical facts that brought about salvation and revealed Jahweh's deity and power."[38] In his essays in the work *Revelation as History*, Pannenberg continues a survey of the history of Israel to demonstrate that the biblical narrative places emphasis on the ways in which God has acted in history. Through Deuteronomy, the prophets, and on into the New Testament as the continuation of God's historical revelation, Pannenberg argues God is indirectly revealed.[39]

Pannenberg emphasizes the indirect nature of revelation in order to provide clarity amidst what he views as a variety of meanings for the term "revelation." Under the category of "the self-revelation of God" fits many competing notions of revelation, which he seeks to clarify.[40] In order for an approach to revelation to be justifiable, Pannenberg argues "the question of the self-revelation of God must somehow be confirmed on the basis of the biblical witnesses if it is to be theologically justifiable."[41] Yet, in affirming a place for the biblical literature in justifying an approach to revelation,

37. Ibid.

38. Ibid., 126.

39. Ibid., 128–29. Pannenberg notes concerning the history surrounding the Exodus, "Although formulated only in words, the glorification of Jahweh through his acts in history is clearly an expression pointing to the indirect revelation of his deity in those acts (see also Ex.16:6)." And again concerning the indirect revelation of God in Jesus, Pannenberg notes, "God is indirectly revealed in the fate of Jesus. The apocalyptic revelation of his glory in the end judgment has come to pass ahead of time in this fate."

40. Pannenberg, "Introduction," 3–4. Among the options at the time of the publication of *Revelation as History* Pannenberg mentions, "Some theologians speak of manifestation and inspiration, of revelation as act and as word, of primal revelation and revelation of salvation; others find revelations not only in God's history with Israel, but also in nature as the underlying phenomenon of all religious experience; still others allow for only the one revelation of God in the person of Jesus Christ. Yet, over and above all of these distinctions is the present consensus that revelation is, in essence, the self-revelation of God."

41. Ibid., 8. Pannenberg goes on to note, "This assertion is not just protestant bias, but accords with the recognition of the biblical scriptures as the fundamental witnesses of the events to which theology relates when it speaks of revelation. However, at first glance, there is no terminological usage concerning the self-revelation of God in the biblical writings."

Pannenberg has something different in mind than viewing the biblical text as inspired and uniquely authoritative.[42]

Rather than view the biblical text as the *direct* revelation of God as personal communication, Pannenberg views the Bible as *indirect* testimony by authors to the works of God. To this end, Pannenberg states, "[w]hile the word authorized by Jahweh or spoken by him had fundamental meaning in the thought of Israel, it still had, in all its manifold functions, concrete contents that are distinct from God. It never had God as its content in any unmediated way."[43] Again, concerning the New Testament authors, Pannenberg states, "When the author speaks of the Word of God, he has in mind the apostolic kerygma. Here, too, is an entity whose content is clearly distinct from God himself."[44] Any notion that the person of God is directly revealed through the biblical text is the result of undue Gnostic influence.[45] In favor of an indirect account of revelation, Pannenberg concludes,

> Now it suffices to insist that if one wishes to understand specifically biblical functions and contents, then the Word of God does not have the character of a direct self-revelation of God. Thus the proclamation of the *Law* on Sinai is not to be understood as a direct self-revelation of Jahweh, namely, a disclosure of the essence of his will which would then be matched as revelation with the New Testament proclamation of the *gospel.*[46]

The implications of Pannenberg's indirect account of revelation is that the Bible itself does not constitute knowledge of God, but is the reflection of God's activity authored by his people.[47] Pannenberg concludes, "Instead of a direct self-revelation of God, the facts at this point indicate a conception of indirect self-revelation as a reflex of his activity in history. The totality of his speech and activity, the history brought about by God, shows who he is in an indirect way."[48]

---

42. Dulles, "Pannenberg on Revelation and Faith," 171.

43. Pannenberg, "Introduction," 10.

44. Ibid., 11.

45. Ibid., 12. Pannenberg argues, "The real problem is the extent to which we may deviate from the biblical understanding of revelation in the use of a gnostic understanding of revelation and a gnostic concept of the Word."

46. Ibid.

47. Pannenberg, *Basic Questions in Theology*, 21.

48. Pannenberg, "Introduction," 13.

The discussion between direct and indirect revelation bears impact on the nature of Scripture and ultimately Pannenberg's hermeneutics. If, for Pannenberg, direct communication "transmits content without a break from the sender to the receiver," and by contrast, indirect communication, "the content first reveals its actual meaning by being considered from another perspective," then the implications are significant for biblical interpretation.[49] Pannenberg makes the significance of indirect communication clear when he states,

> Thus, direct communication would have God himself—without mediation—as its content, analogous to divine epiphanies in the sense of a complete self-revelation, and communication of the divine name would be a direct revelation if it involved a direct disclosure of the being of God himself. The law would be direct revelation if it were identical with God's will, which is itself the essence of God. The Word of God would be direct communication if its content were directly connected with God himself, somewhat in the sense of a self-presentation of the divinity.[50]

Yet by contrast he states, "Indirect communication is distinguished by not having God as the content in any direct manner. Every activity and act of God can indirectly express something about God."[51] Therefore, the event itself does not convey any direct knowledge of God, and similarly so, the textual representation of that event is not direct revelation. Rather, "there is simply a reflection on the event first perceived, and the stimulus to this derives from the event itself, or from the Word fulfilled in it . . ."[52] The acts and the biblical text do not reveal God, but rather cast light back on God through the reflection of those who first apprehended the event.[53]

The hermeneutical significance of indirect revelation through historical acts then is that the method one must take for attaining knowledge of God is to investigate his historical acts to glean what is indirectly revealed.

---

49. Ibid., 14.

50. Ibid., 15.

51. Ibid.

52. Ibid.

53. Ibid., 16. The impact of the discussion of direct versus indirect revelation on the nature of Scripture is clear in Pannenberg's comments, "That does not of course mean that they reveal God or that God reveals himself in them as their originator, for every individual event which is taken to be God's activity illuminates the being of God only in a partial way. God will carry out many things which cannot be foreseen, and they will also point back to their originator, though in different ways."

Pannenberg states it, "If we wish to understand the indirect self-communication that resides in every individual act of God as revelation, then there are as many revelations as there are divine acts and occurrences in nature and history."[54] Through the indirect nature of God's communication, Pannenberg pushes the search for meaning of the Bible behind the text and expands the search into universal history.

Provisional Revelation

The indirectness of revelation leads Pannenberg to assert that all revelation is provisional until the end of history.[55] The acts of God in history partially and indirectly reveal him, so Pannenberg requires the entire sum of history be assembled to perceive God's deity.[56] Pannenberg asserts the connection between the previous discussion and what is to follow with his comment, "placing revelation at the close of history is grounded in the indirectness of revelation."[57] The eschatological horizon for the revelation of God is on two counts. First, "the extent of events proving the deity of God [is] increasing."[58] Through the traditions of the Old and New Testament literature, Pannenberg sees an increasing accumulation of divine acts, which each contribute partially to the indirect revelation of God. Second, "the content of revelation [is] continually revising itself."[59] In other words, what is conveyed about God at one point of religious history is only provisional in light of later and ultimate revelation through history.[60] Rather than an

---

54. Ibid.

55. Pannenberg, "Dogmatic Theses," 131. Thesis two in Pannenberg's systematic presentation of revelation as history states, "Revelation is not comprehended completely in the beginning, but at the end of the revealing history."

56. Pannenberg, "Foreword," in *Basic Questions in Theology*, xv. Pannenberg notes, "Furthermore, if it is true that only with reverence to the *totality* of reality can one speak meaningfully about a revelation of God as the world's creator and lord and that reality (understood as historical) is first constituted as the totality of a single history by the end of all occurrences, then eschatology acquires constitutive significance not only for the question of the knowledge, but also for that of the reality of God."

57. Pannenberg, "Dogmatic Theses," 131.

58. Ibid.

59. Ibid.

60. Dulles, *Pannenberg on Revelation and Faith*, 174.

interpreter taking a text of the Bible as "the final vindication of God [it] is now seen as only one step in the ever-increasing context of revelation."[61]

Pannenberg roots his development of history in what he views to be a disjunction between different parts of the Bible. At one stage of Israel's tradition in Deuteronomy, Pannenberg views the occupancy of the land as the close of God's promises and revelation in history. However, this closure of revelation and history is unsealed by the exile from the Promised Land and the accompanying testimony of the prophets. Pannenberg argues the pattern of disjunction continues throughout the history of Israel and on into the New Testament as his backing for the partiality of revelation until the end of history.[62]

Similar to the indirectness of revelation, the provisionality of revelation in light of eschatological fulfillment bears impact on what one may know now. The goal of hermeneutics is not, and cannot be, to know God in his essence now. Along these lines, Pannenberg states,

> Placing the manifestation of God at the end of history means that the biblical God has, so to speak, his own history. That is, the historical event of revelation cannot be thought of in an outward way as revealing the essence of God. It is not so much the course of history as it is the end of history that is at one with the essence of God. But insofar as the end presupposes the course of history, because it is the perfection of it, then also the course of history belongs in essence to the revelation of God, for history receives its unity from its goal.[63]

Pursuit of meaning in the Bible comes in ascertaining the history of religions by which God is manifesting himself through the history of Israel and in Jesus Christ.[64]

Pannenberg's confidence is that the Christian faith provides the most coherent explanation of reality among world religions and will emerge

61. Pannenberg, "Dogmatic Theses," 131–32.

62. Ibid., 132.

63. Ibid., 133.

64. Pannenberg, *Basic Questions in Theology*, 67. Pannenberg asserts theological and historical inquiry may not proceed at all without the end of history in view. There is no basis for raising the question of whether God has revealed himself in a particular subset of history like that of Israel or the New Testament. Rather, "In order to raise this question it is obviously requisite that one should have history as a whole in view, corresponding to the universality of God, whose revelation is the object of inquiry. Only on the assumption of a universal-historical horizon can there be such an inquiry."

in the end of history to reveal God. Pannenberg makes his confidence in Christianity explicit by stating,

> It is only in the course of this history brought about by Jahweh that this tribal God proves himself to be the one true God. This proof will be made in the strict and ultimate sense only at the end of all history. However, in the fate of Jesus, the end of history is experienced in advance as an anticipation. As we now conceptualize more precisely—it is only in view of the end that we can say God has proved himself in the fate of Jesus as the one true God.[65]

Public Revelation

In contrast to the existentially oriented approaches of many theologians in Pannenberg's setting, he insists on the universal nature of revelation. A critique Pannenberg leveled against his fellow German theologians who were oriented toward existential models of revelation was that immediately and personally received revelation does not pass the criteria of critical reason. Pannenberg notes,

> We are ordinarily urged to think of revelation as an occurrence that man cannot perceive with natural eyes and that is made known only through a secret mediation. The revelation, however, of the biblical God in his activity is no secret or mysterious happening. An understanding that puts revelation into contrast to, or even conflict with, natural knowledge is in danger of distorting the historical revelation into a gnostic knowledge of secrets.[66]

The external and universal character of historical revelation is significant, because "what Jahweh accomplished in history cannot be written off as the imagination of the pious soul, for its inherent meaning of revealing the deity of Jahweh is impressed on everyone."[67]

In the assertion that historical revelation is universal, Pannenberg likewise articulates the grounds upon which he launches all of theological inquiry—world religions. The roots of theological reflection in the universal character of humanity as a religious species demands that the knowledge of the Christian faith be of the same sphere as world knowledge.[68]

65. Pannenberg, "Dogmatic Theses," 134.

66. Ibid., 135.

67. Ibid., 136.

68. Pannenberg, *Basic Questions in Theology*, 38.

Pannenberg is insistent on the universal nature of history, because of the meaning attributed to the word "God" in theology in the emergence of the Christian faith among world religions.[69] The idea of God bears meaning "only if one means by it the power that determines everything that exists," because "[a]nyone who does not want to revert to a polytheistic or poly-daemonistic stage of phenomenology of religion must think of God as the creator of all things."[70] Since all being is in relation to God, theology is of a universal nature and, therefore, must include the entire realm of history.[71]

The uniqueness of Christianity, therefore, is not in a special mediation of meaning from God, but that as universal history, the events of the Christian faith represent a trail from early Israel to the eschatological fulfillment of revelation. Pannenberg states it thus, "The history of Israel all the way to the resurrection is a series of very special events. Thus they communicate something that could not be gotten out of other events. The special aspect is the event itself, not the attitude with which one confronts the event."[72]

The implication of setting biblical history in the context of universal history as Pannenberg does is that "from the universality of the biblical God there emanates a drive to unlimited expansion of historical research. The Christian faith must seek its intellectual confirmation in this just as it was necessary for the ancient church to lay claim to Greek philosophy for its witness to the universal deity of the Father of Jesus Christ."[73]

Historical Revelation in Christ

An indispensable feature of Pannenberg's theology as it concerns revelation and history is his approach to the resurrection of Christ. History represents a development of the indirect revelation of God; the history of Israel is a stage of tradition in which Jahweh is not yet the God of all people. As a

---

69. Ibid., 53. Rather than establish the doctrine of God in reference to the apparent claims of the biblical text as revealing the person of God, Pannenberg holds that the historical process of the emergence of Christianity among world religions is what forms the doctrine of God. Pannenberg states, "It is this history which first corrects the preliminary (and distorted) representations of God—indeed, even Israel's representations of its God! Thus, all statements about the redemptive event remain bound to analogies 'from below,' whose applicability is subject to the procedures of historical criticism."

70. Pannenberg, *Crisis of the Scripture Principle*, 1.

71. Ibid.

72. Pannenberg, "Dogmatic Theses," 137.

73. Pannenberg, *Basic Questions in Theology*, 80.

religious tradition, the narrative of the Old Testament establishes Jahweh as the God of Israel, but not of nations outside of Israel.[74] For those outside of the Jewish tradition, Pannenberg included, the history of the Old Testament "is not proof for us of the deity of Jahweh in its fullest sense, since we are heirs of the Greek philosophical tradition and can give the name of God in an unqualified way only to the one God of all men, and can understand the gods of the religions as at best representations and analogies of the one God."[75] Therefore, the acts of God in the Old Testament remain provisional in view of the final manifestation of God as that which is complete and perfect.[76]

The final manifestation of God at the eschaton to which biblical revelation as history looks is what makes Jesus Christ of special relevance.[77] The special act of Christ in his resurrection from the dead is a unique breaking into history of the reality to be known for all humanity at the eschaton. Pannenberg notes, "In contrast, the witness of the New Testament is that in the fate of Jesus Christ the end is not only seen ahead of time, but is experienced by means of a foretaste. For in him, the resurrection of the dead has already taken place, though to all other men this is still something yet to be experienced."[78]

The eschatological character of Christ's resurrection as the prolepsis for all of humanity's resurrection establishes that "the end of the world will be on a cosmic scale what has already happened in Jesus."[79] In Pannenberg's estimation, the implications for the Christ-event are twofold. First, "While it is only the whole history that demonstrates the deity of the one God, and this result can only be given at the end of all history, there is still one particular event that has absolute meaning as the revelation of God,

74. Pannenberg, "Dogmatic Theses," 139–40. Pannenberg notes, "In the history of Israel, Jahweh had not proved himself to be a God for all men. He had only established himself as the God of Israel. This came about in a way that is quite understandable, although it is hardly applicable to us as non-Israelites."

75. Ibid., 140.

76. Ibid., 141.

77. Pannenberg, *Basic Questions in Theology*, 25.

78. Pannenberg, "Dogmatic Theses," 141; and Pannenberg, *Jesus—God and Man*, 129. Pannenberg further notes in a later work, "Therefore, Jesus' resurrection from the dead, in which the end that stands before all men has happened before its time, is the actual event of revelation. Only because of Jesus' resurrection, namely because this event is the beginning of the end facing all men, can one speak of God's self-revelation in Jesus Christ."

79. Pannenberg, "Dogmatic Theses," 142.

namely, the Christ-event, insofar as it anticipates the end of history."[80] Second, "concerning future development in history that reveals God so long as man is still under way toward the still-opened future of the *eschaton*, the Christ-event is not overtaken by any later event and remains superior to all other concepts and remains superior . . ."[81]

While Pannenberg notes the unique aspect of the incarnation of Christ, the eschatological nature of Christ's resurrection should not be taken as a statement of the finality of revelation in Christ.[82] Pannenberg qualifies his comments concerning the Christ-event as revelation with the presuppositions he has already established. Specifically, "the one and only God can be revealed in his deity, but only indirectly out of a totality of events."[83] Therefore, it would appear, despite the unique nature of Christ's resurrection, true knowledge of God will still only come at the fulfillment of what Christ has provided in foresight.[84]

The Christ-event does not remove the provisional nature of knowledge about God, because it has inaugurated (rather than fulfilled) the end of the process of revelation in history.[85] Hermeneutically, Pannenberg's assertion is to ground understanding of faith in Christ in the setting of Christ as proleptic revelation in the tradition of Israel's faith.[86] The life of Jesus is understood from the place he holds in the unique string of world events that stand in the history and traditions of Israel. The revelational meaning of Christ is not only proleptic in that he represents the eschaton in

80. Ibid., 144.

81. Ibid., 144–45.

82. Pannenberg, *On Historical and Theological Hermeneutic*, 177.

83. Pannenberg, "Dogmatic Theses," 141.

84. Pannenberg, *On Historical and Theological Hermeneutic*, 181. Pannenberg claims revelation in Christ does not provide finality of knowledge when he states, "It is possible to find in the history of Jesus an answer to the question of how 'the whole' of reality and its meaning can be conceived without compromising the provisionality and historical relativity of all thought, as well as openness to the future on the part of the thinker who knows himself to be only on the way and not yet at the goal."

85. Pannenberg, "Dogmatic Theses," 142. Pannenberg states, "Now the history of the whole is only visible when one stands at its end. Until then, the future always remains as something beyond calculation. And, only in the sense that the perfection of history has already been inaugurated in Jesus Christ is God finally and fully revealed in the fate of Jesus."

86. Ibid., 145. Thesis five of Pannenberg's systematic presentation of revelation as history states, "The Christ-event does not reveal the deity of the God of Israel as an isolated event, but rather insofar as it is a part of the history of God with Israel."

developing history, but also in that the history of Israel has progressed toward the eschaton in the Christ event.[87]

The Bible and Hermeneutics

In light of the above survey of revelation as history, in what sense then is the written word of the Bible revelation? Pannenberg raises the issue in the following way, "The biblical traditions are to be related to the same God who brings the events of history into being. Our question is: To what extent are the words, authorized by the God of Israel and Jesus of Nazareth, to be related to the history that he activates?"[88] In response to this question, Pannenberg raises the following three concepts; the Word of God as promise, forthtelling, and kerygma. According to Pannenberg, one gains revelation of God's deity through seeing the way in which he fulfills promise through historical act. The prophetic word plays a special role by setting the stage for the historical act. Establishment of this prophetic word through historical manifestation is necessary before the Word of God may become revelation.[89]

The Word of God as forthtelling is Pannenberg's concept that the Law and commandments "follow as a result of the divine self-vindication. They themselves do not have the character of revelation."[90] The Law and commandments are revelatory only insomuch that they are part of the historical act of God in his self-vindication. Therefore, the biblical text only indirectly reveals God in as much as it is part of the historical act.

The second concept, Word of God as kerygma, is Pannenberg's focus on the New Testament apostolic proclamation. The kerygmatic proclamation is the report of the historic act of God as revelation. The kerygma itself possesses no status as revelation, but has its basis in the historical act. Pannenberg notes:

---

87. Ibid., 146. Pannenberg states the Christ-event is a step in the progression of revelation that stands as something new rather than the fulfillment of past prophecies when he states, "In light of [prophetic literature] it would be possible to connect, in a very particular way, the promises of Israel to the fate of Jesus, just as the primitive Christian proof from scripture has done."

88. Ibid., 153.

89. Ibid.

90. Ibid., 153–54.

The self-vindication of God before all men cannot be thought of apart from the universal notification. However, the kerygma is not by itself a revelatory speech by virtue of its formal characteristic, that is, as a challenge or call. The kerygma is to be understood solely on the basis of its content, on the basis of the event that it reports and explicates. In this sense, the kerygma is not to be thought of as bringing something to the event. The events in which God demonstrates his deity are self-evident as they stand within the framework of their own history. It does not require any kind of inspired interpretation to make these events recognizable as revelation.[91]

Therefore, the kerygma is not revelation, but is an aspect of revelation in that kerygma proclaims the eschatological event as it serves as part of the history of reflection upon the historic acts of God.[92]

Pannenberg's approach to the biblical text through these three concepts of the Word of God bears the marks of his controlling concept of history.[93] Likewise, history as the universal realm of all human activity is the place of God's activity.[94] In contrast to Henry's historiography, Pannenberg does not view the activity and communication of God to be unique within the universal historical setting. Pannenberg's anthropological basis for theology and revelation leads him to conclude,

As the history of man, the history of revelation is always bound up with understanding, in hope and remembrance. The development of understanding is itself an event in history. In their fundamental givenness, these elements are not to be separated from history; history is also the history of the transmission of history. The natural

91. Ibid., 155.

92. Ibid.

93. Pannenberg, *Basic Questions in Theology*, 136. Pannenberg notes concerning his hermeneutical approach to the biblical text, ". . . it appears that an understanding of transmitted texts in their historical differentiation from the present cannot be adequately and methodically carried out apart from universal historical thought which, to be sure, must include the horizon of an open future and with this the possibilities of action in the present."

94. Braaten, *History and Hermeneutics*, 147. Carl Braaten notes, "For Pannenberg, hermeneutics cannot be abstracted out of the all-embracing theology of history which properly locates our contemporary situation in relation to the primitive Christian tradition. The hermeneutical gap is bridged by the continuing history of God's unfolding plan for the world . . . From the Protestant side this would seem to call for a rethinking of the relation between Scripture and tradition with special reference to the *sola scriptura* principle and the hermeneutical value of creeds and confessions."

events that are involved in the history of a people have no meaning apart from the connection with the traditions and expectations in which men live.[95]

The historical focus of Pannenberg's overall theological method and, in particular, his approach to revelation and the biblical text, lead toward a hermeneutical approach of corresponding historical emphasis.[96] Pannenberg notes,

> That every historical process is reciprocally connected to events in its environment entirely forbids theological study of history from taking the biblical witnesses and the events attested by them in isolation by themselves. Israel's testimonies of faith, as historical documents, are to be understood only against the background of the ancient Near Eastern world, and the writings of primitive Christianity only in connection with Judaism and Hellenism.[97]

The nature of Pannenberg's approach leads to a historically oriented hermeneutic by which the interpreter must ascertain the meaning of the biblical text only in relation to the historical situation behind the text as the "norm of all interpretation."[98] This chapter now turns to Carl F. H. Henry's evaluation of this mindset.

Carl F. H. Henry's Appraisal of Pannenberg

In the context of articulating thesis seven concerning the historical nature of revelation, Carl F. H. Henry engages the significant positions different than his own. In this process, one would expect Henry's substantive engagement with the revelation as history view.[99] Henry draws upon Pannenberg in particular as the leading theologian to connect "the revelatory

95. Pannenberg, "Dogmatic Theses," 152.

96. Pannenberg, *Hermeneutic and Universal History*, 99.

97. Pannenberg, *Basic Questions in Theology*, 40–41.

98. Pannenberg, *On Historical and Theological Hermeneutic*, 151; and idem, *Basic Questions in Theology*, 56. Pannenberg further notes, "The reference of the Christian faith to history unavoidably carries with it the demand that the believer must not try to save himself from historical-critical questions by means of some 'invulnerable area'— otherwise it will lose its historical basis. The believer cannot want to prohibit any historical question, no matter how it be fashioned."

99. Revelation as history does not exhaust the alternatives with which Henry engages. Another significant alternative will be discussed in chapter four.

purpose of God's redemptive events with all history as revelational."[100] Following an overview of Pannenberg's approach to revelation, history, and the biblical text, Henry provides an appraisal of Pannenberg's strengths and weaknesses.

Henry's Agreements with Pannenberg

Carl Henry finds three areas of agreement with Pannenberg's approach to revelation, history, and the biblical text. He finds within Pannenberg resonance on the points of the unity of history and revelation, reason-based epistemology, and eschatological focus.

Unity of History and Revelation

Henry observes that in Pannenberg's rejection of existentialist-oriented models of revelation, Pannenberg likewise rejects that meaning is relocated into personal existence.[101] In Henry's view, Pannenberg correctly critiqued existentially-oriented approaches to revelation, because "[a]t the expense of objective external activity in the biblical past [they dilute] history into the events of subjective here-and-now personal experience."[102] In contrast to a split between objective world history and an alternative place for salvation history and revelation, Pannenberg argues for "the objective truth and objective fact of revelation."[103] The fact that Pannenberg presses for the unity of revelation and history resonates with Henry's approach to historiography to a certain extent.[104]

Henry does not stand for the separation of history into separate planes for world history and salvation history. The incarnation possesses its full meaning, for both Pannenberg and Henry, in that God's saving act was accomplished in the universal history of humanity and "not in a ghetto of *Heilsgeschichte* or in an *Urgeschichte* the dimensions of which 'cut across'

---

100. Henry, *God, Revelation and Authority*, 2:294.

101. Henry, "Basic Issues in Modern Theology," 18.

102. Henry, *God, Revelation and Authority*, 2:296.

103. Ibid.

104. The extent to which the principle under discussion resonates with Henry is indeed limited, and will provide grounds for one of Henry's critiques of Pannenberg as well.

ordinary history."[105] Henry's agreement with Pannenberg is that "the most comprehensive horizon of divine revelation is the history of God's relations with man and with his whole creation whose future in Christ is now manifest though hidden from the world."[106] Contrary to the split of the nature of history articulated by existential approaches to revelation, Henry finds agreement with Pannenberg in the unity of history.

Henry supports Pannenberg in his defense of the historicity of the Christian faith against the tendency to minimize historical language, because it is unique and not repeatable. Pannenberg argued that lack of analogy for the resurrection, for example, does not undermine the historical reliability of the event. Consonant with Pannenberg's approach, Henry states, "Although reports of the wholly novel require us to rigidly press for tests distinguishing imagination from responsible attestation, no basis exists for automatically depicting a report of what has never happened elsewhere as merely imaginative."[107]

Reasonable Epistemology

Closely tied to the nature of history is the manner by which one knows history. The agreement between Pannenberg and Henry on the unity of history is likewise manifest in their epistemological emphases. The epistemic point of agreement between the two theologians is that they both view the cognitive abilities of humanity as the means to discerning the meaning of revelation. Pannenberg argues the universal nature of revelation in history means revelation is available for all to discern by the faculties of reason through historical inquiry.[108] While Henry disagrees significantly concerning the path to get to a universally knowable revelation, he arrives at a similar destination.[109]

Again, the similarity between Pannenberg and Henry is in the context of common rejection of existentialist epistemology. Henry is supportive of Pannenberg's rejection that revelation is something to be known through

105. Henry, *God, Revelation and Authority*, 2:297.

106. Ibid.

107. Ibid.

108. Ibid.

109. Ibid., 1:323. Henry's route to the necessity of reason is by way of his emphasis on the biblical text as cognitive-propositional revelation and that man understands such revelation through the faculties of reason endowed in the *imago dei*.

personal intuition or special mediation.[110] Preserving the epistemic unity of knowledge of revelation with knowledge of non-religious content is a rejection of the split between the noumenal and phenomenal, which may be accounted for by Kantian influence.[111] Rather than relegate faith to a basis separated from knowledge, Henry asserts in support of Pannenberg, "Revelation is not ambiguous and obscure but conveys clear and essential information about the grounds of faith as a trust directed to the future."[112]

Eschatological Focus

Henry draws upon his summary of Pannenberg's approach to the eschatological focus of all history to emphasize the nature of historiography. Henry's own approach to history is characterized by God's providential presence in every stage of history to guide it to his desired end. In Pannenberg, Henry finds a theology that asserts, "Universal history is related to the eschatological future provisionally anticipated in the Word of promise and proleptically depicted in the resurrection of Jesus who is the first-fruits of a general resurrection and the coming King."[113] In such a view, history is progressing toward an ultimate and final expression of the person of God and restoration of his creation.[114]

The end of all knowledge in the eschaton resonates with Henry's emphasis that all of world history is characterized by the presence of God and movement toward ultimate fulfillment of promise. While in contrast to Pannenberg, Henry draws the unity of history from the canonical Scriptures rather than religious history, Henry may still state: "[Pannenberg]

110. Henry's agreement with Pannenberg on the basis of epistemology is limited and, likewise, serves as grounds for one of Henry's critiques of Pannenberg.

111. Henry, *God, Revelation and Authority*, 2:298. Of Pannenberg's critique Henry notes he correctly identifies a critique of Kant. Henry states, "It preserves the towering influence of Kant, who considers the limits of reason to be such that man cannot *know* the object of religious faith, namely, God. Hence, on the neo-Kantian premise that the meaning or value of facts is not universally valid but is of the nature of faith, a separation of faith and knowledge is assumed."

112. Ibid.

113. Ibid., 2:294.

114. As with the other points of agreement mentioned in this section, the commonality Henry finds with Pannenberg is only partial. The eschatological emphasis on Pannenberg likewise provides grounds, as will be shown, for Henry to critique Pannenberg on the provisionality of knowledge.

preserves alongside the decisive importance of the resurrected Jesus an emphasis on the objective factuality of historical revelation and the occurrence of salvation events within the totality of this larger revelatory history."[115]

Critiques of Pannenberg

Alongside Henry's appreciation for certain aspects of Pannenberg's theology as a step in the right direction historically, Henry raises four areas of concern. These points of concern are the provisional nature of meaning, an immanentist view of revelation and God, undermining *sola scriptura*, and a historical hermeneutic.

Provisional Meaning

The first point at which Henry takes issue with Pannenberg is on the provisionality of meaning. Stemming from Pannenberg's eschatological focus, his frequent emphasis is that all knowledge remains provisional until the final and ultimate revelation of God in the eschaton. Even the proleptic revelation of God in Christ is subject to the influence of indirect and provisional character of all revelation in history. Henry views the claim that assertions about God may only be made in view of the whole of history to be problematic for faith before the eschaton.[116] In particular, provisionality impacts knowledge of the truth and meaning of the resurrection.[117] If the realities of the resurrection may not be truly known, Henry wonders where this leaves humanity whose salvation through faith in the resurrection reportedly depends on resurrection assurances.[118] In what sense may truth claims be made when "only in view of the whole toward which the process moves can final claims be made."[119]

---

115. Henry, *God, Revelation and Authority*, 2:299, 2:309. Henry further notes, "Historical revelation—universal and particular—looks to an eschatological climax that involves a final judgment and the universal kingship of Christ."

116. Ibid., 2:306.

117. Pannenberg, *Jesus—God and Man*, 397. Pannenberg states, "only the *eschaton* will ultimately disclose what really happened in Jesus' resurrection from the dead. Until then we must speak favorably in . . . metaphorical and symbolic form about Jesus' resurrection and the significance inherent in it."

118. Henry, *God, Revelation and Authority*, 2:300.

119. Ibid., 2:301.

In light of Pannenberg's conclusion that "the revelation knowledge that we have . . . is not universally valid truth," Henry then takes focus on Pannenberg's view of doxological statements.[120] Without a claim to valid absolute truth prior to the eschaton, Pannenberg views theological statements as doxological reflections on indirect historical revelation.[121] As Henry states, the consequence of Pannenberg's view is, "[i]n other words, although creedal statements are historically and logically inappropriate, one can affirm the virgin birth in worship without sacrificing truthfulness."[122]

The devotional nature of doxological reflection on divine events in the Bible removes the ability for textual revelation to convey assertions about God's eternal nature.[123] Rather, such reflection provides limited perspectives on truth to be revealed at the eschaton. Henry views the doxological move in light of provisional revelation to be "twice removing biblical testimony from the status of intelligible revelation."[124] Such reflections in the Bible are first removed in that they are based on events which are indirect (rather than direct) revelation of God, and second removed, because they are merely provisional doxological reflections on the part of authors in the tradition of Christianity.[125]

While supportive of Pannenberg's eschatological focus, Henry argues Pannenberg steps afoul by asserting revelation is only provisional and incomplete until the end. Henry concludes,

120. Ibid., 2:302.

121. Pannenberg, *Jesus—God and Man*, 184–85. To this end, Pannenberg states, "human conceptualization sacrifices itself in adoration" and "the conceptual clarity of the ideas used disappears."

122. Henry, *God, Revelation and Authority*, 2:302.

123. Tupper, *Theology of Wolfhart Pannenberg*, 69. E. Frank Tupper captures the nature of doxological statements for Pannenberg as an abdication of theological clarity and truth when he states, "Since doxological adoration requires the sacrifice of finite language and conception to the infinity of the Biblical God, Pannenberg accentuates the radicality of the mystery, the incomprehensibility, the transcendence of the God revealed in Christ beyond all human understanding and power to conceptualize . . . Pannenberg concludes that Christian theology necessarily embraces a plurality of doctrinal formulations, and that dogmatic options assume the form of 'engaging hypotheses.'"

124. Henry, *God, Revelation and Authority*, 2:294.

125. Tupper, *Theology of Wolfhart Pannenberg*, 297. Tupper articulates the difficulty for a claim to objectivity of truth for Pannenberg when he says, "the objectivity of revelation does not constitute a claim to the rational knowledge of everything; the facticity of revelatory events is not beyond legitimate intelligible debate. However, a fundamental ambiguity exists regarding the primary locus of the claims of revelation's objectivity and universality . . ."

If there is intelligible transcendent revelation at some point before the end—as evangelical orthodoxy insists in regard to inspired Scripture—then one can confidently affirm a great deal about God and his ways. According to the biblical view of revelation, the coming end-time disclosure does not negate the permanent validity of what prophets and apostles were given to know "in part" (1 Cor 13:12, RSV).[126]

In Henry's view, the nature of the Bible is that of divinely inspired literary interpretation of divine acts manifested in universal history. From this Word-centric approach, Henry concludes "Pannenberg does less than justice to revelation as a unity of event and interpretation, especially to the fact that both the past redemptive acts and their meaning are now reliably given to us exclusively in Scripture."[127]

Immanent View of God and Revelation

While supportive of Pannenberg's unification of history and salvation history, Henry views the nature of this unity with concern. Pannenberg rejected the contrast between natural events of history and supernatural events of revelation.[128] Pannenberg's philosophy of history served as a rationale for rejecting the supernatural, as Henry makes clear when he states, "Rejection of the supernatural assures that divine acts and human acts occur in the very same field of activity."[129] Henry then adds "[o]ne is tempted to add that if all reality is marked by historicalness, God too must be a historical event" as a conclusion of Pannenberg's approach.[130]

Concerning the Bible, Henry makes the consequent application when he says, "Pannenberg's rejection of the supernatural is quite another matter and deprives us, in principle, not only of supernatural miracle but

126. Henry, *God, Revelation and Authority*, 2:302.

127. Ibid., 3:297–98. Henry's emphasis appears to be that because revelation is broader than the biblical text as it is inclusive of events and text, the hermeneutical focus of the interpreter should be primarily on the text as the means to full meaning of the historical revelation in events.

128. Pannenberg, "Response to the Discussion," 242. For example, Pannenberg says, "the total reality as history is God's world which he creates and through which he reveals himself. If all reality . . . is marked by historicality, then the divinity of God can only be thought of in relation to the whole of reality understood as history."

129. Henry, *God, Revelation and Authority*, 2:300.

130. Ibid.

also of supernaturally revealed truths."[131] The non-supernatural quality of revelation is reinforced by Pannenberg's insistence that revelation is indirect. Rather than convey content about the person of God in a direct way, the "facts of history in their first intention mean something other than a revelation of God."[132] The removal of supernatural status for revelation ultimately concerns Henry because, in his view, it leaves humanity without true knowledge of who God is and what he has done. In other words, Pannenberg's purely historical approach is at risk of muting God.[133]

Undermining Sola Scriptura

As Pannenberg forthrightly argued, the Enlightenment left no option for Christian theology but to abandon the Reformation Scripture principle view of the Bible (*Sola Scriptura*).[134] It is no surprise then that Henry takes issue with Pannenberg's arguments. Henry writes,

> In wholly emptying the reality of divine revelation into history, Pannenberg deliberately overleaps the ideas and words of the Bible. He contends that traditional evangelical Christianity submerges the distinctive problems of the present in a primitive world view. Instead of repristination of biblical truths, he proposes an exhibition of universal history long and broad enough to span the biblical past and the contemporary scene as parts of one historical process and plateau.[135]

Henry stands at odds with Pannenberg concerning the relation of the Bible to the person of God. Pannenberg's assertion is that the Bible is not direct revelation in the sense of theophany. Henry pushes back at this point by arguing "[f]or while [Pannenberg] rightly emphasizes the indispensability of historical divine revelation for the Judeo-Christian religion, he

131. Ibid., 2:301.

132. Ibid.

133. Braaten, *History and Hermeneutics*, 18. Concerning the hermeneutical impact of Pannenberg's theology of revelation, Braaten notes, "The coupling of revelation with history is an omnipresent feature of modern theology. It is almost unthinkable that revelation could be mediated except through something called historical events or historical existence."

134. As referenced previously in this chapter, Pannenberg argues against the place of Scripture as the specific and authoritative revelation of God as historically articulated in *Sola Scriptura* in Pannenberg, *Crisis of the Scripture Principle*, 1–14.

135. Henry, *God, Revelation and Authority*, 2:299–300.

disengages Scripture from ontological revelation of the essential nature of God . . . and virtually eclipses the self-revelation of God in Jesus Christ."[136] Rather than grant authority to the biblical text, Pannenberg "detaches the category of revelation from the divine Word, and assumes that the external historical events with which he fully identifies divine revelation are self-explanatory."[137]

Henry views Pannenberg's move to an exclusive historical locus for revelation as a hermeneutical move as well. Henry notes, "In this maneuver he blurs the unity of event and interpretation . . . Because of his prior denial of supernatural cognitive disclosure, Pannenberg is compelled to shift the entire focus of divine revelation to history alone."[138] The hermeneutical shift for Pannenberg is one of moving away from the authority of the written Word.[139] Henry is troubled by Pannenberg's willingness to overlook the claims of the Bible itself as divine revelation that contains communication from God to particular prophets and apostles in favor of a basis in history of religions.[140] Henry stands on the other side of Pannenberg with the nature of the Bible as revelation when he concludes: "there is something peculiar about a historical investigation of the Bible that can so readily overlook the Scripture's insistent attestations that God's deeds prominently include the revelation of his Word to chosen spokesmen."[141]

---

136. Ibid., 2:301–02.

137. Ibid., 2:303.

138. Ibid. Henry notes in sympathy the impetus that caused Pannenberg to shift the focus to historical events in the face of prevailing non-cognitive existential revelation. Yet, Henry does not follow Pannenberg into the non-supernatural limitations that result in voiding the Bible of divine authority.

139. Pannenberg, *On Historical and Theological Hermeneutic*, 147. Pannenberg stated concerning authority and the Bible, "In any case, the task of theology is not accomplished in the long run by mythologizing the talk about the Word of God (which was originally a mythological expression, anyway), nor by confronting the hearer, threatened by the *asserted* authority of this divine Word, with the naked demand for obedience."

140. Henry, *God, Revelation and Authority*, 2:300. A similar critique is likewise raised in Grenz, "Appraisal of Pannenberg," 49. Henry challenges Pannenberg's foundation that theology is grounded in historical world religion when he states, "But if universal history reveals God at work, and this disclosure is in fact wholly lucid to man independent of a Bible, then why does Pannenberg not choose Chinese or Greek or Korean rather than Hebrew history to expose the revelation to be found there?"

141. Henry, *God, Revelation and Authority*, 2:305.

Historical Hermeneutic

The hermeneutical implication of Pannenberg's approach to revelation, history, and the biblical text is that the orientation of hermeneutics is exclusively historical. The locus of revelation in event leads to the following hermeneutic: a historical rather than a theological goal for hermeneutics and an interpretive rather than an apologetic role for historical inquiry. These emphases of Pannenberg stand in contrast to Henry's emphases on the locus of revelation in the text, the apologetic role for historical inquiry, and the theological goal of hermeneutics. According to Henry, Pannenberg "insists that revelation is not confined to some single strand or 'ghetto' of history but is given rather in universal history. This general history, he affirms, is self-interpreting and requires no special prophetic illumination."[142] Against Pannenberg, Henry claims the meaning of historical events is not something that may be gleaned from the bare events.[143]

By contrast, Henry asserts the need for a revealed interpretation of history when he argues,

> Although the propositional view affirms that revelation cognitively interprets the special redemptive events, Dulles notes that it nonetheless is not fully committed to historical revelation since it "denies that the events of sacred history are by themselves revelation, at least for modern Christians." Many champions of historical disclosure speak of history as the "primary" arena of revelation, but they do not indicate how events two or three thousand years ago "by themselves" become revelation today.[144]

For Henry, "the meaning of the life and work of Christ is not an inference from redemptive acts, but rather depends upon the scriptural interpretation of these acts."[145] The relationship between history and faith is one in which a unity exists between the text of Scripture and the historical acts of God.[146] In order to make this connection, Henry asserts divine saving

---

142. Henry, "Priority of Divine Revelation," 85.

143. Henry, *God, Revelation and Authority*, 2:308.

144. Henry, "Priority of Divine Revelation," 84.

145. Henry, *God, Revelation and Authority*, 2:308.

146. Henry, "The Identity of Jesus of Nazareth," 130. Henry maintains the meaning of the resurrection is provided not only by the Gospel recounting of those acts, but also in the context of the entire Bible. He states, "It was not their unexpected confrontation by the risen Jesus alone, but the Old Testament prophetic teaching also concerning the coming One that finally illumined Messiah's death and triumph over it in terms of divine

events include as revelation the divine communication of the meaning of those events in inspired Scripture.[147] In the final analysis, Henry's appraisal of Pannenberg and the revelation as history approach is summed up in Henry's statement, "According to historic Christianity, God is universally revealed in history, but this premise does not exhaust the totality of divine revelation, nor does it eclipse God's transcendent supernatural relationship to history, nor minimize Scripture's disclosure of the normative meaning of once-for-all redemptive acts."[148]

Conclusion

Carl Henry's interactions with the revelation-as-history approach established and popularized by Wolfhart Pannenberg have provided clarity as to Henry's own approach to revelation, history, and the biblical text. As an evangelical with historical interest that provides the opportunity for Henry to be perceived as promoting a hermeneutical method oriented toward the history behind the text, the analysis above draws clear distinction between a true historically oriented view and Henry's own approach to historicity. In particular, two elements of Henry's critiques of Pannenberg are essential for understanding his hermeneutic. First, Henry focuses attention on the biblical text as the locus for meaning rather than the historical events that may lie behind the text. Second, Henry points to the sufficiency of the biblical text as the source for theological meaning rather than the realm of history. With Henry's corrective toward a historical hermeneutic established, we now turn to his interactions with Hans Frei as a representative of a different approach.

---

prophecy and fulfillment."

147. Henry, "Basic Issues in Modern Theology," 18.

148. Henry, *God, Revelation and Authority*, 2:309. In making his point, Henry draws upon the criticisms of the revelation-as-history approach in general offered by James Barr. Barr raises multiple criticisms of revelation as history, which may be found in concise form in Barr, "Revelation Through History."

4

Revelation as Narrative for Frei

Hans Frei (1922-1988) bears unique and direct influence over the developments in the theological movement known as narrative theology. As an early pioneer of the movement and colleague of other significant theologians in the movement, Frei's work set the agenda for theological developments in American theology. In particular, Frei's works are formative, because he set a hermeneutical agenda, which influences the structures of theologies derived from his hermeneutic.[1]

As editor of Frei's collected essays, and author of several works about Frei's theology, William Placher notes that while Frei published reluctantly and only a comparatively few works by writing theologian standards, his influence is not diminished.[2] Placher notes that, as a result of Frei's influence, at least in part, "[t]oday, however, biblical scholars increasingly analyze the plot of biblical narratives, the way the literary forms work, the patterns of climax and tension. They often find they have more to learn from, and discuss with, literary critics than with historians; indeed, the literary analysis of the Bible is becoming a minor industry."[3] As a result of Frei's status as representative of the post-liberal movement and the source behind evangelical appropriations of narrative hermeneutics, Carl Henry engages substantively with Frei's works. Before considering Henry's

1. For biographical resources on the life of Hans Frei see, Placher, "Hans Frei and the Meaning of Biblical Narrative," 556–59; Placher, "Introduction," in *Theology and Narrative.*

2. Placher, "Hans Frei and the Meaning of Biblical Narrative," 556.

3. Ibid., 558.

appraisal of Frei, an overview of Frei's approach to revelation, history, and the biblical text is in order.[4]

Hans Frei on Revelation

Hans Frei's methodological starting point is different from Wolfhart Pannenberg and Carl Henry in the sense that he does not begin with a scheme for the doctrine of revelation in the modern setting. Whereas the other two theologians featured in this study sought to establish the major concepts of God, revelation, and religious epistemology at the outset, Frei shows comparatively little direct engagement with such topics. Pannenberg and Henry's approaches to revelation set the theological agenda as discovering and ordering revelation as they had defined it in either history or the Bible respectively, but Frei takes a different approach. Theology is not the discovery and articulation of revelation, whatever its nature, but rather theology is the self-description of Christian belief.[5] Frei says "theology is seen to be completely a matter of Christian self-description. Theology, in turn, is responsible to the Christian community or tradition and seeks to exhibit . . . the informal rules that constitute the common Christian language context."[6]

As a theological aim, Frei's desire was to "break with the entire modern liberal tradition in theology, while still remaining within the purview of that tradition to the extent that he does not wish merely to relapse into the pitfalls of the older orthodoxy."[7] In a sense, Frei seeks to accept pieces

4. In 2004, Mike Higton edited and assembled a collection of unpublished lecture manuscripts, transcripts, notes, and other occasional writings by Hans Frei for the Yale Divinity School archives. This archive provides insight into Frei's published works through the unpublished articles and teaching materials Frei used in his professorship at Yale Divinity School. Individual pieces from this archive will be referenced throughout this chapter. The digital archive may be accessed via the Yale Divinity School library website. Frei, *Unpublished Pieces.*

5. Frei, "Remarks," 33. Frei notes the particular influence of Ludwig Wittgenstein and J. L. Austin on his thinking when he states, "In regard to understanding, (remember: for this particular exegetical task!) I find myself influenced increasingly by Wittgenstein and J. L. Austin rather than by the Idealistic tradition that has dominated the field for so long, whether in its pure form (e.g., in Dilthey), in existentialist form, in a more historical form like that of Pannenberg, or in a more ontological form like that of Heidegger, Gadamer, and among theologians Fuchs and Ebling."

6. Frei, *Types of Christian Theology,* 51.

7. Hunsinger, "Hans Frei as Theologian," 104.

of both the "older orthodoxy" and the liberal Protestant tradition, while also revising both.[8] Frei takes as his starting point the Bible as the central element of the Christian community. As the central literary representation of the Christian faith, Frei seeks to take the Bible on its own terms free from doctrinal and methodological presuppositions.[9]

For Frei, approaching the Bible with a prior framework for the nature of God, revelation, and the biblical text is undermining the descriptive approach he advocates. Only by first surveying the biblical narrative and "rerendering" the descriptions given in the texts may one treat the narrative honestly.[10] As will be demonstrated in Frei's outworking of his method in the Gospels, his stated methodological minimalism is a factor in how a reader of the Bible may view historical reference.[11] Given that the concept of revelation does not fit into a larger theological framework for Frei in the same manner as Pannenberg and Henry, Frei's method is limited more specifically to hermeneutical issues at the outset.[12]

Post-Liberal Approach Applied

In contrast to Henry and Pannenberg, Hans Frei published significantly less material in his lifetime. Yet, the volume of his publishing does not limit Frei's impact on modern theology. The reason for the efficiency of his impact may be due to the persistence and focus of his interests, along with the colleagues who published similar methodological works.[13] A survey of

8. Ibid., 104.

9. Springs, "Between Barth and Wittgenstein," 397. Springs notes, "Frei's aversion to theoretical systems is nowhere more evident than in his approach to the practice of reading scripture . . . Understanding Scripture's account of Jesus, as Frei saw it, could not finally depend upon any particular pre-understanding on the part of the reader—his or her perspective, life-experience or even 'reading through the eyes of faith.' Imposing such categories upon the text would obscure, or dangerously 'anthropocentrize,' its witness."

10. Frei, "Historical Reference and the Gospels," 64.

11. Though published earlier than his methodological writings, *The Identity of Jesus Christ* is Frei's outworking of his method in the interpretation of the Gospels. Therefore, attention will be given to this practical outworking as it provides the best example of Frei's approach to revelation, history, and the biblical text.

12. By contrast, the hermeneutical significance of Pannenberg and Henry comes after a thorough discussion determining the nature of the categories of revelation, history, and the text of the Bible. Frei, by contrast, takes the Bible as the literature of the Christian community and seeks to demonstrate its meaning free from *a priori* considerations.

13. Hunsinger, "Hans Frei as Theologian," 109. Hunsinger likewise attributes Frei's

Frei's writings most appropriately begins with *The Identity of Jesus Christ*, in which he provides the application of his approach to revelation, history, and the biblical text in the way he formulates Christology.[14] Frei's launching point for theological inquiry of the Bible is to take a strictly descriptive approach. What Frei intends by a descriptive approach is that the reader of the biblical text discipline himself to observe only the literary content and features of the text without external inputs of knowledge. *The Identity* is Frei's application of his formal approach, which when read in light of his later publishing on the methodology of his formal approach, demonstrates the outworking of his method in focus on Christology.[15]

The hermeneutical focal point for Frei is to focus on the text as literature. With respect to Christianity, the focal point is Jesus Christ, and thus Christology is highly important for Frei. The task of theology, and Christology in particular, is to provide a descriptive assessment of what the Bible says about Jesus Christ. In his descriptive approach, Frei reacted against the non-cognitive approach to hermeneutics in the Neo-Orthodox tradition.[16] Frei is suspicious of claims to direct encounters of revelation based on the difference of description the common person would articulate between being in the presence of another person and being in the presence of God.[17]

Frei, likewise, does not tolerate a claim to revelation coming to man in an intermediate way on account that this empties revelation of cognitive content.[18] Under Frei's descriptive approach to Christology, the text communicates within its own boundaries rational thought, because

---

impact to his focus on both formal descriptive theological method rooted in the interpretation of the Gospels that Frei in turn asserts as normative for broader hermeneutical theory.

14. Frei, *Identity of Jesus Christ*. *The Identity of Jesus Christ* was first published in article format in the Presbyterian magazine *Crossroads*, in 1967, and later edited into book form for publishing in 1975.

15. Placher, "Hans Frei and the Meaning of Biblical Narrative," 558.

16. Frei, *Identity of Jesus Christ*, 54.

17. Ibid., 54. Frei states, "When you come right down to it, most of us would hesitate to claim that we encounter God or Christ directly, the way we encounter our friends and relations or even the limits of our own potentialities and powers."

18. Ibid., 54. Frei notes, "It is difficult to deny at least a degree of justice to the accusation that 'revelation,' as constructed by neo-orthodox theologians, is a way of intellectualizing the relation between God and man by riveting it to the phenomenon of consciousness or one of its several derivatives. Similarly there is justice in the cognate criticism that even then 'revelation' turns out to be so non-informative as to lack all intellectual content."

literature possesses the ability to do so as a communication tool. The central point of the Gospel narratives for Frei is that the identity of Jesus is as he is described as the one who died, was buried, and resurrected. Given the narrative representation of Jesus Christ, the final view of Jesus is that of the resurrected Christ. As such, the proper identity of Christ is that of his resurrected state.[19]

Descriptive Versus Apologetic Methodology

In his descriptive methodology, Frei draws a sharp distinction between dogmatic theology and apologetic arguments. Frei views modern theology as operating with a preoccupation with apologetics. For Frei, much of theological energy, beginning in the eighteenth century, was focused on showing the significance for Christianity to a secular society. The problem with apologetic concerns is that the attention is necessarily diverted from the biblical text to historical and evidentiary arguments.[20] In contrast to apologetic interests, Frei seeks to base his Christology in the meaning of the biblical literature. Frei holds that the task of the interpreter is not to justify the Bible, but rather to simply state "the logic of Christian belief, i.e. the basis and mutual coherence (though not necessarily the necessary mutual implication) of Christian concepts."[21]

In the sense of descriptive versus apologetic approaches to theology, Frei takes a dispassionate tone about defending the truth of central Christian claims, and views his interpretive task as simply to make plain the logic of Christian belief in Jesus Christ.[22] Frei holds true to this method in the course of exploring the identity of Christ through narrative structure. In the face of objection that the resurrection of Christ may not be unique or factual on account of competing resurrection stories outside Christianity,

19. Ibid., 174.

20. Ibid., 57.

21. Ibid., 58–59.

22. Ibid., 59. Frei describes his non-apologetic approach when he states, "I want to emphasize that I am well aware of, but not terribly distressed by, the fact that my refusal to speak speculatively or evidentially about the resurrection of Christ, while nevertheless affirming it as an indispensable Christian claim, may involve me in some difficult logical tangles. Even so, I believe this a better way than the contrary path (taken, for example, by Wolfhart Pannenberg) and a religiously significant way at that. Dogmatically, belief that Jesus is Lord, grounded in believing Jesus' death and resurrection, is itself the explanation for the enablement of . . . a life of faith, hope, and love."

Frei responds this is not a concern of interpretation.[23] As it relates to history, Frei is willing only to assume what he believes many are willing to assume, "that a man, Jesus of Nazareth, who proclaimed the Kingdom of God's nearness, did exist and was finally executed."[24] Concerning the limited scope of theology as he works through his Christology, Frei states the following,

> In other words, the common cultural backdrop and similarity in themes which the Gospel narrative shares with other redemption stories is bound to raise the question concerning whether the Christian story is at all unique. This being the case, I shall not attempt to evaluate the *historical* reliability of the Gospel story of Jesus or argue the unique truth of the story on grounds of a true, factual "kernel" in it. Instead I shall be focusing on its character as a story.[25]

Frei's concern with the Gospels is solely with them as stories. As Frei approaches discussion of the Bible, he does not utilize the category of revelation in his approach. In contrast to both Pannenberg and Henry who fixed the nature of revelation in relation to God, Frei's concern does not move beyond the Bible as story. The immediate consequence of this move that one notices in reading Frei's Christology is that his method does not include a correspondence between the story and any reality to which it may

23. Ibid., 61. The limited nature of theology as descriptive rather than speculative impacts Frei's definition of hermeneutics in *The Identity of Jesus Christ* as well. Frei notes, "Hermeneutics I define in the old-fashioned, rather narrow, and low-keyed manner as the rules and principles for determining the sense of written texts, or the rules and principles for determining the sense of written texts, or the rules and principles governing exegesis. This is in contrast to the more recent, ambitious, indeed all-encompassing view of hermeneutics as inquiry into the process that goes into understanding or interpreting linguistic phenomena. In the latter instance, hermeneutics becomes practically equivalent to general philosophical inquiry; and the language-to-be-interpreted becomes shorthand for a whole philosophical or theological anthropology, a view of man as language-bearer."

24. Ibid., 106.

25. Ibid.

point.[26] The issue of correspondence to historical or spiritual reality as revelation relates to God is not relevant to Frei.[27]

What is relevant in constructing Frei's Christology is the features of the story, which convey the identity of Jesus Christ through patterns in the text.[28] Further, the narrative presents the same identity for Jesus post-resurrection as it does for Jesus in his life and crucifixion. In light of the narrative flow of the Gospels in their emphasis on the continuity of Christ through the resurrection, Frei concludes any other notion of identity for the risen Christ is misguided. Frei states, "The point is that we misunderstand the narrative if we regard the risen Lord as a phantom of the crucified Jesus or, conversely, if we regard the crucified Jesus as the earthly shadow or perpetual death stage of an eternally rising savior figure . . ."[29]

Limits of Doctrinal Development

An important characteristic of Frei's descriptive approach is the limitation it places on biblical meaning and doctrinal development. Frei's desire is to limit the extent of biblical meaning to what may be plainly described from the narrative. Any amount of drawing meaning by implication or speculative reasoning is inappropriate, because it may not be verified by narrative content. The limited scope for hermeneutics and theology is clear in Frei's discussion of the meaning of Christ's resurrection. The question of whether

26. Frei, "Historical Reference and the Gospels," 68. Frei reinforces his aversion to theological construction over and above pure hermeneutical emphasis when he states, "Now of course I do not deny that the narratives may or may not refer—in fact I believe they do at a crucial point—but I believe this is not their 'meaning' but a judgment made about them. They mean what they say (unlike some other types of narratives) whether they refer or not . . . Whatever I believe the authors believed (and of course I think they believed that what they wrote was true), the meaning of what they wrote is a logically distinct matter and the subject of hermeneutical inquiry."

27. Frei, *Identity of Jesus Christ*, 146.

28. Ibid., 149. Frei's attempt is to show the identity of Jesus solely from the story's description of his intentions and actions. As an example for how Frei draws conclusions about Jesus through his hermeneutical method, the descriptive approach is captured in the following statement: "The characterizing intention of Jesus that becomes enacted—his obedience—is not seen 'deep down' in him, furnishing a kind of central clue to the quality of his personality. Rather, it is shown in the story with just enough strength to indicate that it characterized him by making the purpose of God who sent him the very aim of his being."

29. Ibid., 160.

Jesus raised himself or if he was raised by the Father, or questions as to the exact relationship between Father and Son are beyond the description within the narrative. Concerning the limits of theological conclusions one may draw from the narrative Frei states,

> The nature of the narrative therefore imposes a limit on theological comment. It is not likely that we shall be able to get beyond the descriptive accounts presented in the Gospels concerning the resurrection and the relation of God's and Jesus' actions. And if we do go beyond them in explanatory endeavors, we are clearly on our own and in speculative territory, just as we have suggested that we are in speculative realms when we look beyond the narrative for the writers' and Jesus' own inner intentions.[30]

As a consequence, Frei draws a distinction between what may be properly concluded in a descriptive Christology versus an explanatory scheme, which the tradition of theology has built upon the narrative. By limiting his concerns to the descriptions provided by the narrative itself, Frei effectively limits the possibility of moving from the interpretation of the text to theological construction of Christology. Frei makes this limitation clear when he states,

> But it is never easy and usually not desirable to transform a literary description, such as a narrative sequence, into an *explanatory* scheme using abstract concepts and categories. What is perfectly fitting in a narrative may be banal or absurd in an explanatory scheme drawn from our general experience of occurrences in the world. The task of transforming a narrative into such a scheme may be hardest of all in the case of the Gospels.[31]

In the context of Frei's discussion in *The Identity of Jesus Christ*, to a certain extent theological conclusions about the nature of Christ and his relationship to the Father are considered speculative.[32]

The speculative nature of theological formulation is not limited to Frei's Christological assessments, but manifests itself in his appraisal

30. Ibid., 163.

31. Ibid.

32. Ibid. Frei further notes that while it is inevitable explanatory schemes of theology will develop from the narrative, they do not convey the meaning of the narrative. He notes, "However, necessary as such *descriptive* schemes may be, they cannot provide *explanatory* theories for the narrative's claims and for the various patterns of meaning inherent in it, and inherent in it in such a manner that meaning cannot be detached from the narrative form."

of other theological issues as well. The outworking of Frei's approach to theological formulation may be seen in response to inquiry about how one should interpret passages of the Bible that contain some element of evidentiary argument. In particular, on one occasion Frei pressed the question of the significance for Paul's argument in 1 Corinthians 15 that over five hundred witnesses saw the resurrected Christ as a historical/factual basis for belief.

This account alone is not grounds enough for Frei to affirm a historical basis for the resurrection of Christ. He rests his argument that one ought not speculate as to the nature of Christ's resurrection on an account like this, because "[n]one of us know really what a spiritual body is. We are not given an evidential witness scene of what a resurrection is like, and thus no matter how positive the evidence, the event itself remains, though strongly to be affirmed, an evidentially indescribable, rather than a describable event."[33] A lack of narrative description is the basic principle that leads Frei to argue theological formulation about the resurrection is inappropriate.

Christology and Historical Reference

In the context of Christology, Frei acknowledges the question of historical reference in relation to the Gospel narratives. Frei probes the question to the extent of asking whether the events narrated in the Gospels actually took place and if certain teachings "were actually those of Jesus himself."[34] In answering these questions, Frei holds, "it is quite speculative (in absence of external, corroborative evidence) to ask . . . how much actually happened, what he actually said, and how much is stylized account illustrative of his representational character and the author's beliefs."[35] In light of Frei's descriptive commitments and self-imposed limitations in considering questions that may not be verified by the narrative, the question of historicity does not hold a significant place in Frei's hermeneutical and theological methods. For Frei, "the meaning of these texts would remain the same, partially stylized and representative and partially focused on the history-like individual, whether or not they are historical."[36]

33. Frei, "Scripture as Realistic Narrative," 38.
34. Frei, *Identity of Jesus Christ*, 169.
35. Ibid.
36. Ibid.

As will be discussed later in this chapter through Frei's writings on hermeneutics, his emphasis on the narrative alone in determining his descriptive Christology is reflective of his move past the historical eclipse of narrative that took place in the eighteenth century.[37] The biblical text, whether historically accurate or not, consists of "history-like" literature.[38] Frei defines what he means by "history-like" when he states the biblical narratives qualify as such "precisely because like history-writing and the traditional novel and unlike myths and allegories they literally mean what they say. There is no gap between the representation and what is represented by it."[39] As a representation of the person of Jesus Christ, no requirement is given for correspondence between the text and external reality, whether historical or metaphysical.[40] Frei observes that the investigation into cultural backgrounds for the Gospels, the investigation of the composition of the Gospels, and the investigation of the early church's influence on the theological understanding of the Gospels are the provenance of historical inquiry and do not impact the identity of Jesus Christ in the narrative.[41] In other words, the biblical text is not expected to operate in both a historical and a Christological manner.[42]

As a matter of clarity, Frei is careful to note that bracketing the historicity question of the Gospel narratives is not to reduce the Gospels to myth. In his estimation, the "history-like quality of the narrative" ties the narrative to reality in a way myth or legend does not.[43] The operative idea that Frei employs to make a distinction between myth and history-like narrative is that the Gospels provide "self-warranting fact" concerning the life of Jesus.[44] As such, the Gospel narratives provide the grounds for be-

---

37. The historical dominance over hermeneutics is discussed in *The Eclipse of Biblical Narrative*, and is engaged further in a subsequent portion of this chapter.

38. Ibid.

39. Ibid., 59–60.

40. Higton, *Christ, Providence and History*, 114. Mike Higton notes concerning Frei's Christology, "Such a Christology does not allow the question of the historical reference of the resurrection stories any purchase. In fact, if the accounts of the resurrection were to be considered as making a factual claim, Frei suggests that the whole scheme would be put in jeopardy: it would . . . be at best a distraction from his real message, at worst yet another way of running headlong away from the truth which Jesus has to tell us."

41. Frei, *Identity of Jesus Christ*, 175.

42. Ibid., 176; and Frei, "The Accounts of Jesus' Death and Resurrection," 263–306.

43. Frei, *Identity of Jesus Christ*, 177.

44. Ibid.

lief in Christ's identity and presence by means of the narrative specificity concerning the life of Christ.[45]

The generally realistic nature of the Gospels, whether they are taken to be historical or not, prohibits the interpreter from regarding the narrative as myth.[46] Without external corroboration, considering the historicity of the life of Christ is unnecessary, and rests on shifting grounds in terms of understanding directly the person of Christ.[47] The ahistorical nature of the Gospel accounts, in terms of being history-like but not truly informing of historical referent, is further coupled with Frei's acknowledgment that not all of the content in the Gospels qualifies as "history-like."[48] Frei acknowledges on occasion in constructing certain parts of his Christology that portions of the Gospels are stylized accounts of authors or editors, and that significant portions are even fiction.[49] The question of historicity concerning these texts, which Frei takes to be specifically non-historical, is not relevant to the interpretation of these texts, because of the general history-like nature of the Gospels within which these portions reside.[50]

45. Hunsinger, "Hans Frei as Theologian," 111.

46. Higton, Christ, Providence and History, 107. Higton discusses in detail the criteria Frei uses to distinguish the crucifixion/resurrection narratives from myth. He further identifies the significance of the categories of "repeatability" and "unsubstitutability" as features of the text, which distinguishes history-like text from myth-like text. That is, the nature of the narratives bear features that are public, not repeatable, and cannot be substituted by characters and occurrences and still convey the same meaning.

47. Frei, Identity of Jesus Christ, 177. On the limitation of historical knowledge through biographical accounts Frei says, "Even the most reliable historical or biographical account still leaves us in the situation of a certain amount of mystery, after all the thoughts and actions of an individual have been described."

48. Frei, "Theological Reflections," 263.

49. Frei, Identity of Jesus Christ, 178; and Higton, Christ, Providence and History, 115. According to Frei, one fictional narrative is the scene in the garden of Gethsemane about which he states the story ". . . is more nearly like that of fiction. The main example of that fact is the direct inside understanding of the person of Jesus provided by the scene in the Garden of Gethsemane. Surely one would not want to call this description biographical. It is not even pertinent to the story to ask how this sequence can be historical, if Jesus was alone there and his disciples were sleeping some distance away. It is precisely the fiction-like quality of the whole narrative, from upper room to resurrection appearances, that serves to bring the identity of Jesus sharply before us and to make him accessible to us." Additionally, Higton discusses Frei's perspective that the birth narratives of Christ are not necessarily considered history-like, "because they have a form closer to the legendary."

50. Hunsinger, "Hans Frei as Theologian," 112.

Limits of Frei's Descriptive Approach

Through the application of his interpretive method, Frei identifies Jesus Christ as the:

> man from Nazareth who redeemed men by his helplessness, in perfect obedience enacting their good in their behalf. As that person, he was raised from the dead and manifested to be the redeemer. As that same one, Jesus the redeemer, he cannot *not* live, and to conceive of him as not living is to misunderstand who he is.[51]

This identity is the only one which may be discerned for Jesus Christ if one is to take the Gospel representations as literature under a formal-descriptive approach. As will be discussed in Henry's appraisal of Frei, his affirmation of the identity of Jesus is seemingly fair so far as it goes as a basic description. However, it is important to note a qualification Frei brings to the identity of Jesus as it relates to personal faith and belief in the resurrection. Frei acknowledges that Christian redemption requires faith in the resurrected Jesus, which necessarily raises the question of what is meant by faith. It appears he intends faith as confidence placed in a literary representation of the resurrection rather than faith as the conviction of the theological and historical reality of the resurrection. In considering the identity of Jesus and perhaps expressing faith based on the factual reality of the resurrection, one must have a scheme for devotional commitment and factual acknowledgements in which the two elements coincide.[52] Frei, however, hesitates to allow devotion to Christ and historical factual acknowledgement of the resurrection to coincide based on literary analysis. He states,

> . . . it constitutes a reflection concerning the possibility of making the transition from a literary description to historical and religious affirmation. However, explaining how this transition becomes possible—to say nothing of demonstrating its actual occurrence—is what we claimed from the beginning to be impossible, certainly in the context of our analysis of the unity of Christ's presence and identity, if indeed at all.[53]

---

51. Frei, *Identity of Jesus Christ*, 181–82.

52. Ibid., 180.

53. Ibid.

In these statements, Frei rules the move from a formal descriptive literary analysis of the Gospels to historical affirmation of those texts as beyond the possibility of proper hermeneutical and theological method.[54]

Hans Frei's approach to belief in the resurrection is influenced by the course set in the descriptive literary approach. Belief in the resurrection is not the adoption of personal conviction that Jesus died on the cross and in that act brought redemption, but it is belief in the quality of the literary accounts as depictions of the identity of Jesus. Frei notes, "Having directed attention all along to the descriptive structure of the accounts and not the factual historicity of their contents, we must say that belief in Jesus' resurrection is more nearly belief in something like the inspired quality of the accounts than in the theory that they reflect what 'actually took place.'"[55]

In emphasizing the literary structure over the historical factuality of the Gospel accounts, Frei roots belief "in the resurrection is a matter of faith and not of arguments from possibility or evidence."[56] Frei roots this judgment in the fact that evidence of the extent required for independent confirmation of the resurrection is unavailable. There is "no independent historical or other evidence that lends strong or conclusive support to the likelihood that this event took place or that it belongs to a credible type of occurrence."[57] The move then from literary description to faith judgment is one that requires pure belief, detached from the nature of revelation as divinely intended. By contrast to a divine view of revelation, Frei finds sufficient logic in the evidence of the narrative.[58]

---

54. Frei, "Remarks in Connection," 43–44. Concerning the question of truth in interpretation, Frei articulates the truth-value of a text for a believer lies in its aesthetic value for faith and belief. He notes, "That leaves the question of the transition from the aesthetic, non-apologetic understanding to the truth claim—historical, metaphysical, and existential . . . All I can add is that to the Christian the truth of the story can present no problem, and, therefore, its meaning in formal aesthetic description *is* its truth. To the unbeliever, on the other hand, its meaning and its possible as well as actual truth are two totally different things . . . The possibility of its truth is not often a matter of evidence for it, but of the surprising scramble in our understanding and life that this story unaccountably produces: Understanding it aesthetically often entails the factual affirmation and existential commitment that it appears to demand as part of its own storied pattern."

55. Frei, *Identity of Jesus Christ*, 182.

56. Ibid., 183.

57. Ibid.

58. Ibid.

Narratives and Hermeneutics

Hans Frei's most frequently engaged work is his historical analysis of the shift away from literary interpretation of the Bible toward historical and idealism-based approaches.[59] Frei's concern was that the majority of modern theology took a wrong turn on the interpretation of the biblical text. In one direction, many took a wrong turn by viewing the meaning of the biblical narratives as eternal truths about God or human nature (idealism) or in another direction by viewing the meaning of the stories in their reference to historical events (historicity).[60] The central concern of *The Eclipse of Biblical Narrative* is that a "realistic or history-like (though not necessarily historical) element is a feature . . . of many of the biblical scriptures that went into the making of Christian belief."[61] Yet further, Frei's concern is to show how the proper heading of the biblical narratives became lost through shifts toward historical concerns in hermeneutical methods.[62] As such, the historical shift resulted in a loss of the proper meaning of the Bible.[63]

To translate the issue into the terminology of this study, Frei's assessment is that the emphases were misplaced in eighteenth and nineteenth-century hermeneutics as it relates to revelation, history, and the biblical text.[64] Placher directly contrasts Frei's approach with Pannenberg's and views the enduring influence of Pannenberg to stand in competition with

59. Frei, *Eclipse of Biblical Narrative*.

60. Placher, "Hans Frei and the Meaning of Biblical Narrative," 556.

61. Frei, *Eclipse of Biblical Narrative*, 10.

62. West, "On Frei's *Eclipse of Biblical Narrative*," 299. Cornell West states concerning *The Eclipse of Biblical Narrative*, "Frei's fresh interpretation demonstrates the specific ways in which forms of supernaturalism, historicism, classicism, moralism, and positivism have imposed debilitating constraints on the emergence of modern hermeneutics."

63. Frei's hermeneutical project has come under critique from some, because the Bible contains many genres other than narrative. While not often stated by Frei in his most noted works, Frei does state he does not intend narrative interpretation to be an absolute over all genres. Frei states, "I am deeply concerned about the specificity of narrative texts, but there are all sorts of texts, and the Bible includes all kinds of texts to which different hermeneutical rules may apply. For example, I may want to read a letter in a different way from the way I read a story—non-narratively, that is—even if the same person crops up in the tale and in the correspondence, viz. Jesus Christ. In other words, I hope nobody thinks of something called 'narrative sense' as kind of hermeneutical absolute." Again Frei further acknowledges, "I am not saying narrative is all, or even that narrative texts can't be dealt with by other rules of exegesis." Frei, "The Specificity of Reference," 73. Additionally, see Frei's comments to this end in Frei, "Response to 'Narrative Theology,'" 21.

64. Frei, *Eclipse of Biblical Narrative*, 11.

the legacy of Frei's approach to history and the text. Placher notes, "Fueled by Wolfhart Pannenberg's early arguments for the historicity of Jesus' resurrection . . . some Christians still tend to treat the Bible as a historical source whose value lies primarily in its historical accuracy."[65] Through the course of his historical analysis, Frei makes clear the methodological preferences he holds. Utilizing *The Eclipse* as his closest project to a methodological proposal in monograph form, along with his articles both published and unpublished, we now turn to outlining the principles of his approach to revelation, history, and the biblical text.

Locus of Meaning

Frei consistently represents the locus of the meaning to reside in the biblical text. The task of interpretation is thus to "garner the sense of the narrative and not interfere with it by uniting historical and/or narrative sequence with a logically distinct meaning . . ."[66] For Frei, logically distinct meaning includes meaning provided by the interpreter, external imposition of meaning such a historical referent, or "an amalgam of narrative event and interpretation, in which it is impossible to decide how much 'meaning' belongs to the event, and how much to the interpretive perspective upon it."[67]

Asserting the locus of meaning in the text is to argue the narrative form and meaning are inseparable.[68] The meaning of the text arises from the representation of the characters and circumstances as they are presented in the text.[69] Meaning is "*constituted* through the mutual, specific determination of agents, speech, social context, and circumstances that form the indispensable narrative web."[70] The identification of meaning *as*

65. Placher, "Hans Frei and the Meaning of Biblical Narrative," 556.

66. Frei, *Eclipse of Biblical Narrative*, 36.

67. Ibid.

68. Placher, "Scripture as Realistic Narrative," 41. Placher states the "meaning of a text lies neither in the eternal truth it symbolizes, nor in the way it pictures some independent state of affairs. Rather, the narrative's meaning lies precisely in the story it tells."

69. Frei, *Eclipse of Biblical Narrative*, 280.

70. Ibid. Concerning the locus of meaning, Frei clearly states, "one would want to say that the location of meaning in narrative of the realistic sort is the text, the narrative structure or sequence itself. If one asks if it is the subject matter or the verbal sense that ought to have priority in the quest for understanding, the answer would be that the question is illegitimate or redundant. For whatever the situation that may obtain in other types of texts, in narrative of the sort in which character, verbal communications,

the narrative is representative of Frei's desire for an approach to biblical interpretation that is formally descriptive in which interpretation consists of the re-rendering of the narrative description. Jason Springs points to the exclusively textual locus of meaning for Frei when he states, "We do not need to presume that the author's *true* intention somehow stands hidden within or behind the account that he provides, any more than we need to deduce psychologically the genuine intentions of the characters whose actions the gospel accounts narratively render."[71]

Frei's approach to locating meaning in the text carries with it the implication that the meaning of biblical narrative may not be restated in general statement or conceptual language. Separating the content of narrative from its form will not sustain meaning, because meaning is only instantiated in narrative.[72] By implication, Frei's assertion of the inseparability of meaning and narrative would seem to exclude asserting a propositional correspondence for the theological teachings of the narrative. Restating the Gospel narrative teachings about Jesus in conceptual-theological language is illegitimate on account that it "would approach reducing it to meaninglessness."[73]

Through his critique of correspondence between text and conceptual language, Frei limits the venues in which the biblical text may function. Not only in historical matters, but also in construction of how the Bible refers to spiritual realities, the manner in which the biblical interpreter must think is limited to the content of the narrative.[74] Hunsinger notes the limiting influence Frei's descriptive approach has on the locus of meaning. For example, Hunsinger's account is that the meaning of a text is not found in anything that may be separable from the text, such as the author's intention, "philosophical or theological anthropology, nor in the text's religious or moral impact."[75] The meaning of the narratives, rather, are embedded in the structure of the narratives themselves and, according to Frei, to search

---

and circumstances are each determinative of the other end hence of the theme itself, the text, the verbal sense, and not a profound, buried stratum underneath constitutes or determines the subject matter itself."

71. Springs, *Between Barth and Wittgenstein*, 402.

72. Frei, *Eclipse of Biblical Narrative*, 280.

73. Ibid.

74. Ibid.

75. Hunsinger, "Hans Frei as Theologian," 110.

for meaning separable from the formal features of the text is to commit a categorical mistake.[76]

Goal of Hermeneutics

For Frei, the goal of hermeneutics is specifically identified as discerning the meaning in the text. In this sense, the goal of biblical interpretation is literary rather than historical. Frei's historical burden in *The Eclipse* is to show how within biblical interpretation, the process came to include "incorporating extra-biblical thought, experience, and reality into the one real [biblical] world detailed and made accessible by the biblical story—not the reverse."[77] The foundation upon which the literary/theological goal for hermeneutics is pursued is the narrative shape of the biblical texts themselves. The narratives of the Bible should not be treated as the material for analysis under critical history, because they are not that type of literature. The stories reflect "in their indifference to chronology and their occasional inconsistencies" only a loose relationship to questions of historicity.[78] Focusing on the historical accuracy of the texts will cause the interpreter to miss the "aspects of character and plot development."[79] Therefore, the goal of interpreting biblical narrative is to identify the meaning that results from what certain characters did and the experiences they endured within the framework of the narrative.[80]

The development in the history of hermeneutics to incorporate factors outside of the narrative into the understanding of the narrative was not a healthy development in Frei's estimation. Frei's model is to preserve the world of the text and for the interpreter to enter into that world such that the reality of the narrative overcomes the reality of the reader.[81] A Christian makes sense of his own life by identifying his place in the context

---

76. Ibid.

77. Frei, *Eclipse of Biblical Narrative*, 3.

78. Placher, "Hans Frei and the Meaning of Biblical Narrative," 557.

79. Ibid.

80. Ibid.

81. Frei, *Eclipse of Biblical Narrative*, 3; Placher, "Hans Frei and the Meaning of Biblical Narrative," 557; and Auerbach, *Mimesis*. Placher notes the particular influence of Erich Auerbach on Hans Frei through his work *Mimesis*. Auerbach's influence is seen in the point that biblical interpretation involves entering into the world of the narrative.

of the larger story of the identity of Christ.[82] Frei's estimation is that he is preserving the authority of the text against the external forces of historical criticism by asserting the meaning of a narrative is inseparable from its instantiated narrative form. Frei argues, "The point is that the direction of interpretation now became the reverse of earlier days . . . meaning was detached from the specific story or the world of the text and tied to the reader."[83]

Language and Referent

As a theologian, Frei engages the nature of language and its correspondence to referent. Frei's theology of language provides the backing for his methodological and hermeneutical writings. Frei's concern was that language became, through the influence of modernist philosophy, only a system of reference. He was uncomfortable with the notion that "every word was the precise name for whatever thing it named," when it comes to the biblical text.[84] The result of this mindset through the influence of critical interpretation was a disjunction between the literary description and the historical reality. A gap developed between language and the historical referent. In his historical treatment, Frei traced this development to the end of the seventeenth century.[85]

In contrast to the critical hermeneutic, which severed text from historical inquiry, Frei sought to recover the primacy of the literary account over historical background. He maintained, "The literal sense and the historical sense meant exactly the same thing. If the meaning of what is written is exactly what it says, and if it is not either allegorical or symbolic or anything else but what it says, and if it is a story, then it is a true story, an historical story."[86] No gap exists between linguistic representation and the meaning of that which is conveyed. The claim for the unity of literary experience and meaning is to claim, in Frei's terms, a "realistic quality" to the biblical narratives is present.[87] What Frei intends by his approach to

82. Placher, "Hans Frei and the Meaning of Biblical Narrative," 556.

83. Frei, *Eclipse of Biblical Narrative*, 5–6.

84. Frei, "On Interpreting the Christian Story," 47.

85. Ibid., 48.

86. Ibid.

87. Frei uses the term "realistic narrative" to indicate the nature of narrative, which he takes to represent faithfully the reality intended by the author without obligating him

language and referent as "realistic" is that not everything stated linguistically has a corresponding referent, but it is "as though the author is saying, 'I mean what I say, whether or not something happened.'"[88]

The correspondence of literary construction to external reality is one with no point of exploration, because there is no access to meaning beyond the narrative. Reality comes only under description. Frei states, "We have this reality only as it is rendered under the description, only as it is rendered by this narrative. It is as though the Bible, especially the Gospel story (if I may put it is [sic] this boldly, and following a theological friend of mine) were a non-fictional realistic novel."[89] Frei's concern is not to argue that the linguistic features of the text present something other than the historical reality. On this count, Frei should not be misunderstood as attributing some sort of kerygma to the literary texts that he would not view in the historical facts of the case. Rather, Frei views language as going only so far in its ability to convey historical or metaphysical reality.[90]

Following on his Christological emphasis, Frei emphasizes the disjunction between literature and empirical fact as it relates to the resurrection. While affirming that Christians should rightly believe in the resurrection, Frei also stops short of acknowledging that the resurrection belongs to the same realm of history as other empirical events. He states,

> The resurrection is a fact the truth of which Christians affirm even though they have to say that the nature of it is not such that we are in a position to verify it, because even though we affirm it we do not think of it under the category of an ordinary empirical datum; it is a fact which is rendered effective to us through the story and we cannot have it without the story in which it is given.[91]

As it relates to linguistic expression and historical referent, that which one only has through literary recounting is beyond the affirmation of independent historicity, because empirical verification requires access to the

---

to affirm narrative as historical report.

88. Ibid., 50.

89. Ibid., 51.

90. Frei, "Theology and the Interpretation of Narrative," 110. Hermeneutically, Frei defines the notion of meaning in a non-referential way when he states, "The *sensus literalis*, I have suggested, is deeply embedded in the Christian interpretive tradition of its sacred text, and in that way embedded in the self-description of the Christian religion as a social complex rather than as a set of phenomena cohering in, and manifesting, an underlying essence."

91. Frei, "On Interpreting the Christian Story," 51–52.

repeatable facts of the event. The content contained within the linguistic system is distinct from empirical facts, so Frei concludes the resurrection must be of a different category than "ordinary empirical datum."[92]

With these remarks, Frei conveys a positive test mindset toward historicity. In other words, in order for something to be affirmed as historical, it must be affirmed on the grounds of independent empirical investigation. As will be seen in a subsequent portion of this chapter, Henry's evaluation of Frei's unwillingness to draw correspondence between linguistic, historical, and metaphysical reality leaves the interpreter short on theological truth on which he may base his life. At one point, Frei even acknowledges the historical assumption behind his theory of referent.

The following statement, which is the strongest Frei makes with respect to the historical nature of Jesus Christ, sounds much more congruent with Henry's vision of the importance for historical rootedness for Christian revelation than that conveyed by much of Frei's writings. Frei states,

> On one matter, of which you make much, I plead guilty to a kind of fall-back on common sense, to which someone may say I have no right. I am assuming that somebody roughly fitting Jesus of Nazareth as described in the Gospels really did live. If and when it is shown that this assumption is unwarranted and the person invented, I will no longer want to be a Christian.[93]

Note Frei's interest is not to utilize the text of Scripture in a way that functions as historical proof. Rather, the text is merely description, which operates independent of any factual claims for the historicity of Christ. Historicity is simply a presupposition, which may only be tested by empirical means outside the process of biblical interpretation.[94]

---

92. Ibid., 52.

93. Frei, "Historical Reference and the Gospels," 67.

94. Ibid. In his reliance on the text, Frei falls back to comment in a way not unlike Henry's negative test for historicity when he states, "Until then, I plan to go on being one and saying, 'We know him only under a description, viz., that of the Gospel accounts, and they say that the point at which possibly but not necessarily fictional depiction and factual reality are seen to be fully one is the resurrection. In abstraction from the full connection between them at that point of the depiction, the relation between every description of individual incident and putative factual assertion corresponding to it is simply more or less probable."

Historical Referent and the Resurrection

Given the centrality to Frei's theology of the Gospel narratives in general, and the identity of Jesus Christ in particular, it is illustrative of his approach to language and referent to consider Frei's perspective on the historicity of Jesus. His approach to the historicity of Jesus provides insight into his outworking of the relationship between revelation, history, and the biblical text. Much discussion related to narrative referent and the Gospels in Frei's works do not directly answer the question of how he views the historical Jesus. In a short commentary on the theology of the resurrection, Frei writes more candidly than in many of his other writings. Frei articulates his position concerning the resurrection in contrast to three other positions in modern theology at the time of his writing.[95]

Frei's own view is that the Gospel narratives depict truly the resurrected Christ as a real event. However, literary depiction is inadequate for articulating the resurrection. In other words, a disconnect exists between the biblical text and the reality of the resurrection which may not be bridged. Frei states concerning the biblical text, "The text is not a photographic depiction of reality, for not only are the accounts fragmentary and confusing, but they depict a series of miraculous events that are in the nature of the case unique, incomparable, and impenetrable—in short, the abiding mystery of the union of the divine with the historical, for our salvation from sin and death."[96]

Frei's remarks seem to indicate that the texts of the Gospels do not afford the capability of drawing clear conclusions concerning the incarnation and individual salvation. The primary function of the text is what drives Frei's approach to historical and theological referent. In particular, Frei states the following concerning the primary function of the Gospels,

> [I]n this view the text taken literally is understood primarily as the adequate testimony to, rather than an accurate report of, the reality. Narratives such as the empty tomb and accounts of the resurrection appearances are understood to be the indispensable means for grasping, even though not explaining, the mystery of Christ's resurrection as a real event. This, and not their credibility

95. Frei, "Of the Resurrection," 201–02. These alternate positions are: (1) that of Bultmann, (2) "the historicist view" of Pannenberg and conservative evangelicals, and (3) the historical-critical approach of Tillich.

96. Ibid., 203.

as evidence for the factuality of the event, is their primary function as texts.[97]

In the above passage, Frei makes use of the nuance of distinguishing between the primary function as literature and the possible function of historical referent for the biblical text. While this nuance may portray Frei as closer to Henry in how the text functions, the lack of affirmation for historical referent in the breadth of Frei's writings prevents viewing Frei with this balance. Frei's approach to the nature of the text's purpose then, at a minimum, minimizes the Gospels as historical basis for belief in the empty tomb.[98]

Frei's approach to the resurrection leads one to ask if Frei is willing to take the biblical accounts as factual reason to believe in an empty tomb, even if this is not the primary function of the Gospels. As is perhaps typical for Frei, he remains hesitant to commit to a historical-factual resurrection. He states,

> This is not to deny the possibility, in this point of view, that the story of the empty tomb may have the tentative secondary role of rendering historical evidence, but the argument in its favor is at best likely to be as good as, but no better than, the contrary position, namely, that the textual account is not likely to have been derived from genuinely early or reliable accounts. Faith in the resurrection of Jesus Christ cannot be articulated except by way of the resurrection narratives; but though indispensable, they are not the sufficient condition of the faith that Jesus himself (not merely faith in him) is the subject of the resurrection. That Jesus, and not merely faith in him, is raised from the dead is the mysterious gift of the one God who accomplished both and linked them together. Seeking to understand the primary and secondary, major and minor, functions of texts (such as that of the story of the empty tomb) in this larger context of faith, we can perhaps do no better than to endorse the cautious words of a recent writer: "[The empty tomb

---

97. Ibid.

98. Ibid. In order to reinforce the purpose of the text Frei states, "In other words, to take the account of the empty tomb (for example) to have primarily the status of a factual report used as evidence is from this point of view to mistake its textual function. It is to turn it from a witness of faith into a report, from testimony to the truth of the mystery that unites the divine and the human into a report of a simply and solely natural-type event that is supposed to demonstrate its divine character by running counter to customary natural experience."

story] functions as a negative condition which contributes to the overall shape and character of the resurrection."[99]

Despite making allowance for the possibility of a historical referent to the empty tomb, Frei remains agnostic that the textual accounts are any more likely to provide factual witness than they are to provide faith reflections of the authors.[100]

What is ultimately important for Frei is that the Jesus depicted in the Gospels still stands in solidarity with his people as their savior. Yet, without a willingness to articulate a factually empty tomb based on the biblical texts, Frei is left with a questionable foundation for having confidence in the eternal rule of Christ when he states, "In his eternal rule Jesus Christ maintains that solidarity with us that he established in the days of his flesh."[101] While eternal advocacy before the Father is a role theologians have attributed to the resurrected Christ, Frei stops short of acknowledging the historical-factual importance of Christ's resurrection as the expression of God's power in space and time to raise Jesus Christ to his place of solidarity to humanity's benefit.

Hunsinger raises questions as to the nature of Frei's Christology—not only as it relates to the historicity of Christ, but to the divinity of Christ. The outcome of Frei's hermeneutic appears to be a relatively low Christology as it relates to affirming the divinity of Christ. Hunsinger notes that no specific exegesis of a passage is used in Frei's writings to support the full divinity of Christ. He notes affirmation of such is the product of dogmatic assertion rather than hermeneutical conclusion.[102] This relatively low Christology of the person of Christ is a result, according to Hunsinger, of the methodological limitations Frei places on his hermeneutical method. Hunsinger notes, "Frei needs a larger set of concepts and a wider hermeneutical base to sustain what he says about Christ's saving work. Yet he is prevented from openly acquiring them insofar as he strives for deliberate methodological austerity and independence from dogmatic theology."[103]

---

99. Ibid., 203–04. Frei is quoting from Fergusson, "Interpreting the Resurrection," 303.

100. Higton, *Christ, Providence and History*, 116. Higton summarizes Frei's mindset concerning the resurrection as "Frei affirms the resurrection, but he does so with a deep reserve."

101. Frei, "Of the Resurrection," 206.

102. Hunsinger, "Hans Frei as Theologian," 116.

103. Ibid., 117.

The Nature of History

Hans Frei does not give systematic treatment to the nature of history in his major writings in the same way as Pannenberg and Henry. Given Frei's emphasis on minimizing historical referent as the criteria for interpretation, he emphasizes the literary features of the text much more. In so doing, Frei does not exhibit the same interest in whether history is unified or a duality as part of his scheme for revelation, history, and the biblical text. On one occasion, Frei did engage the topic of "sacred and profane history" in a symposium manuscript preserved in the Yale Divinity School archives.[104]

Frei engages the question of whether Christian history is to be subsumed under world history or if Christian history constitutes something altogether unique. In Frei's words, "Which, if either, is logically subordinate to, or a sub-species of the other? General history or salvation history?"[105] What is peculiar about Frei's framing of this question and treatment in the 1981 symposium is that he remains agnostic as to the answer to the question. Frei hesitates to commit, but instead remarks, "It's hardly fair to raise a question and then refuse to answer it, but unless I am very much mistaken there is no compelling Christian theological reason to solve this matter, not even perhaps to think of it in terms of either/or."[106] Instead of declaring for either a unified or a duality approach to history, Frei appears to avoid answering the question in an effort to articulate a position in between the two options. Frei seeks to avoid what he judges to be two extremes on this issue. On one side, he refuses to view history as the mere outworking of a secular materialism through world history.[107]

On the other side, Frei is concerned the existentialist view that the consciousness of the human being provides meaning to historical events falls short. These two prevailing philosophical notions set the framework for Frei's consideration of the nature of history. Distinct from Pannenberg and Henry, Frei does not offer a theological explanation rooted in the doctrines of God, creation, and revelation.[108] Rather, Frei looks to provide a way of viewing history and revelation, which does not fit the traditional categories, but is rooted in a notion of teleology. The closest Frei comes to

104. Frei, "History, Salvation-History, and Typology," 76–88.
105. Ibid., 77.
106. Ibid.
107. Ibid., 78.
108. Ibid., 79.

stating the synthesis of his dialectical consideration of unified or duality history comes in the following statement,

> Though not directly manifest in extrinsic or immanent teleology of the natural process or consciousness process, God sustains his creatures, non-human as well as human, whom he has called into being, one creation in two realms, cosmos and history, the revealed unity of their administration being not the collapse of either into the other but Jesus Christ as the all-governing providence of God.[109]

In this statement, Frei seems to indicate a unity of history under the principle of God's providential governing of all aspects of creation.

This unity does not involve collapsing the realms of theological truth and history, but rather maintaining a distinction amongst unity. Unfortunately, in his ambivalence for answering the question of the nature of history, Frei does not elaborate upon these ideas to provide insight into how this unity functions and what impact it may have upon hermeneutics. Further, while he affirms the role of Jesus Christ as the "all governing providence of God," which would seem to point to a unified theory of history, Frei is ultimately hesitant against overtly metaphysical articulations of the nature of history. Further, while the statement above indicates some sort of unity, subsequent discussion will demonstrate Frei operated with a functional duality of history.[110]

Carl Henry's Appraisal of Hans Frei

Carl Henry specifically engaged the nature of narrative theology in a way that yielded a series of articles containing an interchange between Henry and Frei published in the *Trinity Journal*.[111] Henry's focus in his evaluation of Frei in particular (and narrative theology broadly) was on the issues of revelation, history, and the biblical text. Henry begins his analysis by situating the rise of narrative hermeneutics in the shifting hermeneutical times of modernity. With the passing of the "assumption of assumptionless interpretation" and the setting of "existential and neo-orthodox" emphasis on internal faith beyond cognitive verification, the door was open for a new

109. Ibid.
110. Ibid., 85.
111. Henry, "Narrative Theology," 21–24.

alternative in Henry's opinion.[112] In this setting, narrative theology entered as the new alternative. Henry's definition of the movement is that it is composed of "influential scholars who have proposed narrative hermeneutics and canonical hermeneutics as constructive alternatives to these rival contemporary approaches."[113]

In Henry's estimation, the crux of the narrative approach is the relationship between history and the text. Henry states, "The newer options reject the higher critical dismemberment of the Bible into segments of differing historical value."[114] The narrative approach does so with the aim that "the Bible should be taken as it stands and not partitioned and reconstructed in search of some primitive version of which we have only a prejudiced late redaction."[115] The implication of setting aside occupation with the historical inquiry of the Bible is that the "authority of the biblical text is independent of confirmation or disconfirmation by historical critics."[116] The chief champion of the narrative hermeneutic in Henry's estimation was Hans Frei; therefore, he applied his focus to evaluating those views which find their source in Frei. In particular, Henry is concerned to reveal the strengths and weaknesses of Frei's narrative approach as it relates to the divine authority of the biblical text.

Carl Henry's Points of Agreement with Hans Frei

The points of agreement between Henry and Frei are twofold. The first significant point of agreement rests upon Hans Frei's text-oriented hermeneutic. As much as Frei offered a substantive critique against the power historical-critical theory came to hold over the biblical text, Henry expressed appreciation.[117] Henry's writings are in agreement with Frei in

---

112. Henry, "Narrative Theology: An Evangelical Appraisal," 3–4.

113. Ibid., 4.

114. Ibid.

115. Ibid.

116. Ibid.

117. Ibid., 8. Concerning the value of narrative theology for emphasizing the divine authority of the text Henry remarks, "Does this orientation approach the evangelical emphasis on the authority of the text? The evangelical belief in the divine redemptive acts does not depend on verification by historical criticism but rests on scriptural attestation. The Bible conveys the meaning of God's redemptive acts; since it is the divine salvific acts it interprets, the acts are indispensable presuppositions of that meaning. Or does the emphasis on a destiny-laden truth-claim have more in common with David

that the meaning of divine redemptive acts do not depend on historical confirmation, but rather are interpreted and given through the biblical texts. Henry's second significant point of agreement with Hans Frei rests upon their common critique of the tendency of existentialist approaches to hermeneutics to locate meaning in personal, intuitional knowledge of the divine. Through Frei's text-oriented emphasis, he sought to make a way forward after the influence of modern historicism and existentialism that would return the proper place to the text as the locus of meaning. Henry takes up similar concerns in his treatments on revelation and history.[118] Henry notes that existential approaches, expressed specifically by Barth and Bultmann, place human decision as "creatively formative in interpreting historical events, whose meaning is therefore not universally valid and objectively accessible to all men but gains significance for individuals only through subjective inner decision."[119]

Carl Henry's Points of Critique toward Hans Frei

Carl Henry expressed appreciation for Hans Frei for his emphasis toward hermeneutics that are textually oriented and for his critique of the existentialist tendency to supply personal meaning for the text. While Henry and Frei find common ground in their critiques on the two preceding points, their differences are more significant and may be summarized in the three following categories: universality of narrative, value of historical referent, and the Bible and truth.

Universality of Narrative

Henry's first point of critique for Frei's approach to revelation, history, and the biblical text is a challenge that literary categories are sufficient to unify the biblical text.[120] Henry observes that the foundational principles of Frei's

---

Kelsey's emphasis on the life-transforming function of Scripture in the believing community, than with historical evangelical formulations of its objective cognitive authority that vouchsafes and validates such personal dynamisms?"

118. In particular see *God, Revelation and Authority*, chapter twenty of vol. 2 entitled *Revelation and History: Barth, Bultmann, and Cullman*, in which Henry specifically addresses the existentially oriented approaches to revelation and history.

119. Henry, *God, Revelation and Authority*, 2:284.

120. Henry, "Narrative Theology: An Evangelical Appraisal," 15. While the debate

approach to the nature of Scripture stem from literary theory. Frei's reliance on literary theory stands in contrast to utilizing a scheme of revelation to account for the nature and unity of the Bible. Henry queries, "On what rational basis does narrative theology insist that the biblical narrative reflects a unified theme and orderly content?"[121] Further, Henry remarks, "But does narrative theology offer a credible alternative to classic Protestantism's emphasis on intelligible divine revelation and the creator-redeemer God's cognitive inspiration of chosen prophets, an emphasis that narrative theologians dilute or subordinate?"[122]

The lacuna of an account for revelation in relation to the personhood of God leaves an appeal to the unity of Scripture based on the literary category of narrative inadequate in Henry's mind. The significance of inspiration as the mode of God's revelation leaves the nature of the Bible inadequate to support the weight of competing arguments for the disunity of Scripture. In other words, in contrast to the historical-critical mindset Frei intends to counter, it is questionable what gives his articulation of biblical unity advantage over the argument from critical scholars that the Bible is fundamentally a disunity of assembled texts.

The response articulated by Henry is that without rooting biblical authority in divine authority through revelation, the unity of the Bible is weakened. The theological foundation for biblical unity rooted in the notion of revelation leads Henry to argue, "Evangelicals insist that authorial intention and grammatico-historical interpretation do not exclude a single divine Author and a single sense that permeates the diverse genres and constitutes an undergirding and overarching unity. They do so, however, on the premise that the Bible is a singularly inspired book."[123] Henry raises the concern that narrative theology, as Frei articulates it, does not make effort to account for the idea of revelation as it relates to the Bible. Taking

---

between Henry and Frei illustrates the differences between their views, Henry does note the points of congruence with his own view of revelation, history, and the biblical text. In particular, Henry states appreciation for the emphasis Frei's work has brought to the place Scripture should hold independent of historical criticism. Henry states, "Whatever its differences from evangelical orthodoxy, narrative theology reaffirms that the Bible persists as a harmonious unity towering above cultural and historical differences; that historical criticism has not invalidated the relevance of Scripture; that the biblical world spanning creation to consummation is the real world . . . that affirmation of Jesus as the indispensable Saviour remains on the human agenda as an imperative decision."

121. Ibid., 9.

122. Ibid., 10.

123. Ibid.

Henry's concern for a lack of rooting biblical unity in the divine author together with the fact that the category of narrative does not account for significant portions of the Bible, Henry raises the question of how might not the same text Frei judges to be a unity be judged a disunity based on the same evidence of genre variety and disparate sources?[124]

Value of Historical Referent

Henry's second significant concern with Frei's approach to narrative theology is the nature of textual claims to historical fact.[125] As a potential friend of evangelical hermeneutics, Frei seeks to liberate textual interpretation from the pressure of historical-critical confirmation. Henry's view discussed in chapter two was that textual interpretation is separate and not contingent upon historical reconstruction. Despite the similar affinities of a hermeneutic that is textually-based, Henry expresses concern over Frei's views of the text and history. At the heart of the matter is the nature of history as unified or duality. Henry states that narrative hermeneutics does not affirm,

> [W]hat confessional orthodoxy does when the current theory accepts the literary authority of the narrative and embraces appropriate factual implications of the text independently of historical criticism. Unless the historical data are assimilated not only to faith but also to the very history that historians probe, the narrative exerts no claim to historical factuality.[126]

Henry's concern is that Frei's approach, which systematically hesitates to make any detailed affirmations regarding the relation of the text to historical claims, fosters a duality in the nature of history.[127] Ultimately, Frei has relegated biblical-historical narrative to a self-referential closed language system separate from historical reference. In a passage which bears

124. Ibid.

125. Ibid. Henry's assertion is that "by focusing on the meaning of the divine acts Scripture does indeed carry an independent testimony to the factuality of the redemptive acts for faith."

126. Ibid., 11.

127. Ibid. Henry notes, "The notion that the narrative simply as narrative adequately nurtures faith independently of all objective historical concerns sponsors a split in the relationships of faith to reason and to history that would in principle encourage skepticism and cloud historical referents in obscurity."

resemblance to the duality of nature between *historie* and *geschicthe*, Frei states,

> Is Jesus Christ (and here I come across the problem of miracle) a "fact" like other historical facts? Should I really say that the eternal Word made flesh, i.e., made fact indeed, is a fact like any other? I can talk about "Jesus" that way, but can I talk about the eternal Word made flesh in him that way? I don't think so, just as I don't think that I can say "God created the world" and mean by that a factual referent like any other.[128]

In contrast to the hermeneutics based on the unity of history in Henry and Pannenberg, the historical agnosticism of Frei presents opportunity for duality of history.[129] In light of apparent affirmations by the biblical text itself to the historical occurrences, one of which is the focus of Frei's work on the resurrection, the biblical interpreter must preserve a place for genuine historical inquiry.[130] Insofar as the unique redemptive acts of God are thought to be historical, Henry reasons, "must they not fall into the same category of history that legitimately concern contemporary historical investigation? The narrative indeed gives the meaning of the acts which, as interpreted, elicit saving faith."[131]

John Johnson provides a similar assessment of the importance of historical referent based on the idea that the "*narratives themselves* in the New Testament are used to undergird the historicity of Christ's resurrection from the dead in bodily form."[132] Johnson points to texts such as Acts 17:31, Acts 26, and 1 Corinthians 15:12-19 as textual warrants for faith based on the resurrection of Christ as "an objective event in time-space history

---

128. Frei, "Response to Narrative Theology," 24.

129. Henry, "Narrative Theology: An Evangelical Appraisal," 11. It should be noted that Frei does not specifically articulate a duality for history. Yet, as has been demonstrated through analysis of his writing in this chapter, Frei methodologically resists affirmations which stem from a unified approach to biblical and universal history. On this point, Henry states that the "Representations of biblical history by many narrative theologians leave one with the uneasy sense that their commendable reservations about the historical method are correlated with a view that important aspects of biblical history belong to a different historical category than the history that contemporary historians investigate."

130. Ibid. Henry states it thus, "Surely the NT does not present the resurrection of the crucified Jesus without explicit historical claims to which it attaches first-order importance (1 Cor 15:3–8, 17)."

131. Ibid.

132. Johnson, "Hans Frei as Unlikely Apologist," 140.

that verified the claims of the new faith the disciples were preaching."[133] Importantly for Henry, affirming historical reality does not push him into the search for biblical meaning in universal history as does Pannenberg. Rather, the Bible is taken by Henry to be adequate testimony to historical reality in universal history. He conveys this view when he states, "The Bible thus provides a line to historical redemptive acts independently of historical critical investigation."[134]

The heart of the issue for Henry is that if Frei's scheme requires setting aside the reality of events historically revealed, then this requirement carries implications for one's view of God. The epistemic implication of Frei's view of historical reference is such that the biblical narrative does not refer to the events in historical reality that were the sovereign choice of the creator God for how to reveal himself.[135] Of potential concern as a derivative of Frei's methodology is that the historical reality would be considered unnecessary for the interpretation of any narrative literature.[136] Henry is supportive of Frei's assessment that historical-critical interpreters had suspended the "validity of the biblical witness upon confirmation by the historical method."[137] However, he is simultaneously concerned that Frei's methodological presuppositions have compromised "a vital commitment to the historical trustworthiness of Scripture."[138]

The question of validity as it relates to historical reference for Frei is "whether faith elicited by the biblical narratives as narrative theologians encourage it involves an epistemic split, one that allegedly would retain salvific efficacy even if historical investigation were to discredit the empty

133. Ibid., 140–41. Johnson's intention in his article is to make use of Frei's argument for textual sufficiency in addition to the foundation of referent provided by a traditional evangelical doctrine of revelation. Johnson is overly sanguine about the compatibility of Henry and Frei's theoretical approaches and does not sufficiently acknowledge the alterations necessary to Frei's approach in order to accomplish this cooperation.

134. Henry, "Narrative Theology: An Evangelical Appraisal," 11.

135. Ibid., 12. In support of his point Henry asserts, "Evangelical theism insists that God reveals himself in external history and nature, and supremely in redemptive history, although man's predicament in sin locks him up to the biblical revelation for the authentic meaning of the redemptive acts."

136. Ibid.

137. Ibid., 13.

138. Ibid. Henry further expounds, "The narrative approach unacceptably minimizes Luke's expressed concern (1:1–4) for historically reliable sources and Paul's affirmation that our faith is vain unless Christ arose factually from the dead (1 Cor 15:17)."

tomb and Jesus' bodily resurrection?"[139] While Frei has not stated that the Christian faith produced the resurrection (in fact, he criticizes such a view throughout his writings), he has demonstrated a hesitance to make any categorical statement that if Christ had not indeed raised from the dead, the Christian faith would be weakened.[140]

The Bible and Truth

Henry's third point of critique of Frei's approach to revelation, history, and the biblical text focuses on Frei's approach to truth. In particular, Frei's approach to reference affects not only how the Bible refers to historical datum, but also how the Bible refers in any sense. Frei acknowledged the influence of language philosophy in general, and Ludwig Wittgenstein in particular on his theology.[141] The influence of viewing language as a self-contained system of meaning is evident in Frei's hesitance to acknowledge any text-transcendent referent. This lack of referent is evident not only in historical matters but in metaphysical matters as well.[142] Henry's concern is that Frei's approach to language and referent ultimately compromises the category of truth, which Henry views indispensable to the theological appropriation of Scripture.[143]

Along these lines Henry notes, "The notion that truth is a feature only of language determined solely by grammatical rules actually presupposes

139. Ibid.

140. This type of hesitance to historical affirmation toward the resurrection may be specifically seen in Frei, "Of the Resurrection." Johnson notes a similar assessment when he states, "So Frei apparently was inclined to see the resurrection *perhaps* as a real event in history, although he did not fully commit himself to its historicity." Johnson, "Hans Frei as Unlikely Apologist," 146.

141. Clark, "Narrative Theology and Apologetics," 500. As noted previously in this chapter, Frei acknowledged the influence of Wittgenstein on his thinking. Clark likewise notes, ". . . pure narrativists like Hans Frei, George Lindbeck, and Stanley Hauerwas are antifoundational, cultural-linguistic, Wittgensteinian-inspired descriptivists."

142. Henry, "Narrative Theology: An Evangelical Appraisal," 13.

143. Henry, *God, Revelation and Authority*, 3:451. Henry viewed the language philosophy influence on Narrative Theology in context of the movement's historical development. He notes, "As often happens, a strong corrective of one error sways to an opposite extreme. As positivism resulted in a reductionism that disallowed the inherent cognitive integrity of metaphysics, theology, and ethics, the emerging ordinary language movement issued in a relativism that knew no standard of truth or adequacy for philosophical discourse other than that given in the ordinary workings of language."

that there is no reality beyond language itself, or that, if there is, we cannot know it."[144] To state the issue in terms consistent with the vocabulary of this study, the goal of hermeneutics for Frei is neither historical or theological, but literary, and without a focus on the category of truth.[145] This point of critique is not surprising in light of Henry's emphasis on the truth claims of the biblical text in relationship to the text's ability to refer in a true way to matters that are worldly or metaphysical.[146] Yet, in constructing critique concerning Frei's approach to the nature of language and referent, Henry does not compromise a textually-oriented hermeneutic. He specifically notes, "The locus of the meaning and truth of Christian language is to be found, not in the empirical correlates of words, nor in an inner existential response to which words are said to point, but in the Bible as an inspired literary deposit of divinely revealed truths."[147]

In light of the above discussion concerning language and referent, a basic difference between Henry and Frei emerges in how the two theologians account for the legitimacy of language and referent according to grounding in epistemic claims. The methodological emphasis Henry requires is exactly the opposite of the methodological minimalism that Frei desires. The legitimate question stemming from this contrast is whether Frei's methodology is, indeed, a fair claim to minimizing presuppositions in terms of prior epistemic commitments.[148] For what claims to be a minimalist structure philosophically has been critiqued as grounded in philosophical commitments.[149]

144. Ibid., 3:448–49.

145. Ibid., 3:351. Frei's literary focus without explicit concern for truth stands in contrast to Henry's apologetic concern for historical validity.

146. Henry, *God, Revelation and Authority*, 3:342; 352–56; and 386–402. While expounding upon Henry's constructive approach to the source and nature of language is not directly within our scope, he does provide a theistic view of language rooted in the concept of language as a necessary component for God's self-revelation. For Henry's discussion, see *God, Revelation and Authority*, 3:230–47.

147. Ibid., 3:452.

148. Springs, *Between Barth and Wittgenstein*, 404. While philosophical categories are the focus of critique in this section, it is significant that Frei's ruling literary category of narrative was on occasion of concern for himself, and others supportive of his method, on account it may have been given undue priority over the biblical text to a general literary category.

149. A significant critique that demonstrates Frei's philosophical commitments may be found in Wolterstorff, "Will Narrativity Work as the Lynchpin?". Wolterstorff argues Frei's hermeneutic lacks a place for revelation as the Word of God when he states,

Hans Frei's Response to Carl Henry's Appraisal

Hans Frei responded specifically to Carl Henry's critique of narrative theology. This response from Frei grants the opportunity to observe that Henry's critique is not one of unfair assessments, but rather an honest analysis that illustrates the differences between two approaches to revelation, history, and the biblical text. With significant candor, Frei draws attention to the epistemic differences, which drive the distinctions between him and Henry on the issue of text and referent.

Frei acknowledges, as does Henry, "how we refer is not language neutral."[150] Consistent with his basis in language philosophy, Frei asserts the limitation of external referent for a text when he states, "We are, and are able to think, only by way of the language in which we think. Our referencing, especially in cases where empirical objects are not involved, like God (who, St. Thomas tells us, is beyond genus and species) is language-bound."[151] Frei's implication is that there is no legitimate place for discussing the reality of the claims made by the text outside of the closed system of reference provided within the text. Without a category for reference that corresponds to a reality outside of the biblical text, Frei is seemingly content to abstain from any inquiry into the validity of the claims of Scripture as true or false. Before voluntarily making definitive statements on language and referent Frei states,

> I am going to listen in on a conversation that I am going to request among Wilfred Sellars, Alvin Plantinga, Willard Quine, John Stuart Mill, Immanuel Kant, and Aristotle. I am going to listen in, and when they agree on what they mean by logic, and when they agree on the transcendental categories that get them started on their way to formal certainty and clarity, and on their epistemologies or lack of them, then I'll have a starting point for a natural theology . . . or for an appropriate theological "prolegomena."[152]

"[T]he traditional view that proper reading of the scriptures is a mode of revelation in the present (and was a mode of revelation in the past) is as absent from Frei's line of thought as it was from Locke's. That [the Bible] is 'the Word of God' does not function in his argument." Ibid., 101.

150. Frei, "Response to Narrative Theology," 22.

151. Ibid.

152. Ibid., 22–23.

Frei's assertion is that the lack of a clear epistemology in modern philosophical terms leaves the interpreter best off not attempting to work in the realm of reference.[153]

To be even-handed, Frei does not claim he is free from epistemic concerns. He acknowledges the need for such underpinnings and arrives at them in a way consistent with postmodern epistemology. Frei states, "I indeed can't do without some philosophical equivalent to natural theology, some philosophical equivalent to epistemology, let's say, but I have to piece it together eclectically and provisionally."[154] For Frei, the nature of reference is not that the text communicates transcendently true information about God through events that are historically true. Rather, the biblical text provides the language for the life of the church, and questions of reference are outside the scope of the Bible. Taking Frei at his own words in length on this point is helpful when he states,

> I proceed on the conviction that there is a genuine continuity in the language of the Christian church as it readapts itself in every age to the paradigmatic language of Scripture, particularly to the story of the gospel and to reading the OT as the "figure" leading toward fulfillment in that story. I have to go on the conviction that there is more continuity in the language of the church and the Scripture than there is in the philosophical languages and their use of "knowledge," "God," and so on and so on. And again, let me simply refer here to what I said earlier. For example, using the term "God" christianly is in some sense referential. But that doesn't mean that I have a theory of reference to be able to tell you *how* it refers. It is also true in some sense other than a referential one: it is true by being true to the way it works in one's life, and by holding the world, including the political, economic and social world, to account by the gauge of its truthfulness.[155]

Frei's desire is to assert the sufficiency of the biblical text in contrast to dependence on philosophical or historical-critical categories.[156] However,

153. Perhaps some irony exists in that the importance of religious epistemology is what compels Henry in his approach to divine revelation and to reach conclusions very different from Frei on textual meaning and reference. The two theologians are similar in their understanding of the importance of noetic prolegomena, but divergence in conclusions highlights the difference in their epistemic foundations.

154. Ibid., 23.

155. Ibid.

156. Ibid. Frei's desire to assert biblical authority and sufficiency is clear, yet the question arises from this affirmation, if he is willing to affirm textually sufficiently in such a

REVELATION AS NARRATIVE FOR FREI

as genuine and beneficial as Frei's text-based hermeneutic may be in regard to challenging historical-criticism, his reticence concerning reference limits his ability to assert a culturally transcendent authority for Scripture. Frei makes the statement that, if he were pressed into the language of factuality and truth, he would speak of a literal resurrection.[157] However, he continues by stating the terms on which truth is based is limited by the nature of language. In order to accomplish this, he must make moves in the following way by stating,

> If I am asked to use the language of factuality, then I would say, yes, in those terms, I have to speak of an empty tomb . . . But I think those terms are not privileged, theory-neutral, trans-cultural, an ingredient in the structure of the human mind and of reality always and everywhere for me, as I think they are for Dr. Henry.[158]

In other words, it appears Frei is asserting that there are not sufficient grounds from the biblical text and epistemological resources to affirm that the resurrection is factual in a way that it is universally true for all cultures at all times.[159] Frei has sought to put forward the biblical text as self-referential and sufficient in itself for providing the language of Christian faith. Yet, his epistemological background prevents universal truth claims from arising from Scripture, whether of metaphysical or historical importance.[160]

---

way then, why not affirm historical reality of the text as well? Frei states, "The truth to which we refer we cannot take apart from the biblical language which we employ to do so. And belief in the divine authority of Scripture is for me simply that we do not need more. The narrative description there is adequate. 'God was in Christ reconciling the world to himself' is an adequate statement for what we refer to, though we cannot say univocally how we refer to it."

157. The hermeneutical importance of the Christian community as the cultural linguistic setting and source of authority in which the biblical texts are used may be particularly seen in: Frei, "The 'Literal Reading' of Biblical Narrative," 117–53.

158. Frei, "Response to Narrative Theology," 24. Frei's ambiguity and statements that approximate denial of the historical reality of the resurrection have been previously noted in this chapter.

159. Clark, "Narrative Theology and Apologetics," 509. In this regard, Clark views the case as "Frei is insisting on the postmodern mode of thinking—a holistic, linguistically flexible, pragmatic style."

160. Frei, "Response to Narrative Theology," 24. Frei acknowledges his adoption of a metaphysical theory different from premodernity or modernity when he states, "But it may also be that I am looking for a way that looks for a relation between Christian theology and philosophy that disagrees with a view of certainty and knowledge which liberals and evangelicals hold in common."

Contemporary Discussion
Concerning Henry and Frei

As an attempted contemporary extension of Henry's critique of Frei, Gregory Alan Thornbury offers "A Henry-Esque Critique of Frei's Approach to Hermeneutical Methodology and the Theological Task."[161] Of concern to Thornbury is that Frei seems to have traded one set of epistemic principles for another and labeled it as hermeneutical minimalism.[162] The first point in distinction Thornbury identifies is on the nature of truth. As demonstrated in chapter two, Henry held to a realist position concerning the nature of truth. In contrast, Frei demonstrated a hesitance to acknowledge truth as a category relevant for biblical interpretation and hermeneutics. In essence, Frei subordinates truth claims he does not view favorably under those he does view favorably, yet he identifies this as removing unnecessary philosophical elements in biblical interpretation. Frei is most clear on the nature of his philosophical commitments when he states, "Stick to your guns, treat the truth question also under the auspices of your theme, otherwise you will point us back to the theological past rather than to the future."[163]

Thornbury rightly observes Frei's moves on the nature of truth when he states, "This points to the fact that despite Frei's equivocation, he does argue for truth claims on a rational, logical basis much like his putative hermeneutical villains of *Eclipse*. He does so not only by hiding behind the obscurity of his concept of realistic biblical narrative."[164] In a fashion similar to that of Henry, Thornbury takes Frei's hesitance to acknowledge textual referent to ontological truth and applies it to the matter of historical reference. Thornbury notes that "while it is not always the case, often the author gives clear indication that his historical concerns are concomitant with his theological and narrative concerns, as with Luke's stated intention in his Gospel and adjoining account of the early church."[165] The ambiguous nature of historical reference in Frei leads Thornbury to respond, "for Frei, the Christian understanding of truth need not correspond to a reality to

161. Thornbury, *Recovering Classic Evangelicalism*, 91.

162. Thornbury's assessment is helpful to my analysis of Henry and Frei, even though he takes a different approach to the issues. Thornbury's analysis is conducted based on the differences between Henry and Frei's epistemology, whereas I have conducted analysis on the interpretive strategies of the two theologians.

163. Frei, "Epilogue," 279.

164. Thornbury, *Recovering Classic Evangelicalism*, 92.

165. Ibid., 94.

which everyone and everything is held accountable."[166] Thornbury views
Frei's hesitance to affirm correspondence between text and metaphysical
truth or text and historical truth as a weakness, which leaves Frei's hermeneutic open to the charge of failing to provide a way through competing
authorities.[167]

Thornbury has provided helpful assessment of the distinctions between Henry and Frei through making clear their differences on the philosophical underpinnings for their approaches to reference. Thornbury does
not take a specifically hermeneutical approach to assessing Henry's critique
of Frei, but is concerned with the epistemic consequences of Frei's non-referential philosophy. Nonetheless, the philosophical underpinnings Thornbury highlights are related to the hermeneutical points raised through the
fivefold rubric such that Thornbury's analysis provided above is helpful for
demonstrating the efficacy of Henry's critique of Frei.

George Hunsinger provides an alternative perspective that Frei is not
completely denying ostensive reference from the biblical text based on the
idea that Frei's approach to meaning and truth is most often misunderstood. The basic claim that Frei finds in the Gospels is that Jesus is rightly
identified as the one who is resurrected. Taking this claim as the ultimate
meaning of the Gospel narratives, Hunsinger views Frei's system of reference as genuinely referring to a "self-warranting fact."[168] The self-warranting facts of the narrative are rightly taken by faith on account of the merit of
the narrative text rather than independent verification from other sources.
Hunsinger notes, "In this light it becomes clear that Frei is not claiming
that the Gospel narratives make no ostensive reference. He is rather claiming that they make no ostensive reference to an object to which we have
independent epistemic access and whose factuality can be affirmed on any
grounds other than faith."[169] In essence, Hunsinger views Frei's moves on
reference to claim that the true reference of the narrative is to the "mystery
of the presence of Jesus Christ" whose true identity the narrative depicts.[170]

166. Ibid., 95.

167. Ibid. Additionally, concerning the importance of textual referent Thornbury
notes, "The debate over external referents is a debate over biblical authority and ultimately whether one must believe in the claim that the Christian gospel is ontologically
true."

168. Hunsinger, "Hans Frei as Theologian," 125.

169. Ibid.

170. Ibid.

Mike Higton is another theologian who favorably appropriates the work of Frei and seeks to apply his approach to history. Yet, in contrast to Frei's claim to minimalist philosophical commitments as he compares his approach to that of Henry, Higton acknowledges Frei's underlying epistemic commitments. Higton notes,

> Nevertheless, it is clearly not the case that Frei's categories and claims have been read direct from the New Testament. It has been clear in the course of this chapter that the distinctions Frei has made have involved him in philosophical discussions with the likes of Gilbert Ryle, or with the German idealist and existentialist tradition, and that he has produced in their favour some dense and complex passages of technical argumentation which make no claim to be biblical exegesis. These are clearly not "New Testament concepts," and they are clearly not elements of an esoteric language open only to Christians. They are elements of public language, open and available to anyone—yet they are learnt, according to Frei, from the New Testament.[171]

Thus, in light of these theologians who favorably receive Frei's legacy concerning the nature of the biblical text and history, it is clear there are philosophical assumptions concerning Frei's mindset about the nature of the biblical text which influence his approach just the same as for Henry and Pannenberg.

What one finds in comparing the Henry/Thornbury and Hunsinger/Higton assessments of reference in Frei are that Hunsinger/Higton's definition of reference is different than that of Henry/Thornbury. Henry identifies reference in terms of faithful correspondence between textual description and the historical reality the text is describing. In contrast, Hunsinger's definition of reference subsumes the idea of reference under the category of realistic narrative description as Frei limits the theological task to formal re-description. To this point, Hunsinger notes, "In the case of the Gospel narratives, meaning-as-ostensive-reference is conceptually dependent on and subsequent to meaning-as-realistic-narrative-identity-depiction."[172]

Conclusion

Henry's sum assessment of Frei is that he "in the broader sense offers us a hermeneutical theory that affirms the comprehensive authority of Scripture,

---

171. Higton, *Christ, Providence and History*, 110–11.

172. Hunsinger, "Hans Frei as Theologian," 125.

yet suspends the question of its ontological truth and historical factuality
. . . a theory that insists on the plenary-verbal integrity of the story form, yet
concedes that large portions of the Bible do not fit that form."[173] The ultimate concern for Henry is that Frei's approach to truth and correspondence
stems from a metaphysic foreign to the biblical paradigm for revelation that
Henry finds to be basic for the Christian faith.[174] As it relates to evangelical
appropriation of narrative hermeneutics, Henry expressed concern about
the mixing of presuppositions on critical categories like truth and reference.[175] Henry states to this end,

> Scholars who employ narrative exegesis for theological ends se-
> lectively engage its hermeneutical presuppositions. They supple-
> ment its use, moreover, by advancing doctrinal considerations
> initially derived from reading the Bible on traditional orthodox
> premises, rather than from a consistent application of the narra-
> tive approach.[176]

Through analysis of the hermeneutical approaches to revelation, history, and biblical text, it is clear that Carl Henry provides a balance of the
historical realism of Wolfhart Pannenberg and the textual focus of Hans
Frei. Uncritical appropriation of either hermeneutical approach opens the
way to emphases that are not consistent with what Henry views to be the
essential convictions evangelicals should hold concerning the doctrines of
God and revelation. In this role, Carl Henry's approach provides what Pannenberg and Frei do not—a textually oriented *and* apologetically engaged
approach to revelation, history, and the biblical text.

173. Henry, "Narrative Theology: An Evangelical Appraisal," 19.

174. Ibid. Henry notes, "It eclipses transcendent divine authority and revelatory truth
that initially spurred immense interest in scriptural exegesis. The narrative approach
therefore seems not fully befitting the historic Christian faith, nor fully serviceable to the
need for an intellectually compelling argument with modernity."

175. Johnson, "Hans Frei as Unlikely Apologist," 147. Johnson notes concerning the
relevance of Henry's critiques of Frei, "But Henry raises a question that Frei cannot avoid:
are the truths found in the narrative portions of scripture based on actual events of history? And if they are not, why should anyone take them seriously in terms of the truth
they allegedly convey? . . . To this Frei gave no real answer, and his position that truth
is not 'univocal' (whatever that may mean) is not helpful when faced with the type of
unavoidable question that Henry asks."

176. Henry, "Narrative Theology: An Evangelical Appraisal," 19.

5

Carl Henry's Insights and Today's Evangelical

The previous three chapters have surveyed Carl Henry's approach to revelation, history, and the biblical text in light of his interactions with the approaches of Wolfhart Pannenberg and Hans Frei. The purpose of this chapter is to articulate that Henry has provided a way through the issues under discussion that is text-driven, yet apologetically engaged and, therefore, is a preferred model for approach to such issues in contemporary evangelicalism. Henry's approach is faithful to a view of the biblical text as God's revelation, while also bearing the nuances of Pannenberg and Frei's strengths. Accordingly, the redemptive acts of history are meaningful and fully revelatory only through the inspired interpretations of the events provided in Scripture. The endorsement of Henry as a paradigm for contemporary evangelicals on the issue of revelation, history, and the biblical text is not absent of observation about how Henry's approach may be improved. Thus, this chapter will provide critical analysis to demonstrate Henry provides the best path forward, while also identifying points where Henry's articulation may be improved.

Prior to considering the individual concerns of the fivefold rubric, it is appropriate to note the foundational value of Carl Henry's contribution to the matter of revelation, history, and the biblical text. The overarching contribution Henry has made is that he provides grounds for establishing the role of the authority of the Triune God as the undergirding for textual interpretation. Concerning the nature of Scripture, Henry states,

> The first claim to be made for Scripture is not its inerrancy nor even its inspiration, but its authority. Standing in the forefront

of prophetic-apostolic proclamation is the divine authority of Scripture as the Word of God. The main emphasis of the apostolic kerygma in its use of Scripture is that it is divinely authoritative. As in proclaiming the incarnate Word, so in regard to the epistemic Word, the fact of a divine reality holds center stage; related details of birth and growth and underlying psychology have lesser prominence.[1]

With this statement, Henry pushes the consideration of issues concerning revelation, history and hermeneutics to a state where the person of God is preeminent. Through his theology of revelation, Henry directs the attention of biblical interpreters upstream from debates about the nature of history and the biblical text, and he points them to the central conviction that there is a "triune personal God behind all biblical affirmations and attestations."[2]

Through this approach, Henry makes debates over the nature of the biblical text as narrative and the historicity of divine redemptive events a matter of God's ability to speak to his people and the reliability of God's divine communication. The central idea that gives Henry's approach privilege over those of Pannenberg and Frei is that his approach is rooted in the biblical picture of the Triune God as authoritative. Gregory Thornbury notes to this end,

> Christianity, in Henry's view, must root itself firmly in the assertion that the definitive and final revelatory word for all Christian belief and action is wholly contained in the authority of Scripture. This is the essential disjunction of Henry's entire argument and what he perceives as the fundamental question of modern theology; either the Bible is the transcendentally objective, divinely inspired, God-ordained authority and final word for all standards of truth and value, or the Bible is not and all of life is thus relative and culturally conditioned and thus incoherent.[3]

For Henry, all of the subsidiary debates concerning revelation, history, and the biblical text—locus of meaning, nature of history, goal of hermeneutics, and so forth—are essentially arguments of authority, and specifically the authority of biblical revelation. The hermeneutical details stemming from this central idea about the biblical text as revelation

---

1. Henry, *God, Revelation and Authority*, 4:27.

2. Thornbury, *Recovering Classic Evangelicalism*, 127.

3. Ibid., 129.

provide advantage for his treatment of history. Conversely, it is Pannenberg and Frei's divergence on the nature of the Bible's relationship to the Triune God that produces the weaknesses in their approaches to history and hermeneutics.

The Fivefold Rubric Revisited

Throughout this book, five points of evaluation have been used to consider the approaches of Henry, Pannenberg, and Frei. The diversity regarding the nature of revelation among the three theologians is clearly seen in the analysis of their approaches in the fivefold rubric below. In each of these five points, it will be demonstrated Carl Henry's approach to hermeneutics is an appropriate paradigm for text-centered and historically affirming interpretation compared to Pannenberg and Frei.[4]

Locus of Revelation: Text or Event

Surveying the theology of revelation upon which the three theologians in this study have built their hermeneutics has revealed three distinct approaches to the locus of revelation. Wolfhart Pannenberg has identified the locus of revelation to reside specifically in universal history. While emphasizing a text-oriented hermeneutic, Hans Frei does not provide a specific answer as to the locus of revelation. In general, Frei's concern was not to provide an explanation for how God has made himself known beyond basic emphasis on a few narratives found within the Gospels. Through implication, it could be stated Frei takes the text as the locus of revelation, because the text is the exclusive concern in his hermeneutics, but this implication for Frei is quite different from Henry's approach. In contrast to Frei, Carl Henry devoted much attention to the task of articulating a doctrine of revelation that is encompassing of many dimensions, yet specifically focused on the Bible as written revelation. For Henry, revelation may include God's activity in history through redemptive acts, but the Word of God defined as Scripture is the particular revealed meaning of these spiritual interventions

---

4. For a summary of the fivefold rubric, see chapter one.

of God in world history.[5] In light of these three approaches, which is to be preferred?[6]

The tension a historically oriented approach such as Pannenberg's produces is evident in the critiques put forward by Henry and Frei. As both Henry and Frei noted in their distinct ways, the ultimate fruit of a historically oriented approach is that it undermines the function and authority of the biblical text. The noted effect of historically oriented hermeneutics, both within and outside those who claim the evangelical label, is a pressing behind the biblical text for meaning. In its fullest form, the historical hermeneutic manifests itself in thorough and exclusive historical-critical interpretation. Among those who claim the evangelical label, one finds a spectrum of influence from the historical mindset.[7] This influence spans from hermeneutics that are functionally historical-critical to those that, in

---

5. Sailhamer, *Pentateuch as Narrative,* 56. Henry's mindset on the locus of revelation reflects helpful clarity concerning the term "history" in a similar fashion to the distinction Graham Cole provides when he states, "*History* as a term is, of course, ambiguous. It may refer to what actually happened (words spoken, deeds done, circumstances leading up to, consequences arising from). Or it may refer to our account of what actually happened (an interpretation of words spoken, deeds done, circumstances leading up to, consequences arising from)." Likewise, Sailhamer notes his terminological preference for clarity when he states, "Thus the term *event* offers a more precise way of speaking about history when we want to distinguish it from a written record about history."

6. Henry, "Narrative Theology: An Evangelical Appraisal," 12. Henry has provided a concise summary of the two approaches that are represented by Pannenberg and Frei in the following passage. "The revelation/history/Scripture tensions will be illuminated if one contrasts Frei's *Eclipse of Biblical Narrative* (1974) with G. Ernest Wright's *God Who Acts* (London: SCM Press, 1952). Wright insisted that an objective divine revelation was conveyed not in the Bible, but rather in external historical redemptive events that the prophets and apostles devoutly, but fallibly, interpret in Scripture. By contrast, narrative theologians hold that the revelation is conveyed in and through Scripture, which, however, they categorize as realistic narrative that has a loose and unsure connection with historical actuality."

7. Sailhamer, *Pentateuch as Narrative,* 17. Sailhamer notes the influence of the historically oriented model for revelation on evangelical hermeneutics when he notes, "Evangelical biblical scholars have not always been clear on this point. Although holding to a view of Scripture as God's revelation, they have tended to interpret the formula 'revelation in history' in such a way that the term *history* refers not to the text of Scripture but rather to the past events themselves. In other words, the locus of revelation is taken to lie not in the text of Scripture but in the events witnessed by the text. In such an approach, the events lying behind the text of Scripture are read as a salvation history within which God makes known his will to humanity."

a more measured manner, promote an interpretive process that is incomplete without some component of historical inquiry.[8]

Hans Frei is illuminating in the way he draws attention to the commonality of liberal and conservative evangelical historical tendencies to press beyond attention to the biblical text for meaning in some plane other than the text.[9] As part of the interpretive process, Frei does well to pull attention away from concerns "behind the text" to focus attention on the particulars of the biblical literature itself. The historical turn in hermeneutics brought with it a tendency to look past the biblical text to find meaning elsewhere. Whether meaning is sought in historical detail, a psychological consciousness-centered view of the author's intention, or doctrinal principles propositionally restated, severing revealed meaning from the text ultimately undermines the role of the Bible in the Christian church.

With preference established for a text-based locus for revelation that excludes Pannenberg as a viable approach to the locus of revelation, the question arises as to which approach is more fruitful between Henry and Frei. While features of Frei's approach are helpful to evangelicals, as will be argued in more detail later in this chapter, it is evident Frei does not provide a doctrine of revelation sufficient for an approach to the locus of revelation that is theologically robust. Frei's writings on the nature of revelation—minimal as they may be—are in line with the articulations of the broader post-liberal approach to revelation and doctrine. In particular, George Lindbeck has provided insight into a narrative approach to revelation, which views doctrine as the articulation of the grammar of the Christian community rather than direct revelation of reality.[10] Without providing a full evaluation of the post-liberal approach to doctrine, one may state in summary that post-liberal theology does not conceive of textual revelation as a fundamental theological source for meaning.[11] Without a distinct role for revelation in a broader theological sense, Hans Frei is unable to provide clear argument for a preference of the locus of revelation in either history or the text.

---

8. For a summary of the influence of the historical approach of evangelical hermeneutics, see chapter two in Sailhamer, *Old Testament Theology*.

9. Frei articulates a correlation between liberal and conservative evangelical hermeneutical method in Frei, *Types of Christian Theology*.

10. Lindbeck, *Nature of Doctrine*.

11. For summary and critical interaction with post-liberal theological method, see Phillips and Okholm, *The Nature of Confession*.

The claim above that Frei is not the preferred text-oriented approach concerning the locus of revelation may appear out-of-step with certain perspectives on Frei because of his text-focused hermeneutic. Does not Frei's emphasis on the biblical text hermeneutically indicate his view is that the text is the locus of revelation? The answer lies in that Frei provides the right solution (text-oriented hermeneutic) without the right foundation (a theology of the Bible as revelation). For Frei, the biblical text does not generally function to provide true knowledge of God and his will. As a narrative, the Bible is not a revelation of the truth of God, and the reality God created because portions are classified as *history-like* and other portions as *fiction-like* by Frei. A foundation of revelation such as Frei provides is insufficient as the theological backing for a text-oriented hermeneutic.[12]

The argument of this section is that Carl Henry's description of the locus of revelation provides a surer foundation for text-oriented hermeneutics than Pannenberg and Frei. Concerning Pannenberg, it has been demonstrated that his strong emphasis on revelation as history leads the interpreter past the text to methods of historical inquiry for meaning. Henry's advantage over Frei is not so transparent given Frei's reputation of text-centeredness, but analysis demonstrates Frei does not offer a substantive doctrine of revelation. The notion of textual authority requires grounding, and Frei leaves this authority untethered from a specific foundation outside of the community. In contrast, Henry roots textual authority in divine revelation.[13] The rooting of textual authority in the nature of divine authority through revelation as the doctrinal formulation is the overarching theme of Henry's theology.[14] Henry reasons that if God himself is authoritative as

---

12. It is for this reason that when appropriated by modern evangelicals, Frei's methodology is best utilized in a careful supplementary manner to a more classical form of evangelical doctrine of revelation. Frei's textual emphasis is employed as a corrective toward certain approaches to revelation and hermeneutics, but not as a full replacement for the view that the Bible is personally revealed by God. Frei is drawn upon to restore attention to the biblical text precisely because the Bible is viewed as God's revelation.

13. Henry, "Narrative Theology: An Evangelical Appraisal," 16. The strength of Henry's approach comes through in his affirmation of both God's activity in history and in the unique nature of textual revelation as the divine meaning of revelatory events. Henry states to this end, "Revelation is grounded in the history of God's reconciling acts but is not exhausted by them. The events are attested and interpreted by inspired writers."

14. Henry, *God, Revelation and Authority*, 2:8. Specifically, thesis one of *God, Revelation and Authority*, sets the tone for rooting textual authority in divine revelation. Henry states, "Revelation is a divinely initiated activity, God's free communication by which he alone turns his personal privacy into a deliberate disclosure of his reality."

the sovereign creator and sustainer of all reality, then his communication is authoritative as well.

In the context of chapter two, it was demonstrated that Henry viewed the locus of this revelation to be the biblical text. While his theology of revelation encompasses issues broader than the biblical text, Henry was clear that humanity's access point to God's revelation is uniquely located in the biblical text. Much is congruent between Henry and Frei on the priority of the text in interpretation, yet Henry provides grounding for his text-driven approach with a clear articulation of the locus of divine revelation in the text, whereas Frei is not so explicit.

Nature of History: Duality or Unified

Considering the relationship of faith and historical events presses one to consider the nature of history. Of concern as it relates to the nature of history is if world history and biblical history are one and the same in a unity or whether they are distinct as a duality. The significance of defining the nature of history resides in the fact that the nature of history is a matter of how textual revelation and history relate. In a sense, the nature of history is a matter of if and how the notion of historical revelation impacts one's faith and life. History that is divided between the occurrences of world history and the accounting of faith reflections of the people of God drives a separation between historical fact and religious significance. An approach to history that holds world history and biblical history in unity provides the opportunity for the objective facts of history to bear direct relevance on the life of the believer. Stated negatively, a scheme for the nature of history in which biblical history and world history are a duality leaves the biblical narrative untethered from the plane of life on which humanity experiences history and needs redemption from its personal sinful history. However, it is possible to articulate a unity of history that undermines the transcendence of God and tends toward panentheism as one finds in Pannenberg.

Wolfhart Pannenberg drafted a scheme for revelation that is based on a strong notion of the unity of history. For Pannenberg, no division existed between the plane of God's historical revelation and the details of common world history. Revelation and history are so integrated, according Pannenberg, that knowledge of God is to be sought in the details of world history. Pannenberg's radicalized unity of history is driven by his mindset that the locus of revelation is in history. The net effect of Pannenberg's variety of historical unity is an approach to biblical interpretation that presses for meaning in independent inquiry of historical events, leaving the biblical interpreter with little grounding for the text-oriented hermeneutics, and in many cases with a critical view of the Bible.[15] A further concern with Pannenberg's unity of revelation and history is the tendencies toward panentheism that it opens, because the revelatory activity of God is taken to be imminent in the unfolding of history.

In contrast to Pannenberg, Frei in his aversion for detailed theoretical frameworks takes an approach to the nature of history that may be most accurately categorized as a duality of history. As has been demonstrated in chapter four, Frei did not seek to articulate a clear position on the nature of history. While he does not make clear statements on this issue, Frei makes clear in his writings that the narrative is a world all its own independent of historical facts. Frei does not present the world of the text to be in competition with historical factuality but views them as two separate matters of concern.[16] Relegating biblical history to a matter of self-referential narratives that produce faith without a theory for correspondence to reality fosters a functional duality of history. On one plane is the *history-like* piece of literature, which remains in its own sphere, and on the other plane is the world of historical factuality. These two planes—literature and historical occurrence—constitute a functional duality of the nature of history for Frei.

A duality of history is significant and problematic for Christian hermeneutics, because it leaves the claims of the biblical text untethered from the

---

15. Harrisville and Sundberg, *Bible in Modern Culture*, 1. Harrisville and Sundberg articulate the full effect of a critical approach to the unity of history. "Historical-critical study of the Bible is a necessary component of responsible theology. To employ historical-critical method is to subject the putatively factual material and literary structure of the Bible to independent investigation in order to test their truthfulness *and to discern their original historical meaning.* This independent investigation assumes that the outcome of research will not be predetermined by a guarantee of the Bible's infallibility. The student of Scripture, using historical-critical method, is placed under the imperative of the historian who must seek the facts no matter where they lead" (emphasis added).

16. Springs, "But Did It *Really* Happen," 279. Springs reinforces this interpretation of Frei when he states the following separation of history and kerygma. "Where does this leave historical reference? It means that the positive contribution historical reference makes to the *kerygmatic* efficacy of these accounts, while necessary, is secondary and dependent. The proper ordering of this relation led Frei to add that 'the text is witness to the Word of God, whether it is historical or not.' Frei's point with this claim is that, whether or not each detail happened as described in the Gospel accounts, these accounts nonetheless convey the identity of Jesus Christ by portraying what he was like and what he accomplished."

real activity of God in space and time. If matters of biblical meaning do not communicate about reality external to the text because they are on separate planes of history, then the claims of the text lack objective epistemological grounding. John Sailhamer notes,

> It is not enough to say that the biblical narratives are only "history-like" and to relegate them to the level of "realistic narrative." . . . one can say with reasonable certainty that the authors of the biblical narratives give every indication of intending their works to be taken as history rather than fiction. Their aim, they imply throughout, is to record what actually happened in human history. One can also say today with confidence that there is reasonable evidence that the history recorded in these narratives corresponds to the events themselves.[17]

Pannenberg's revelation as history doctrine allowed for the discovery of divine revelation through appropriate historical methods, even if meaning was confined to historical event.

In contrast, Hans Frei functionally distinguished narrative truth from revelation that is historically grounded, leaving the reader to discern a separate linguistic reality. Harrisville and Sundberg note the effect of creating a duality of history.

> This has resulted in the creation of complicated hermeneutical procedures in which the content of the Bible is separated from what stands behind it. What the Bible reports and what it means are conceived to be two different matters, the latter especially to be determined by scholarship operating under presuppositions of modern culture. The result has been to assess the Bible according to measures that scholars deem fit and to treat church tradition and its reading of biblical texts with a hermeneutic of suspicion.[18]

Critique of a duality is not to argue that interpretation is suspended on historical inquiry. The purpose of preference for a unity of history is not to derive a historically oriented hermeneutic as Pannenberg did. Rather the benefit of a proper approach to the nature of history is to provide grounding for the biblical narrative in the personal God who works in human history. The strength of Henry's approach is a unified nature of history that produces a text-oriented hermeneutic, provides theoretical grounding for

---

17. Sailhamer, *Pentateuch as Narrative*, 16.
18. Harrisville and Sundberg, *Bible in Modern Culture*, 2.

the presence of God in history, and maintains the transcendence of God in the unity of revelation and history.

Henry articulates a unified nature of history rooted in the theological assertion that the same God who has created, sustained, and revealed provides such a unity. As was noted about Henry in chapter one, he could not take the issue of revelation and knowledge of God separate from the person of God as creator, sustainer, and communicator over all creation. With this theological backing in the doctrine of God, Henry provides a distinct approach to the nature of history as unified. History is not unified due to epistemic consequences of the Enlightenment as it is for Pannenberg; rather, it is unified, because that is the logical implication of the biblical view of God. Whereas Pannenberg sought to assert the unity of history as the best explanation for reasonable foundations for religious knowledge, Henry asserted the unity of history as a product of the biblical view of God as transcendent and imminent.

Henry's assertion of a unified history under the sovereignty of God situates the Bible in an important way. The Bible then is the particular and special communication of God that is situated in the context of his relationship over all of creation and history. The meaning of history is specially articulated in the biblical text. The theological step of situating the Bible as the meaning of history communicated by God rests textual authority on the personal authority of God. To contrast the effect each approach to unified history has for Pannenberg and Henry is important. For Pannenberg, the unity of history is produced by the idea that history provides the legitimate universal source of religious knowledge for humanity. The effect then is that history is the realm in which meaning and knowledge of God is sought, producing a historically driven hermeneutic.

By contrast, Henry has unified history under the idea of God as sovereign creator and reconciler. The effect is the biblical text is uniquely important and, therefore, a text-driven hermeneutic is required. At the same time, he avoids a historically driven hermeneutic, Henry likewise provides theological and apologetic backing for biblical authority that is lacking in Frei's duality of history. The historical events and references of the biblical text are significant, and the reality of the Christian faith is dependent on God's faithful activity in history just as it is in his textual revelation of himself. The biblical text is the only required verifying principle for Christian faith in historical matters, but historical reality matters in light of the character of God as revealer.

Role of Historical Inquiry: Apologetic or Interpretive

Each of the three theologians surveyed clearly articulated a role for histori-cal inquiry in biblical interpretation. Wolfhart Pannenberg viewed histori-cal inquiry as the exclusive driver in biblical interpretation. Hans Frei did not view historical inquiry as a legitimate part of the interpretive process, but he reserved a place for it as legitimate in apologetic inquiry. For Frei, pursuing questions of historical veracity did not serve to provide literary understanding of the text, but Frei did not entirely rule historical inquiry out-of-hand in the field of theology. Henry is perhaps most at risk for be-ing misunderstood on the point of the role for historical inquiry. On one hand, Henry has provided multiple statements as to the value of historico-grammatical interpretation. Further, Henry willingly cast his allegiance with evangelical articulations of historically oriented hermeneutics.[19] Ultimately, Henry's propositionalism makes him vulnerable in perception, and perhaps at certain points in reality, to making affirmations of an in-terpretive role for historical inquiry. In balance to what appears to be a historically oriented hermeneutic are Henry's clear affirmations in favor of textually oriented hermeneutics.

Henry's dual affirmations of textual hermeneutics and apologetic in-terest raise the question as to the actual nature of his hermeneutic with the significance that this question impacts how one might use Henry as a model. That Henry viewed all historical matters with an apologetic drive is sufficiently clear. The breadth of Henry's concern to provide a justifiable "world-life" view that comprehensively explains God and human experi-ence to the surrounding culture is foundationally an apologetic theology. Thornbury has noted the apologetic drive in Henry's theological interests when he states, "[Evangelicalism's] leading theologians, with Henry at the vanguard, concerned themselves not only with right doctrine, but also with establishing how the concept of the reliability and authority of the Scrip-tures could be established and maintained in the modern world."[20]

This apologetic concern pervaded Henry's writings, whether from his ethical, cultural engagement, revelation, or his popular level writings.[21]

---

19. For example, Henry was a participant in the ICBI Summit II articulation on hermeneutics, which makes affirmation of a historico-grammatical approach to interpretation.

20. Thornbury, *Recovering Classic Evangelicalism*, 40.

21. Representative examples include the following works: Henry, *The Uneasy Conscience of Modern Fundamentalism*; Henry, *Twilight of a Great Civilization*; Henry,

With the breadth of his writings, Henry sought "to convince skeptics that the Christian world-and-life view operates from a position of genuine philosophical credibility. Stated differently, it was understood that there is a pattern to truth."[22] With Henry's apologetic concern in view, his approach to biblical interpretation likewise takes on a clear apologetic interest of justifying the historical claims of the Bible. This apologetic interest leads to Henry not separating the apologetic and interpretive process as clearly as does Hans Frei. At the same time, in his theological affirmations as to the nature of the text and biblical history, Henry likewise does not advocate for an interpretive role for historical interpretation as does Pannenberg.[23]

Does Henry's emphasis on historical reference require an interpretive role for history? This question is the point at which Henry's interpretive priorities are most susceptible to critique. As is clear from Henry's disagreements with Frei, Henry views historical reference as a non-negotiable feature of the biblical text. This may cause Henry to appear, in contrast to Frei, to be ascribing interpretive significance to historical inquiry. However, this critique by Frei belongs much more in an apologetic category, because Henry's point is not that one is incapable of interpreting the biblical text without historical inquiry. His point is that, in interpreting the text as literature, if the text is not taken to refer truly to metaphysical and historical realities, then the Christian faith may be undermined.[24]

Despite the mingling of apologetic and interpretive interests by Henry, it is sufficiently clear from his affirmations that Henry seeks to articulate an apologetic role for historical inquiry. Utilizing Henry's insight in light of Pannenberg and Frei requires a nuanced and clarifying step that Henry did not always make. Healthy appropriation of Henry's hermeneutic will preserve the place of the importance of apologetic concern for validating the Christian faith on all matters, including the historical. Yet, care should be taken to clarify that the principal concern of historical inquiry is not an interpretive function. Stemming from a theology that affirms the text as the

---

Toward a Recovery; and Henry, "Fortunes of the Christian World View," 163–76.

22. Thornbury, *Recovering Classic Evangelicalism*, 38.

23. Sailhamer, *Old Testament Theology*, 63. Sailhamer views Henry in this light as well in his assessment of evangelical reactions against historically oriented hermeneutics.

24. Sailhamer, *Pentateuch as Narrative*, 27. Sailhamer provides clarity to the proper relationship between the interpretive and apologetic roles for historical inquiry when he states, "One cannot overemphasize the importance of the apologetic task of demonstrating the accuracy of Scripture, but that is no reason to push the hermeneutical question of the meaning of the text aside. Both questions are of utmost importance."

revealed meaning of historical events, historical inquiry is best categorized as an apologetic endeavor to support the truth claims of the text rather than a formal step in discerning textual meaning.

In conclusion, Henry's emphasis on historical and metaphysical referent is not a giving-over to interpretive strategies that undermine the role of the text. Rather, the text is part of a larger revelatory scheme that includes meaningful connection between the text, the God of the text, and his activity in history. This defense of a theological foundation for textual meaning is an expressly apologetic point, and so one benefit of Henry's approach is he accomplishes a textually oriented hermeneutic that is simultaneously apologetically engaged.

Goal of Hermeneutics: Theological or Historical

What is one searching for as the result of the hermeneutical process? The answer to this question need not be entirely monolithic, but value is present in determining what the basic or ultimate purpose for engaging the biblical text is for a reader. Wolfhart Pannenberg's theology of revelation conflated history and revelation leading to a hermeneutic in which the goal of interpretation is historical. Henry's critique of the revelation-as-history approach outlined in chapter three demonstrated the incongruence of an approach that is historically oriented with a text-oriented interpretive approach. The key factors that place a historical goal for hermeneutics out of bounds in an evangelical approach to Scripture are the categories of inspiration and canon. Under a historically oriented goal, the purpose of the interpretive process is to press beyond (or behind) the text in order to discern meaning for the biblical text.

Further, what is contained in the biblical text becomes treated as a historical report merely to be evaluated for veracity. Such a historical approach moves past the idea that the biblical text is the inspired meaning ascribed to historical events, which have been assembled and preserved in the Bible.[25] The distinction between Pannenberg and Henry's goal of hermeneutics is summed up in the idea that "the goal of a text-oriented approach is not

25. Ibid., 19. Sailhamer helpfully notes, "It is true that when God works in history he inevitably makes himself known, and thus revelation in history is a natural consequence of God's working in history. But the category of revelation alone is not sufficient to deal with the problems raised by the idea of salvation history . . . The important distinction lies in the final evaluation of the status of the text of Scripture as revelation. Here Scripture, as a text, is more than a mere record of God's revelatory acts—it is itself revelation."

revelation in history in the sense of an event that must be given meaning. Rather, the goal is a revelation in the history as it is recounted in the text of Scripture."[26]

The historical emphasis is challenged by Hans Frei's call to return to textual meaning. Chapter four demonstrated the effect of Frei's influence is to demonstrate that the goal of reading Scripture was not historical prior to the eighteenth century, and it should not be historical today. On this point Carl Henry and Hans Frei agree, but this is also the point at which their agreement ceases. Though Frei's goal for hermeneutics was not historical, it was not necessarily theological either. The lacuna of a theology of revelation in Frei's writings, coupled with his closed literary-focused system, which resists theological formulation, prevents one from concluding Frei held a theological goal. While Frei emphasized the text over historical inquiry, his emphasis was on the text as a literary unity. The text itself, with Frei's theory of non-reference, does not stand in direct relation to theological realities. In light of Frei's own writings, the best conclusion then is that Frei asserts a literary goal for hermeneutics.[27]

The goal then of Frei's interpretive approach is not to discern the meaning of the text as revelation of reality, but is simply to take the literature on its own terms.[28] Lacking a scheme for a theological goal for interpretation does not undermine Frei's usefulness if the theological element of textual revelation is supplied as backing for textual focus. Functionally by calling for a focus on the biblical text, even though Frei himself did not articulate this, he has provided evangelicals with the means to focus on a theological purpose for interpretation. This textual focus received in an evangelical context of revelation is one of the fruits of Frei's writings. Is Frei then the preferred resource to which evangelicals should look for a text-oriented hermeneutic?

26. Ibid., 22.

27. Frei, *Types of Christian Theology*, 79. One such passage which illustrates Frei's literary goal for hermeneutics follows: "[W]e don't have more than our concepts of God. We don't have a separate intuition, a preconceptual or prelinguistic apprehension or grasp of God in his reality . . . But we don't need it either; for the reality of God is given in, with, and under the concept and not separably, and that is adequate for us."

28. A topic that warrants further discussion and clarity from Hans Frei's approach is what distinguishes biblical interpretation from the interpretation from other realistic narratives. If the goal of interpretation is literary because of the nature of the text, then it is unclear as to what warrants granting authority differently to the Bible versus other history-like literature.

The basic goal for a reader who approaches the Bible as authoritative communication from God should be to know God and respond in faithful living. This articulation of the goal of hermeneutics is expressly theological and not unlike what B. B. Warfield has stated.

> Scripture records the direct revelations which God gave to men in days past, so far as those revelations were intended for permanent and universal use. But it is much more than a record of past revelations. It is itself the final revelation of God, completing the whole disclosure of his unfathomable love to lost sinners, the whole proclamation of his purposes of grace, and the whole exhibition of his gracious provisions for salvation.[29]

This theology of revelation does not allow for the bracketing of historical concerns, because historical concerns are part of the context for revelation—revelation in its fullness is located in the biblical text.[30]

I have argued that in the writings of Carl Henry reside the resources to interpret the Scripture theologically with the backing of a robust doctrine of revelation. Whereas Frei's approach leaves him without an articulation for how the biblical text relates to theological formulation, Henry has provided the resources for both a literature-driven interpretation and theologically robust insight about God. While Henry and Frei find common ground on the centrality of the biblical text, they depart on the nature of reality and its relation to the text. As it concerns the goal of interpretation, Frei is useful to shaping a text-oriented hermeneutic, but Henry provides a more encompassing view of how one may access divine revelation through textual interpretation.

Test of History: Negative or Positive

In order for the biblical text to be received as reliable, must there be positive attestation by independent historical research, or is the biblical text sufficient witness for biblical faith? Wolfhart Pannenberg constructed a

---

29. Warfield, "The Idea of Revelation," 48.

30. Rae, "Creation and Promise," 283. Rae identifies the goal of hermeneutics to be theological, because of the unique theological nature of the biblical text. Rae states, "We may say, therefore, that the Bible is a theological account of history. It is an account that is shaped by the conviction that all that takes place does so within the context of God's providential care for the created order. That it is a theological account, employing categories peculiar to its own concerns, does not render it illegitimate as history . . ."

hermeneutic under which the facts that may be verified through empirical historical inquiry constitute reliable religious knowledge. In chapter one, it was argued the faithful position for biblical hermeneutics ought to be a negative test for historicity. This preference for a negative test is on account that demanding a positive test for historicity requires the interpreter to seek history as the goal of interpretation. The practical effect of a positive test is the interpreter is overly compelled to engage in identifying the historical veracity of the biblical text rather than taking the text on its own terms.[31]

The effect of Pannenberg's orientation toward a positive test for history is that his hermeneutic is concerned with historical inquiry. The biblical text is not treated as reliable witness to historical events with the effect that the Bible is not authoritative apart from verification by an empirical method. Likewise, Hans Frei provides a positive test for historicity in practical terms. While he does not engage the question in terms of positive-versus-negative test as specifically outlined in the fivefold rubric, Frei functionally constructs a hermeneutic that clearly leads to the positive test position. Frei is forthright in his assertion that biblical interpretation stands independent from historical referent. In his affirmations of biblical sufficiency, Frei articulates significant reserve for taking the biblical text as reliable witness to historical events. Yet, Frei likewise expressed contentment on apologetic grounds with independent inquiry into the historicity of the text. Practically, Frei's resistance to the biblical text providing reliable historical reference and openness to independent historical inquiry leads to the implication that to take the historical matters of the Bible as history, an independent positive test is necessary for historical affirmations.

In contrast to Pannenberg and Frei, Henry has articulated an approach to hermeneutics that is explicitly based on a negative test for historicity.[32] Historical reliability of the Bible is significant for Henry in an apologetic sense, because aspects of the Christian faith depend on historical reality. As significant as the historical reality of biblical events may be,

31. Henry, "Narrative Theology: An Evangelical Appraisal," 13. Henry has observed concerning the effect of requiring a positive test for biblical interpretation, "If one suspends the validity of the biblical witness upon confirmation by the historical method he frustrates a vital commitment to the historical trustworthiness of Scripture."

32. Ibid., 8. Henry articulates the negative test for historicity in the following manner: "The evangelical belief in the divine redemptive acts does not depend on verification by historical criticism but rests on scriptural attestation. The Bible conveys the meaning of God's redemptive acts; since it is the divine salvific acts it interprets, the acts are indispensable presuppositions of that meaning."

Henry acknowledges independent confirmation is not necessary to affirm biblical historicity. As long as independent historical research has not disconfirmed a particular historical claim, then it is reasonable in Henry's view to accept the biblical text as sufficient grounds for historical reliability. This release of the biblical text from a positive test for historicity is, likewise, a release from the empirical expectations of modernist epistemology.[33]

Both Frei and Henry presented the argument that one effect of modernist epistemology was a requirement that the biblical text be treated contrary to its nature. According to the two theologians, this treatment was to require an empirical verification in historical terms for interpretation. Frei brought corrective to the positive test that was empirically driven as a part of interpretation by leaving questions of historicity and reference outside the bounds of theological formation. Henry accomplished the corrective of empirical verification by restoring the notion of textual revelation that is reliable interpretation of and witness to historical events as the communication of God. Henry's theological foundation for a negative test of history and text as faithful historical witness make his approach preferable to Pannenberg and Frei on the point of positive-versus-negative test for historicity in biblical hermeneutics.

Navigating Henry and Frei

The Henry-Frei interchange served to crystalize many issues and set the course for subsequent discussions between theologians of each persuasion. The conversation that has stemmed from their initial debate includes an important conversation as to how evangelicals should approach revelation, history, and the biblical text. The relationship between revelation, history, and the biblical text is one of determining the role of biblical authority in the life of the church along the way of determining the proper hermeneutical approach fitting to the nature of the biblical text. There have been multiple responses to the question of what the best approach should be from the evangelical-narrative theology dialogue.[34] Given the significance

33. Ibid., 5. Henry notes, "Evangelicals consider the gospels not as mere historical chronicles but as a distinct genre that combines history and interpretation; moreover, they lean upon inspired Scripture more than on historical research for assurance of past salvific acts. They insist, however, on the historical factuality of the divine redemptive acts, and they are confident that historical research will not disprove the factuality of redemptive history."

34. Thornbury, *Recovering Classic Evangelicalism*, 124. The relevance of refining

of various ways in which the Henry-Frei interchange has been utilized to make proposals related to history, revelation, and the biblical text, attention to these various options is necessary.

One approach is narrative theologians who seek to influence evangelical theology based on similar points of emphasis. George Hunsinger and Jason Springs are theologians who represent this category. The feature of their argument that unites them is that they require a basic change in Henry's doctrine of revelation in order to achieve compatibility between Henry and Frei. Following his summary of Henry and Frei's mutual critiques, Hunsinger states his purpose in analyzing the interchange.

> In trying to discern what Evangelicals and Postliberals might learn from each other about Holy Scripture, I will try to uncover various points where concessions might be made from each side. I will look especially for concessions that can be made without compromising the basic convictions that seem definitive of either position. I will therefore be looking for areas of possible convergence rather than for areas of complete or outright agreement. In this thought-experiment, I will grant Frei's point that Henry seems bound by an excessive commitment to modernity.[35]

Despite his even-handed comments at the beginning of the article, Hunsinger's goal is to demonstrate that if Henry were modified with certain postmodern accommodations, he would be much more congruent with Frei. Hunsinger's desire is for evangelicals to drop the need for correspondence and reference in defining theological truth. He states, "Once the encumbrances of excessive modernity are shed and left behind, the real theological issues can emerge with greater clarity, and the differences between Evangelicalism and Postliberalism—though still strong—begin to look more like a matter of degree than a matter of kind."[36]

---

one's theology of revelation, history, and the biblical text in light of Henry, Pannenberg, and Frei is illustrated in modern evangelicalism by the discussion surrounding the doctrinal importance of a historical Adam and Eve. A full discussion of this topic is not possible here. However, Thornbury's comments illustrate the significance of the discussion, "Indeed, with the historicity of Adam in question, almost nothing else is sacred. Christology appears to be the next commonplace of the system to go." For further reading on the contemporary discussion concerning the historicity of Adam and Eve, see Barrett, *Four Views on the Historical Adam*; Enns, *The Evolution of Adam*. On a more popular level, the BioLogos Foundation promotes a non-historic view of Adam and Eve.

35. Hunsinger, "What Can Evangelicals and Postliberals Learn from Each Other," 163.

36. Ibid., 163.

The points of congruence Hunsinger is able to take for granted in Henry's own stating are the unity of Scripture, the hermeneutical inadequacy of historical criticism, the centrality of the biblical depiction of the world, and the indispensability of Jesus Christ as savior.[37] For both theologians, the biblical text is authoritative "independent of confirmation or disconfirmation by historical critics."[38] Beyond these agreements, Hunsinger seeks to reconcile the differences between Henry and Frei by modifying Henry's commitments to referent.[39] In order to bring the two theologians together, Hunsinger seeks to strip Henry of what he perceives to be his commitment to modernism.[40]

In the course of critiquing Henry, Hunsinger states, "Unlike Henry, Frei thinks that we properly grasp the truth of the gospel not just with our heads, but also with our hearts and our hands."[41] This perspective about Henry's approach to the truth and role of Scripture in the life of the church is untenable considering Henry's many emphases on the life-encompassing role of Scripture and Christian doctrine.[42] In favor of clear claims to the nature of truth, Hunsinger prefers a "low key epistemology" in the variety of what Frei provided.[43] Ultimately, Hunsinger calls for moving "beyond excessive modernity" to which Henry is entrapped according to his assessment.[44] A response to the charge that Carl Henry was a modernist has

37. Henry, "Narrative Theology: An Evangelical Appraisal," 15.

38. Hunsinger, "Henry/Frei Exchange Reconsidered," 164.

39. Ibid., 169. There are points at which Hunsinger appears to have taken Henry inappropriately, as when he perceives Henry as advocating for a positive test for historicity. I have demonstrated that Henry, in fact, argued against a positive test for historicity. It is likely a lack of full reading of Henry that has provided Hunsinger's perspective on Henry, since he cites only one article by Henry and does not include any reference to *God, Revelation and Authority* in support of his point. Hunsinger makes his points by stating, "However, if faith were to forego a systematic reliance on historical critical method as a secondary means of verification and certainty, then the consequences as Henry understands them would be dire indeed. For in that case skepticism would not only be encouraged, but the foundations of a stable faith would remain clouded in obscurity."

40. Ibid., 172.

41. Ibid., 174.

42. The breadth of Henry's publications demonstrates how encompassing his idea of truth was. His works include a history of a mission effort, social and personal ethics, the organization of an international evangelistic initiative, and popular level periodical articles intended to equip the North American church for social action, based on personal biblical interpretation. For the breadth of these works, see the bibliography.

43. Hunsinger, "Henry/Frei Exchange Reconsidered," 174.

44. Ibid., 177.

been provided in chapter two. For this discussion, what is significant is that Hunsinger's call to evangelicals consists of setting aside concern for the nature of truth and reference in favor of the methodological underpinnings promoted by Frei.[45] This call to modification of Henry, based on certain reading of his works, appears to be incomplete.

Jason Springs seeks to draw evangelicals and postliberals together through mediating the Henry and Frei interchange. Similar to George Hunsinger, Springs's method for navigating this unity is to require evangelical approaches to lay aside commitments to historical and metaphysical reference. Springs states his intention to navigate past Henry's critiques when he says, "Based upon close examination of the full range of resources available in his writings, I argue that Frei makes available means by which to successfully navigate both of these challenges, even if he himself never managed to articulate such means with sufficient clarity."[46] Springs's attempt is to show the superiority of Frei's approach and that he did not accommodate postmodern philosophical priorities as much as has been characterized by some.[47]

Springs finds Frei to be a more faithful resource than Henry on interpreting Scripture according to its nature. He argues Frei is effective because, while his approach "incorporates historical investigation, it refuses to reduce or finally constrain the integrity and efficacy of the biblical witness to the criterion of historical verifiability."[48] Springs takes Henry to be arguing, according to an empirical mindset, that the Bible is in its general nature a historical fact book. The opportunity for Henry and Frei to merge is dependent upon Henry revoking his theory of reference. This formula typically applies the same to those who hold positions resembling these two theologians.[49]

---

45. Ibid., 181.

46. Springs, "But Did It *Really* Happen," 273.

47. Ibid., 275. Springs notes, "With this provisio Frei sought to question the normative assumptions by which some event might be determined historically verified or verifiable. And, initially, it sounds like Frei is making a move customary of the so-called 'postmodern' turn away from the very possibility of 'objectivity.' I want to suggest, however, that this is the wrong way to characterize Frei's reservation."

48. Ibid., 276.

49. It is debatable according to the material presented in chapter two that Henry views the Bible in the manner that Springs characterizes, but it is understandable that Springs takes Henry this way in light of the common critiques of Henry.

Springs joins Frei's narrative approach to ideas he gleans from Karl Barth in order to present his model for affirming reference in a way to assuage Henry-esque evangelicals, while not altering Frei's basic program. Springs makes clear it is Henry's program which must bend to accommodate Frei's priorities when he states,

> [Frei] did gradually come to an increasingly clear realization that it is not possible to describe the Christian world of disclosure as anchored in a static set of representations conveyed in Scripture, and to which all understanding must conform. Rather, the claims and patterns conveyed in Scripture are caught up in the continuing set of cultural and historical practices, and second-order scrutiny, which they orient.[50]

The bridge between Henry and Frei here is not that Frei should have developed more clarity on reference (despite Springs's own acknowledgement that Frei was elusive on the topic), but that Henry should have been content to minimize reference in favor of viewing the claims of Scripture as second-order patterns of community orientations.

In conclusion, Springs believes he has succeeded in bringing together what has been demonstrated in the previous chapters to be quite distinct. Springs claims, "Moreover, as my parsing of Frei's response to Carl Henry should make clear, they are consistent with his views on the nature of scriptural authority."[51] He has not accomplished this harmony by allowing each theologian to stand on his own terms, but by redefining Henry to alter significant elements of his doctrine of revelation.

The approach of Hunsinger and Springs does not represent the only method for bringing Henry and Frei together. The alternative approach is found among those who identify as evangelicals who seek to soften Henry's notion of reference, and require theological accommodation in the direction of affirming more about revelation and reference than Frei was willing to embrace. Gabriel Fackre and Roger Olson have published this approach in varying degrees.

Gabriel Fackre has constructed his theological method on the basis of articulating an evangelical theology in narrative form. Fackre has specifically addressed the issue of narrative and revelation.[52] Fackre defines the

---

50. Springs, "But Did It *Really* Happen," 296–97.

51. Ibid., 299.

52. For his theology of revelation in narrative form, see Fackre, *Doctrine of Revelation*.

significance of narrative for theology when he states, "For one, Scripture is full of narratives, definitively those of Jesus, living, dying, risen. But more than that, the Bible is a book that tells an 'overarching story.' While imaginatively portrayed, it is no fictive account, having to do with turning points that have 'taken place' and will take place, a *news* story traced by canonical hand."[53]

Fackre's boldness and clarity concerning the role of reference in narrative as compared to Frei is noteworthy. Highlighting the hermeneutical importance narrative description provides, Fackre notes the prevalence of narratives as a genre in the Bible and also notes the overarching narrative of the Bible as significant for interpretation. Fackre's attention to narrative affords him the opportunity to articulate seven points of appreciation for Hans Frei's methodology.[54] Fackre's intended balance is that while he emphasizes the role of narrative, he seeks to maintain the commitment of conducting theology as the exploration of divine revelation that may be organized in a logical fashion, whether that is theological loci or according to the narrative framework of Scripture. Fackre notes,

> The understanding of Scripture in these terms comes from its canonical shape and thus from the early process of the Christian community's self-definition-vis-á-vis its surroundings. Concurrently, it developed its "rule of faith" and subsequent creedal refinements including its doctrine of the Trinity, economic and imminent, all formulations of the biblical Storyline from creation to consummation.[55]

Similar to Henry, Fackre situates the doctrine of revelation in the broader context of God as revealer and the subsequent authority of the text.[56] As a result of this approach to revelation, Fackre maintains commitment to a theological basis for revelation that includes historical and metaphysical reference.[57] Fackre notes, "Story by no means excludes his-

---

53. Ibid., 3.

54. For this seven-point list, see Fackre, *Doctrine of Revelation*, 5.

55. Ibid., 6.

56. Ibid., 13. Fackre notes to this end, "In each case, therefore, a *doctrine of revelation* is the underpinning of a concept of authority and its interpretive principles." Again, "Every claim to know something about ultimate states of affairs entails a leap of faith into an epistemological circle of this sort. As such, the circle is not vicious, but universally functional and logically necessary."

57. Fackre, *Ecumenical Faith*, 101. Fackre observes, "That inspiration is integral to revelation is crucial to evangelical witness. Evangelicals also agree on why such

tory. The Christian recital could not exclude empirical narrative or it would cease to be Christian, for its central events presuppose hard empirical claims—Jesus did live, Jesus did die on the cross."[58] Thornbury provides affirmation of Fackre's integration of narrative insights, while maintaining the evangelical distinctive of the doctrine of revelation. Thornbury states, "Gabriel Fackre, who considers biblical narrative the central element in positioning a Christian theology, contends that, for example, a proper doctrine of verbal inspiration helps establish the truth claim of Scripture."[59] Thornbury comments further, "Fackre understands that propositional truth claims undergird the narrative witness: they add to, rather than take away from, the primary missiological thrust of the biblical accounts."[60] Finally, concerning the place of historical inquiry in biblical interpretation, Fackre arrives at a similar description as Henry in which both theologians are text-oriented, while reserving a limited role for textual criticism for the apologetic and theological implications of historicity.[61]

Fackre's definition of narrative within the category of divine revelation places him closer to Henry in terms of willingness to draw connections of reference from the biblical text and willingness to construct first-order statements of doctrine from the biblical text.[62] Fackre, in fact, finds resonance with Henry on the hermeneutical impact of the redemptive narrative of Scripture.[63] In addition to supplying a canonical narrative, Fackre credits Henry with providing a necessary emphasis on textual inspiration to the narrative approach.[64]

inspiration is necessary; they contend for its role in making propositional/affirmational truth claims of a universal nature."

58. Fackre, *The Christian Story*, 27.

59. Thornbury, *Recovering Classic Evangelicalism*, 92–93.

60. Ibid., 93.

61. Fackre, *Ecumenical Faith*, 185.

62. Henry, "Narrative Theology: An Evangelical Appraisal," 15–17. Carl Henry acknowledged merit in Fackre's approach to revelation, history, and hermeneutics by virtue of Fackre's maintaining of truth claims and a revelation-based authority of Scripture; yet, Henry also cautioned that more specificity is needed on a narratively informed evangelical approach to reference, biblical authority, and revelation. Further, Henry is discontent with Fackre's theology of revelation, which allows for biblical fallibility.

63. Fackre, *Doctrine of Revelation*, 161–62. Fackre finds Henry's orientation of narrative to be succinctly stated in Henry's tracing of God's purposes from creation through eschatological fulfillment.

64. Ibid., 162. Fackre notes concerning the foundation of biblical authority, "Taking up a much-neglected theme in contemporary theology, Carl Henry gives the evangelical

While appreciating Henry's emphases that are absent in the narrative approach, Fackre departs from Henry's distinct propositionalism. Fackre finds Henry to overstate the certainty of theological statements in light of the provisional nature of knowledge until the eschaton. Fackre notes concerning Henry,

> His contribution to the understanding of the doctrine is the defense of the revelatory significance of biblical assertions about the real order of things, human and divine. However, his understanding of them as "sentences" protected from error by the Holy Spirit affiliates the human words themselves with the clarity of Light reserved alone for the End.[65]

Fackre seeks to chasten the potential for doctrinal autonomy he views Henry's propositional approach to foster, though he does not accuse Henry of this error directly.

Fackre's second point of critique for Henry is a chastening of what he perceives to be the autonomy of human reason. He notes that Henry maintained biblical propositions must pass the test of humanity's universal capacity for reason. The way biblical assertions pass such a test is through logical principles like the law of contradiction and other theorems of formal logic.[66] Fackre stops short of accusing Henry of a modernist epistemology as others have, but he is uncomfortable with the notion that Scripture falls under the rules of human reason.[67] Ultimately, biblical assertions should

---

answer: inspiration. As such, he makes an evangelical contribution to the understanding of the narrative of revelation."

65. Ibid., 170–71. Fackre further notes, "While Henry cannot be charged with the identification of a detailed time-bound theological formulation with inspiration, the stress on revealed 'timeless truths' lends itself to that kind of mistake. For example, the penal substitutionary theory of the atonement regularly reaches this level of authority in evangelical preaching and teaching. However, this view of the atonement is a human construct rising out of New Testament stories of Christ's death and apostolic metaphors of interpretation of the death."

66. Ibid., 174.

67. Ibid. Fackre states of Henry's approach to reason, "While reason is certainly not designated by Henry as the 'source' of authority—for definitive knowledge of God comes only through inspired Scripture—it is assigned the role of adjudicating all truth-claims, those of Scripture included. In principle, if Scripture's claims do not pass muster before the canons of reason, they are failed propositions, although none such are discovered. In fact, Henry does use the standards of reason to determine what Scripture can and cannot say, for 'paradoxes' are ruled out as a violation of the principle of non-contradiction."

DID IT REALLY HAPPEN?

not be tested by their coherence to the law of human reason, but by their coherence within the narrative of the biblical canon.[68]

Roger Olson is a second example of an evangelical theologian who seeks to allow shaping by Hans Frei. Olson identifies post-liberal theology as a form of postmodern theology that roots "Christian faith on the identity and presence of Jesus Christ in the narrative-shaped community of God's people."[69] Olson finds the influence of Hans Frei to be helpful for an evangelical emphasis on the authority of the biblical text in the Christian faith.[70] Frei's value for contemporary theology is that he places the form of the narrative central to the Christian faith.[71]

While seeking to draw the benefits from Frei's methodology, Olson remains cautious about the broader theoretical commitments of narrative hermeneutics. Olson views Frei as generally disinterested in categories such as objective truth and referent. Olson notes, "To most of us, the Yale theologians seem to go too far with postmodernism's 'incredulity toward metanarratives.' That is, they appear ambiguous and ambivalent regarding the question of Christianity's universal truth status relative to competing accounts of 'the ultimate nature of reality.'"[72] Olson simultaneously appeals to Frei's accounting of doctrine as restatement of narrative and second-order rules for faith in the community. He notes, "Doctrine cannot replace the narrative-shaped revelation of God in Scripture."[73]

Olson places the onus for modification on Hans Frei when he desires an articulation of truth, reference, and community transcendent meaning. Concerning the nature of textual meaning and theological truth, Olson notes,

---

68. Ibid., 175. For a response of the critique of Henry as a rationalist, see chapter two.

69. Olson, "Back to the Bible (Almost)."

70. Ibid.

71. Ibid. Olson notes according to Frei, "[The Bible] is irreducibly literature. Literature, like art, must be kept separate from explanatory schemes and theories for the sake of its integrity." Further, Olson notes, "Many postliberal theologians, however, see the majority of evangelicals as 'premodern' in their attachments to objective, propositional revelation and literal historicity of Scripture's stories. They fear that this leads inevitably to a divorce between Scripture and the explanatory schemes and theories that get built up into systematic theologies and rational apologetics based on propositional truth claims that end up replacing the literary form of Scripture."

72. Ibid.

73. Ibid.

On the other hand, we want to know more about the truth-status of affirmations in this postliberal account of doctrine. To date, anyway, postliberal theologians have not explored sufficiently the nature of heresy. When a self-identified "Christian" denies the sole lordship of Jesus Christ and affirms "other lords and saviors," is he merely "breaking a rule" or violating truth and affirming a lie?[74]

Concerning the nature of reference, Olson notes, "If the bodily resurrection of Jesus Christ as historical and not just historylike is essential to the structure of the gospel story, why are not other events so closely linked with his identity in that story? The postliberals' answer to this remains unclear and unconvincing."[75] Olson's analysis concludes with a call to incorporate judiciously the text-oriented insights of Frei's approach, while critically pushing back with the evangelical distinctives of doctrinal truth, historical and metaphysical referent, and community transcendent meaning.[76]

Fackre and Olson have provided examples of evangelical appropriation of Hans Frei that require significant modification of Frei's approach. This section has illustrated the two directions the conversation following the Henry-Frei interchange has followed. One observation worth noting is that each approach requires significant changes to the opposing position, because of differing doctrinal presuppositions. Contrary to Hunsinger's stated desire, it is not possible to make the difference between Henry and Frei's merely a "matter of degree than a matter of kind."[77] While learning from the emphases of each side of the conversation is a fruitful exercise, it is clear the underpinnings of each theologian are different enough that substantive alteration is required.

Gregory Thornbury makes a similar argument that significantly fusing the methods of evangelical and narrative theology will lead to an inevitable compromise on commitments that are essential to the views of either Carl Henry or Hans Frei. Concerning the departure from the basic metaphysical

74. Ibid.

75. Ibid.

76. Ibid. Olson states it thus, "As a 'back to the Bible' movement in contemporary mainline Christianity, postliberal theology is to be valued and applauded by evangelicals. Perhaps we can even learn something about the natures of Scripture and doctrine from it. At the same time, we ought to reach out cautiously to these brothers and sisters across the mainline-evangelical divide and challenge them with the insights and wisdom of our own tradition."

77. Hunsinger, "Henry/Frei Exchange Reconsidered," 163.

commitments required to take a favorable view toward narrative theology, Thornbury notes,

> If that is what a new generation of evangelicals claims as the nature of theology, that is their business. But it really should be understood that one cannot easily modify the conclusions of twentieth-century philosophical hermeneutics for the purposes of theology without doing violence to the work of those theorists who advanced these concepts. With a few notable exceptions, they clearly did not believe that Christian doctrines referred themselves to anything like a transcendent metaphysical reality beyond our natural world.[78]

The observation that significant alteration is required for full-scale integration of the two approaches serves as a caution for considering the implications of modifying another's approach. While this caution is necessary, it does not mean the two positions are unable to benefit from the conversation. Whether contemporary evangelicals have proclivities toward Henry or Frei, the conversation stemming from their interchange illuminates the path forward for utilizing the insight of Carl Henry. The next section will consider how the two paths descending from Henry and Frei inform utilizing Henry as the preferred paradigm on revelation, history, and the biblical text.

Henry and Frei for Contemporary Evangelicals

While this study serves as a vindication of Carl Henry as a resource for revelation, history, and the biblical text in contrast to Pannenberg and Frei, his interchange with Hans Frei has drawn to the forefront two issues critical for the use of Henry. In addition to utilizing Henry as the paradigm for making decisions of interpretive method according to the fivefold rubric, Henry and Frei have provided insight into the need for a nuanced propositionalism and a move all the way back to the Bible. The former is a corrective to Henry, and the latter is a corrective to Frei.

---

78. Thornbury, *Recovering Classic Evangelicalism*, 100–101.

Nuanced Propositionalism

Chapter two engaged the critique that Henry's propositionalism is a form of rationalism. It was demonstrated that while Henry sought to affirm reason as a resource divinely given for understanding revelation, he did not promote rationalism. Further, passages of Henry were identified, which make it appear the text of Scripture was not so important to Henry as is the propositional restatement of the biblical assertions. A fuller reading of Henry demonstrated Henry sought to primarily engage Scripture according to its nature and overall narrative shape. Yet, the need exists to nuance Henry's approach to propositional reference. The intention of this point is not to diminish the importance Henry ascribes to reference and the truth of the Christian faith, but is intended to make the point of priority and emphasis.

In spite of his ambiguity on reference, Hans Frei did rightly critique interpretive schemes that foster a move beyond the Bible. Frei's primary concern was historical, but his point is equally relevant for systems of propositional restatement that move too easily past the biblical text for the sake of propositional restatement. Henry himself sought to protect against a premature move beyond the text, but without balanced attention to Henry's writings, he may be used as a resource for that which he sought to avoid. Lashing historical and metaphysic referent to the text does not undermine the priority of textual interpretation as the foregoing analysis of the fivefold rubric has demonstrated. Yet, priority and emphasis must remain on practicing a hermeneutic that is truly text-oriented and not falling into an interpretive practice of seeking meaning outside the biblical text. A proper doctrine of revelation will provide the theoretical underpinnings for interpreting historical narrative faithfully. Sailhamer notes to this end,

> Historical narrative is the re-presentation of past events for the purpose of instruction. Two dimensions are always at work in shaping such narratives: (1) the course of the historical event itself and (2) the viewpoint of the author who recounts the events. This dual aspect of historical narrative means that one must look not only at the course of the event in its historical setting but also for the purpose and intention of the author in recounting the event.[79]

As Henry stated of Frei, biblical interpreters should be sure "the Bible prods us to assess our experience in terms of the biblical world, instead of

---

79. Sailhamer, *Pentateuch as Narrative*, 25.

forcing and fitting the biblical narrative into another world on the assumption that alternatives that we construct actually constitute reality."[80]

The second point for nuancing Henry's approach to reference is his insistence on univocal language as the exclusive manner in which language functions.[81] Henry's emphasis is that the purpose of language is to inform, and he takes departure from language as univocally informative as departure from determinate textual meaning toward equivocation of language. Henry notes,

> [O]nly univocal assertions protect us from equivocation . . . All man needs in order to know God as he truly is, is God's intelligible disclosure and rational concepts that qualify man—on the basis of the *imago Dei*—to comprehend the content of God's logically ordered revelation. Unless man has epistemological means adequate for factual truth about God as he truly is, the inevitable outcome of the quest for religious knowledge is equivocation and skepticism.[82]

The capacity of language to refer and inform is inseparable from biblical interpretation and belief in the Christian faith. Yet, as Henry states it, grounds exist for challenging Henry's mindset for the nature of language based on insight from Frei's narrative approach. Since the biblical text is the locus of revelation, the language of the text bears the ability to inform about God's reality, though the informative function does not eliminate the possibility that there are functions language may serve in addition to referential informing.

Does anything other than strict univocal language result in equivocation of language as Henry states? While affirming that the biblical text is undergirded by reality, Ashford and Whitfield note a strictly univocal nature of language is not capable of encompassing the reality of God. Ashford and Whitefield note, "Human language about God cannot be equivocal because God is the triune God who is personal, purposive, and communicative and because he created us to live in fellowship with him. But neither

---

80. Henry, "Narrative Theology: An Evangelical Appraisal," 6.

81. A full discussion of the nature of language as univocal, equivocal, or analogous is complex. While a full evaluation of the nature of language is not possible here, there is warrant in noting that a view toward strict univocal language is not as necessary as Henry thinks to preserve the Christian truth claim.

82. Henry, *God, Revelation and Authority*, 4:118–19.

is our knowledge and language about God univocal because God is both quantitatively and qualitatively different from his creation."[83]

Language about God, while capable of faithfully referring and inform- ing of reality is capable of functioning in a way that is not strictly univocal due to the transcendence of God. The challenge to the nature of knowledge as flatly univocal presses the need for evangelical hermeneutics to be shaped according to the particular genre of the text and the overall narrative shape of the biblical story.[84] Ashford and Whitfield note the benefit of narrative influence in this regard when they state,

> Indeed, the narrative approach is helpful because of the narrative quality of Scripture. Not only does the majority of the canon con- sist of narrative, but even the nonnarrative books (e.g. the epistles) are in constant conversation with the Old Testament narrative(s) and the life of Christ (e.g., 1 Cor 10:1-13) . . . it is helpful because it helps us read the text within its totality (*tota Scriptura*).[85]

Henry is correct in affirming the rational nature of God's revelation and human ability to understand revelation through God's creative grace in endowing humanity with the *imago Dei*. The effect of this evaluation is that revelation is not less than a univocal description of God's true nature, but it may be more as revelation of the transcendent God.

Two points have been made that provide nuance to Carl Henry's ap- proach to revelation, history, and the biblical text. These points are first: care to maintain the proper priority of textual exegesis and narrative aware- ness in biblical interpretation, and second: accommodating theory of lan- guage to allow the nature of language to be shaped by textual details and context, while acknowledging the transcendence of God.[86] These nuances

83. Ashford and Whitfield, "Theological Method," 40–41.

84. Thornbury, *Recovering Classic Evangelicalism*, 114. Thornbury provides a simi- lar assessment of Henry's assertion that language is strictly univocal when he states, "Vanhoozer makes a good point that Henry was so focused on maintaining evangelical affirmations that he downplayed the richness of language and its setting in canonical linguistic form. Vanhoozer is also correct that language does more theologically than Henry allows."

85. Ashford and Whitfield, "Theological Method," 48.

86. Bartholomew and Goheen, *The Drama of Scripture*, 21. Bartholomew and Goheen note the influence on evangelical hermeneutics to operate with the biblical metanarrative when they state, "Over the past few decades, one of the most exciting developments in biblical studies has been the growing recognition among scholars that the Bible has the shape of a *story* . . . It functions as the authoritative Word of God for us when it becomes the one *basic* story through which we understand our own experience

strengthen Henry's text-oriented hermeneutic without going so far as Hunsinger and Springs in their requirement to set aside the notion of referent. Further, these nuances incorporate Hans Frei's insight without adopting the features of his theoretical framework that are contrary to the theology of revelation put forward by Carl Henry.

Back to the Bible . . . All the Way

The positive influences of Hans Frei on evangelical hermeneutics have been noted in the previous section. With these positive influences noted, the legacy of Carl Henry's critique of Hans Frei is that any movement back to the Bible must go all the way. Fackre and Olson both noted that Frei's resistance to the correspondence of textual description of reality leaves biblical interpretation ungrounded as revelation of God. Fackre notes, "Those who hold that the Bible and its classical exposition in Christian tradition are authoritative do so because of their answer to the Why?: the triune God by the light and power of the Holy Spirit has revealed defining truth through them."[87] It is at the point of answering the question *why* the biblical text holds authority that Frei and Henry are irreconcilable.

Frei's answer to the *why* of biblical authority rests in the nature of literature and the formation of the community, all the while resisting a notion of revelation that draws correspondence between the words of the Bible and the reality of God. Henry's answer for the *why* of biblical authority is a revelatory design of the sovereign creator-God who bestows his authority on his communication. In the process of pressing for text-oriented hermeneutics, adopting Frei's approach to reference and abandoning Henry's brings significant consequences. The idea that biblical interpretation is inseparable from the undergirding of God's revelation of reality is at risk without Henry's corrective to Frei.[88] A similar notion leads Olson to claim,

> Evangelicals need to encourage postliberal theologians to reconsider and rediscover the historical nature of the "mighty acts of God" recorded and interpreted in the biblical narratives. While the Scriptures' main purpose may be to identify God and their major contribution may be to create the interpretive world out of which God's people live and move and have our being, they also purport to tell us that our God is intimately and immediately

and thought, and the foundation upon which we base our decisions and actions."

87. Fackre, *Doctrine of Revelation*, 12.

88. Ashford and Whitfield, "Theological Method," 41.

involved in our time and space and cannot be reduced to the main character in a wonderful epic story.[89]

The textual emphasis of Frei is valuable and may be helpful to an evangelical emphasis on the biblical text as the locus of meaning. The emphasis of textual interpretation of historical event, however, does not of necessity undermine the role for historical referent. Concerning Frei's hermeneutic, Johnson notes, "[h]is thesis of Christ as the unsubstitutable one would have lost nothing of its power had he been open to other types of evidential support for the historicity of the resurrection. Indeed, this openness would have only made his position stronger."[90] Contrary to Frei's rebuttal of Henry, minimalism on the theoretical nature of revelation, reference, and language is not a virtue that restores biblical authority.[91] Rather, a movement Frei began in returning to the Bible is only complete when the Bible is taken to reveal God in a faithful manner.

Conclusion

How God has revealed himself and how humanity understands the revelation of God are issues of utmost importance throughout history. One element of the issues of God's revelation and humanity's knowledge of God is the relationship between revelation, history, and the biblical text. I have sought to demonstrate merit for the thesis that Carl F. H. Henry's doctrine of revelation contains the necessary resources for a text-oriented, yet apologetically driven, view of the relationship between revelation, history, and the biblical text. To accomplish this pursuit, this work has explored the connection between revelation, history, and the biblical text in the writings of Henry, Pannenberg, and Frei with subsequent analysis. The resultant analysis demonstrates that, in contrast to Pannenberg and Frei, Henry's approach contains the resources for text-oriented hermeneutics and apologetic undergirding for Christian historical-truth claims. As such, Henry serves as a preferred resource for contemporary evangelicals in constructing an approach to revelation, history, and the biblical text.

89. Olson, "Back to the Bible (Almost)."

90. Johnson, "Hans Frei as Unlikely Apologist," 150.

91. Frei, "Response to Narrative Theology," 22. Concerning the need for a theory of revelation and referent Frei states, "And belief in the divine authority of Scripture is for me simply that we do not need more. The narrative description there is adequate. 'God was in Christ reconciling the world to himself' is an adequate statement for what we refer to, though we cannot say univocally how we refer to it."

In light of the fact that Hans Frei is typically taken to be a model for text-oriented approaches to hermeneutics, considerable attention has been given to the points of congruence and departure between Henry and Frei. Their congruence may be seen in the text-oriented approach to hermeneutics articulated by both theologians. Specifically, it has been demonstrated Henry is able to appreciate several elements of Frei's approach to textual interpretation, including the unity of the biblical text, the limitation of historical-criticism, and the primacy of attention on the biblical text for interpretation. Concerning the departures between Henry and Frei, the indispensable insight Henry provides concerning Frei is that without an interaction with reality that lifts the interpreter above the narrative, "one may bask day and night in the literary affirmation of an incarnation involving eyewitnesses, and insist also that John the beloved argues that even to a historian the tomb would have been empty, yet simply on that basis not necessarily rise above dramatic literary depiction."[92] Likewise, "the scriptural narrative is not content to reduce questions of authorship and of relationships to universal history to second order questions."[93]

Of particular concern is the manner in which one approach should relate to the other. The alternatives were classified into two categories, both of which involved significant accommodation of one theologian to another. Caution has been issued against pressing either theologian into compromise in order to bring the two together. Yet, while I have argued Henry provides the preferable resources over Frei, the contrasting of their two approaches has informed the reader on how Henry might be nuanced in light of contemporary scholarship.

Wolfhart Pannenberg was the other theologian evaluated in the foregoing pages who is representative of an alternative approach to Henry. Henry provides a corrective to the historically oriented hermeneutic produced by Pannenberg's theology of revelation as history. The historical reality of the biblical text should not push biblical interpreters to seeking meaning beyond the text, as Pannenberg has fostered through his revelation as history doctrine. Henry's influence is a reminder that evangelical biblical interpreters must be diligent to point to the biblical text in matters of interpretation rather than beyond the text. In his critiques of revelation as history hermeneutical approaches, Henry affirms a unique role for the biblical text as the fullness of meaning for historical events. Henry's affirmations at points

92. Henry, "Narrative Theology: An Evangelical Appraisal," 13.
93. Ibid., 11.

appear to communicate the biblical text is the exclusive revelation of God, yet in his broader scheme of revelation, he seeks to affirm other dimensions as revelatory.

From a hermeneutical perspective, Henry's approach raises the question as to whether Henry thinks Scripture should be viewed as primarily revelatory or exclusively revelatory in contrast to historical event. By means of the synthesis provided in the fivefold rubric above, this chapter has articulated the perspective that the redemptive events become revelatory through the inspired interpretations of Scripture. While this distinction is a slight departure from Henry's view that Scripture is primarily revelatory, Henry is a valuable resource as an evangelical who has affirmed the historicity of the redemptive events, while simultaneously affirming the special revelatory quality of biblical texts. Henry has maintained the apologetic relevance of affirming the historicity of the biblical text, while avoiding the immanentist implications that stem from Pannenberg's locus of revelation in history. This balance in Henry allows him to provide a theology of revelation that places emphasis on text-oriented hermeneutics.

The topic of revelation, history, and the biblical text is no mere exercise in the details of hermeneutics. Rather, the issues undertaken strike at the importance of the central claims of the Christian faith. The Christian faith rests on a textual depiction that supplies the revealed meaning of historical events. Without the historical elements of the Bible—not the least of which are Adam and Eve as the first people created in God's image, Christ born of a virgin and identified as the second Adam, and the empty tomb of Christ—the textual depictions leave faith untethered from the world in which deliverance from sin is needed and accomplished. Additionally, without the textual revelation of God in Scripture, which provides the meaning of the historical events, humanity would be left without the meaning and personal application of those events as part of God's outworking of redemption.

In conclusion, Carl Henry has provided an approach to revelation, history, and the biblical text that is worthy of attention, because he articulates God's involvement in history and humanity's ability to know this history, all the while focusing the interpreter's hermeneutical efforts on Scripture as the authoritative and truthful accounting of God's historical activity. As a result of Henry's influence, may it be that Christians read the Bible as God's faithful communication concerning himself and the true revelation of his magnificent accomplishment of saving sinners for his glory.

Bibliography

Albrektson, Bertil. *History and the Gods: An Essay on the Idea of Historical Events as Divine Manifestations in the Ancient Near East and in Israel*. Lund: CWK Gleerup, 1967.

Alter, Robert, and Frank Kermode. *The Literary Guide to the Bible*. Cambridge: Harvard University Press, 1987.

Ashcraft, Morris. "Response to Carl F. H. Henry, "Are We Doomed to Hermeneutical Nihilism?" *Review & Expositor* 71, no. 2 (1974) 217–23.

Ashford, Bruce Riley. "Wittgenstein's Impact on Anglo-American Theology: Representative Models of Response to Ludwig Wittgenstein's Later Writings." Ph.D. diss., Southeastern Baptist Theological Seminary, 2003.

———. "Wittgenstein's Theologians? A Survey of Ludwig Wittgenstein's Impact on Theology." *Journal of the Evangelical Theological Society* 50, no. 2 (2007) 357–75.

Ashford, Bruce, and Keith Whitfield. "Theological Method: An Introduction to the Task of Theology." In *A Theology for the Church*, edited by Daniel Akin, 3–66. Nashville: B & H, 2014.

Auerbach, Erich. *Mimesis: The Representation of Reality in Western Literature*. Princeton: Princeton University Press, 1953.

Barr, James. "Revelation Through History in the Old Testament and in Modern Theology." *Princeton Seminary Bulletin* (1963) 4–14.

Bartholomew, Craig. "Introduction." In *"Behind" the Text: History and Biblical Interpretation*. Scripture and Hermeneutics Series, edited by Craig Bartholomew et al., 1–16. Grand Rapids: Zondervan, 2003.

Bartholomew, Craig, and Michael Goheen. *The Drama of Scripture: Finding Our Place in the Biblical Story*. Grand Rapids: Baker, 2004.

BioLogos Foundation. Questions Categorized as "The First Humans." Accessed December 21, 2014. http://biologos.org/questions/category/the-first-humans.

Bloesch, Donald G. *The Battle for the Trinity: The Debate Over Inclusive God-Language*. Ann Arbor: Vine, 1985.

———. *A Theology of Word & Spirit: Authority & Method in Theology*. Downers Grove: InterVarsity, 1992.

Braaten, Carl E. *History and Hermeneutics: New Directions in Theology Today*. Vol. 2. Philadelphia: Westminster, 1966.

Braithwaite, R. B. "An Empiricist's View of the Nature of Religious Belief." In *A. S. Eddington and the Unity of Knowledge: Scientist, Quaker & Philosopher: A Selection of the Eddington Memorial Lectures*, edited by Volker Heine, 101–28. Cambridge: Cambridge University Press, 2013.

Brand, Chad Owen. "Is Carl Henry a Modernist? Rationalism and Foundationalism in Post-War Evangelical Theology." *Trinity Journal* 20, no. 1 (1999) 3–21.

Brown, Colin. "History & the Believer." In *History, Criticism, & Faith*, edited by Colin Brown, 147–224. Downers Grove: InterVarsity, 1976.

Brown, Jeannine K. *Scripture as Communication: Introducing Biblical Hermeneutics.* Grand Rapids: Baker, 2007.

Bultmann, Rudolf. *The Presence of Eternity: History and Eschatology.* New York: Harper, 1957.

Carson, D. A., and John D. Woodbridge, eds. *God and Culture: Essays in Honor of Carl F. H. Henry.* Grand Rapids: Eerdmans, 1993.

Carswell, Robert Justin. "A Comparative Study of the Religious Epistemology of Carl F. H. Henry and Alvin Plantinga." Ph.D. diss., Southern Baptist Theological Seminary, 2007.

Cerillo, Augustus, Jr., and Murray W. Dempster. "Carl F. H. Henry's Early Apologetic for an Evangelical Social Ethic, 1942-1956." *Journal of the Evangelical Theological Society* 34, no. 3 (1991) 365–79.

Chapman, Stephen. "Reclaiming Inspiration for the Bible." In *Canon and Biblical Interpretation*, edited by Craig Bartholomew, 167–206. Grand Rapids: Zondervan, 2006.

Chewning, Richard C., and Carl F. H. Henry, eds. *Biblical Principles and Public Policy: The Practice.* Colorado Springs: NavPress, 1991.

"The Chicago Statement on Biblical Hermeneutics." In *Hermeneutics, Inerrancy, and the Bible: Papers from The ICBI Summit II*, edited by Earl D. Radmacher and Robert D. Preus, 881–87. Grand Rapids: Zondervan, 1984.

Childs, Brevard. *The New Testament as Canon: An Introduction.* Philadelphia: Fortress, 1985.

Clark, David K. "Narrative Theology and Apologetics." *Journal of the Evangelical Theological Society* 36, no. 4 (1993) 499–515.

Cole, Graham. "The Peril of a 'Historyless' Systematic Theology." In *Do Historical Matters Matter to Faith: A Critical Appraisal of Modern and Postmodern Approaches to Scripture*, edited by James K. Hoffmeier and Dennis R. Magary, 55–70. Wheaton: Crossway, 2012.

Connor, Walter Thomas. *Revelation and God: An Introduction to Christian Doctrine.* Nashville: Broadman, 1936.

Coon, George Michael. "Recasting Inerrancy: The Doctrine of Scripture in Carl Henry and the Old Princeton School." Ph.D. diss., University of St. Michael's College, 2009.

Davies, P. R. "Whose History? Whose Israel? Whose Bible? Biblical Histories, Ancient and Modern." In *Can a 'History of Israel' Be Written?*, edited by L. L. Grabbe, JSOT Sup 245, 104–22. Sheffield: Sheffield, 1997.

Dempster, M. W. "The Role of Scripture in the Social Ethical Writings of C. F. H. Henry." Ph.D. diss., University of Southern California, 1969.

Doyle, G. Wright. *Carl Henry, Theologian for All Seasons: An Introduction and Guide to God, Revelation, and Authority.* Eugene: Pickwick, 2010.

Dulles, Avery. *Models of Revelation.* Garden City: Doubleday, 1983.

———. "The Place of Christianity Among the World Religions: Wolfhart Pannenberg's Theology of Religion and the History of Religions." In *The Theology of Wolfhart Pannenberg*, edited by Carl Braaten and Philip Clayton, 287–312. Minneapolis: Augsburg, 1988.

Duvall, J. Scott, and J. Daniel Hays. *Grasping God's Word: A Hands-on Approach to Reading, Interpreting, and Applying the Bible.* Grand Rapids: Zondervan, 2001.

Erickson, Millard. "Narrative Theology: Translation or Transformation?" In *Festschrift, A Tribute to Dr. William Hordern,* edited by Walter Freitag. Saskatoon, 29–39. Canada: University of Saskatchewan, 1985.

Fackre, Gabriel. *The Christian Story: A Narrative Interpretation of Basic Christian Doctrine.* Vol. 1. Grand Rapids: Eerdmans, 1996.

————. *The Doctrine of Revelation: A Narrative Interpretation.* Edinburgh: Edinburgh University Press, 1997.

————. *Ecumenical Faith in Evangelical Perspective.* Grand Rapids: Eerdmans, 1993.

Farley, Gary Eugene. "Authority in Contemporary Christian Ethics: A Study in How One May Know the 'Will of God' as Discussed in the Writings of Carl F. H. Henry, Jacques Maritain, Emil Brunner, Reinhold Niebuhr, and Nels F. S. Ferre." Ph.D. diss., Southwestern Baptist Theological Seminary, 1966.

Fee, Gordon. "History as Context for Interpretation." In *The Act of Bible Reading,* edited by Elmer Dyck, 10–32. Downers Grove: InterVarsity, 1996.

Fergusson, David. "Interpreting the Resurrection." *Scottish Journal of Theology* 38 (1985) 287–305.

Frei, Hans. "The Accounts of Jesus' Death and Resurrection." *Christian Scholar* 40, no. 4 (1966) 263–306.

————. *The Eclipse of Biblical Narrative: A Study in Eighteenth and Nineteenth Century Hermeneutics.* New Haven: Yale University Press, 1974.

————. "Epilogue: George Lindbeck and the Nature of Doctrine." In *Theology and Dialogue: Essays in Conversation with George Lindbeck,* edited by Bruce Marshall, 275–82. South Bend: University of Notre Dame Press, 1990.

————. "Historical Reference and the Gospels: A Response to a Critique of the Identity of Jesus Christ" [1981]. Hans W. Frei Unpublished Pieces. Edited by Mike Higton. Yale Divinity School Archive, Yale University, New Haven.

————. "History, Salvation-History, and Typology" [1981]. Hans W. Frei Unpublished Pieces. Edited by Mike Higton. Yale Divinity School Archive, Yale University, New Haven.

————. *The Identity of Jesus Christ: The Hermeneutical Bases of Dogmatic Theology.* Philadelphia: Fortress, 1975.

————. "The 'Literal Reading' of Biblical Narrative in the Christian Tradition: Does it Stretch or Will it Break?." In *Theology and Narrative: Selected Essays,* edited by George Hunsinger and William C. Placher, 117–53. New York: Oxford University Press, 1993.

————. "Of the Resurrection." In *Theology and Narrative: Selected Essays by Hans Frei,* edited by George Hunsinger and William C. Placher, 201–06. New York: Oxford University Press, 1993.

————. "On Interpreting the Christian Story" [1976]. Hans W. Frei Unpublished Pieces. Edited by Mike Higton. Yale Divinity School Archive, Yale University, New Haven.

————. "Remarks in Connection with a Theological Proposal." In *Theology and Narrative: Selected Essays,* edited by George Hunsinger and William C. Placher, 26–44. New York: Oxford University Press, 1993.

————. "Response to 'Narrative Theology: An Evangelical Appraisal'." *Trinity Journal* 8, no. 1 (1987) 21–24.

———. "Scripture as Realistic Narrative" [1974]. Hans W. Frei Unpublished Pieces. Edited by Mike Higton. Yale Divinity School Archive, Yale University, New Haven.

———. "The Specificity of Reference." Hans W. Frei Unpublished Pieces. Edited by Mike Higton. Yale Divinity School Archive, Yale University, New Haven.

———. "Theological Reflections on the Gospel Accounts of Jesus' Death and Resurrection." *Christian Scholar* 49 (1966) 263–306.

———. "Theology and the Interpretation of Narrative." In *Theology and Narrative: Selected Essays*, edited by George Hunsinger and William C. Placher, 94–116. New York: Oxford University Press, 1993.

———. *Theology and Narrative: Selected Essays.* Edited by George Hunsinger and William C. Placher. New York: Oxford University Press, 1993.

———. *Types of Christian Theology.* Edited by George Hunsinger and William C. Placher. New Haven: Yale University Press, 1992.

———. Unpublished Pieces. Edited by Mike Higton. Yale Divinity School Archive, New Haven. Accessed November 17, 2014. http://divinity-adhoc.library.yale.edu/HansFreiTranscripts/.

Galloway, Glenn Monroe. "The Efficacy of Propositionalism: The Challenge of Philosophical Linguistics and Literary Theory to Evangelical Theology." Ph.D. diss., Southern Baptist Theological Seminary, 1996.

Goldsworthy, Graeme. *Gospel-Centered Hermeneutics: Foundations and Principles of Evangelical Biblical Interpretation.* Downers Grove: InterVarsity, 2006.

Green, Garrett, and Hans W. Frei. *Scriptural Authority and Narrative Interpretation.* Philadelphia: Fortress, 1987.

Grenz, Stanley. "The Appraisal of Pannenberg. A Survey of the Literature" In *The Theology of Wolfhart Pannenberg*, edited by Carl Braaten and Philip Clayton, 19–52. Minneapolis: Augsburg, 1988.

Grenz, Stanley, and Roger E. Olson. *20th Century Theology: God & the World in a Transitional Age.* Downers Grove: InterVarsity, 1992.

Halsey, Jim S. "History, Language and Hermeneutics: The Synthesis of Wolfhart Pannenberg." *Westminster Theological Journal* 41 (Spring 1979) 284–89.

Haney, D. P. *Carl F. H. Henry: A Critical Appraisal of Fundamentalism.* Richmond: Earlham School of Religion, 1965.

Harrisville, Roy, and Walter Sundberg. *The Bible in Modern Culture: Theology and Historical-Critical Method from Spinoza to Childs.* 2nd ed. Grand Rapids: Eerdmans, 2002.

Harvey, Van A. *The Historian and the Believer: The Morality of Historical Knowledge and Christian Belief.* Philadelphia: Westminster, 1966.

Hays, Christopher M., and Christopher B. Ansberry, eds. *Evangelical Faith and the Challenge of Historical Criticism.* Grand Rapids: Baker, 2013.

Helseth, Paul Kjoss. "'Re-Imagining' the Princeton Mind: Postconservative Evangelicalism, Old Princeton, and the Rise of Neo-Fundamentalism." *Journal of the Evangelical Theological Society* 45, no. 3 (2002) 427–50.

Henry, Carl F. H. "American Evangelicals in a Turning Time: A Theology Perpetually on the Make Will Not Do; How My Mind Has Changed." *Christian Century* 97, no. 35 (1980) 1058–62.

———. *Answers for the Now Generation.* Chicago: Moody, 1949.

———. *Aspects of Christian Social Ethics.* Grand Rapids: Eerdmans, 1964.

———. "The Authority and Inspiration of the Bible." In *Expositor's Bible Commentary*, edited by Frank E. Gaebelein, vol. 1, 3–38. Grand Rapids: Zondervan, 1979.

———., ed. *Baker's Dictionary of Christian Ethics*. Grand Rapids: Baker, 1973.

———., ed. *Basic Christian Doctrines*. Contemporary Evangelical Thought. New York: Holt, Rinehart, and Winston, 1962.

———. "Basic Issues in Modern Theology: Revelation in History Part I." *Christianity Today* 9, no. 5 (December 4, 1964) 17–20.

———. "The Bible and the Conscience of Our Age." *Journal of the Evangelical Theological Society* 25, no. 4 (1982) 403–07.

———., ed. *The Biblical Expositor: The Living Theme of the Great Book*. 3 vols. Philadelphia: A. J. Holman, 1960.

———. "Canonical Theology: An Evangelical Appraisal," *Scottish Bulletin of Evangelical Theology* 8 (Autumn 1990) 102–08.

———. *Carl Henry at His Best: A Lifetime of Quotable Thoughts*. Portland: Multnomah, 1989.

———. *Christian Countermoves in a Decadent Culture*. Portland: Multnomah, 1986.

———. "Christian Education and the World of Culture." *Mennonite Quarterly Review* 32, no. 4 (1958) 307–13.

———. *The Christian Mindset in a Secular Society: Promoting Evangelical Renewal & National Righteousness*. Portland: Multnomah, 1984.

———. *Christian Personal Ethics*. Grand Rapids: Eerdmans, 1957.

———. "Christian Theology and Social Revolution." *Perkins School of Theology Journal* 21, nos. 2–3 (1968) 13–23.

———. "The Church in the World or the World in the Church: A Review Article." *Journal of the Evangelical Theological Society* 34, no. 3 (1991) 381–83.

———. *Contemporary Evangelical Thought*. Great Neck: Channel, 1957.

———. *Confessions of a Theologian: An Autobiography*. Waco: Word, 1986.

———. *Conversations with Carl Henry: Christianity for Today*. Lewiston: Edwin Mellen, 1986.

———. "Divine Revelation in the Bible." In *Inspiration and Interpretation*, edited John F. Walvoord, 253–78. Grand Rapids: Eerdmans, 1957.

———. *The Drift of Western Thought*. Grand Rapids: Eerdmans, 1951.

———. "Ecumenical Age: Problems and Promise." *Bibliotheca sacra* 123, no. 491 (1966) 204–19.

———. "Evangelical Profits and Losses." *Christian Century* 95, no. 3 (1978) 69–70.

———. *Evangelical Responsibility in Contemporary Theology*. Grand Rapids: Eerdmans, 1957.

———. *Evangelicals at the Brink of Crisis: Significance of the World Congress on Evangelism*. Waco: Word, 1967.

———. *Evangelicals in Search of Identity*. Waco: Word, 1976.

———. *Faith at the Frontiers*. Chicago: Moody, 1969.

———. *Fifty Years of Protestant Theology*. Boston: W. A. Wilde, 1950.

———. "Fortunes of the Christian World View." *Trinity Journal* 19, no. 2 (1998) 163–76.

———. "Frontier Issues in Contemporary Theology in Evangelical Perspective." *Bulletin of the Evangelical Theological Society* 9, no. 2 (1966) 63–80.

———. *Frontiers in Modern Theology*. Chicago: Moody, 1966.

———. *Giving a Reason for Our Hope*. Boston: W. A. Wilde, 1949.

———. *Glimpses of a Sacred Land*. Boston: W. A. Wilde, 1953.

————. *God, Revelation and Authority.* 6 vols. Wheaton: Crossway, 1976–83.

————. *The God Who Shows Himself.* Waco: Word, 1966.

————. *Gods of this Age or—God of the Ages?.* Nashville: Broadman, 1994.

————. *Has Democracy Had Its Day?* Nashville: ERLC, 1996.

————. *The Identity of Jesus of Nazareth.* Nashville: Broadman, 1992.

————. "The Identity of Jesus of Nazareth." *Criswell Theological Review* 6 (1992) 91–130.

————. "Interpretation of the Scriptures: Are We Doomed to Hermeneutical Nihilism?" *Review & Expositor* 71, no. 2 (1974) 197–215.

————. "Justification: A Doctrine in Crisis." *Journal of the Evangelical Theological Society* 38, no. 1 (1995) 57–65.

————. "Justification by Ignorance: A Neo-Protestant Motif?" *Journal of the Evangelical Theological Society* 13, no. 1 (1970) 3–13.

————. "Looking Back at Key 73: A Weathervane of American Protestantism." *Reformed Journal* 24, no. 9 (1974) 6–12.

————. "Narrative Theology: An Evangelical Appraisal." *Trinity Journal* 8, no. 1 (1987) 3–19.

————. "Natural Law and a Nihilistic Culture." *First Things*, no. 49 (1995) 54–60.

————. *New Strides of Faith.* Chicago: Moody, 1972.

————. *Not by Bread Alone: Wheaton Chapel Talks.* Grand Rapids: Zondervan, 1940.

————. *Notes on the Doctrine of God.* Boston: W. A. Wilde, 1948.

————. *Pacific Garden Mission: A Doorway to Heaven.* 6th ed. Grand Rapids: Zondervan, 1942.

————. *Personal Idealism and Strong's Theology.* Wheaton: Van Kampen, 1951.

————. *A Plea for Evangelical Demonstration.* Grand Rapids: Baker, 1971

————. "Postmodernism: The New Spectre?." In *The Challenge of Postmodernism: An Evangelical Engagement*, edited by David S. Dockery, 34–52. Wheaton: Victor, 1995.

————. "The Priority of Divine Revelation: A Review Article." *Journal of the Evangelical Theological Society* 27, no. 1 (1984) 77–92.

————. *The Protestant Dilemma: An Analysis of the Current Impasse in Theology.* Grand Rapids: Eerdmans, 1949.

————. *Quest for Reality: Christianity and the Counter Culture.* Downers Grove: InterVarsity, 1973.

————. "Reflections on the Kingdom of God." *Journal of the Evangelical Theological Society* 35, no. 1 (1992) 39–49.

————. *Remaking the Modern Mind.* Grand Rapids: Eerdmans, 1946.

————. *Revelation and the Bible: Contemporary Evangelical Thought.* Grand Rapids: Baker, 1958

————. "Science and God's Revelation in Nature." *Bulletin of the Evangelical Theological Society* 3, no. 2 (1960) 25–36.

————. "The Spirit and the Written Word." *Bibliotheca Sacra* 111, no. 444 (1954) 302–16.

————. *Successful Church Publicity: A Guidebook for Christian Publicists.* 2nd ed. Grand Rapids: Zondervan, 1943.

————. "The Tensions Between Evangelism and the Christian Demand for Social Justice." *Fides et Historia* 4, no. 2 (1972) 3–10.

————. "Theology and Biblical Authority: A Review Article of the Uses of Scripture in Recent Theology by D. H. Kelsey." *Journal of the Evangelical Theological Society* 19, no. 4 (1976) 315–23.

———. "Theological Reflection on Bicentennial Concerns." *Religious Education* 71, no. 3 (1976) 288–303.

———. *Toward a Recovery of Christian Belief: The Rutherford Lectures.* Wheaton: Crossway, 1990.

———. *Twilight of a Great Civilization: The Drift toward Neo-Paganism.* Westchester: Crossway, 1988.

———. *The Uneasy Conscience of Modern Fundamentalism.* Grand Rapids: Eerdmans, 2003.

———. "What Is Christianity?." *Bibliotheca Sacra* 123, no. 490 (1966) 104–14.

———. "Where Is Modern Theology Going?" *Bulletin of the Evangelical Theological Society* 11, no. 1 (1968) 3–12.

Henry, Carl F. H., and Gordon Clark. *Fundamentals of the Faith.* Grand Rapids: Zondervan, 1969.

Henry, Carl F. H., and J. Oliver Buswell. *Christian Faith and Modern Theology: Contemporary Evangelical Thought.* New York: Channel, 1964.

Henry, Carl F. H., and W. A. Criswell. *Prophecy in the Making: Messages Prepared for Jerusalem Conference on Biblical Prophecy.* Carol Stream, IL: Creation House, 1971.

Higton, Mike. *Christ, Providence and History: Hans W. Frei's Public Theology.* London: T. & T. Clark, 2004.

Hirsch, E. D. *Validity in Interpretation.* New Haven: Yale University Press, 1967.

Hoffmeier, James K., and Dennis R. Magary, eds. *Do Historical Matters Matter to Faith?: A Critical Appraisal of Modern and Postmodern Approaches to Scripture.* Wheaton: Crossway, 2012.

Hunsinger, George. "Hans Frei as Theologian: The Quest for a Generous Orthodoxy." *Modern Theology* 8, no. 2 (1992) 103–28.

———. "What Can Evangelicals and Postliberals Learn from Each Other? The Carl Henry/Hans Frei Exchange Reconsidered." *Pro Ecclesia* 5, no. 2 (1996) 161–82.

Jensen, Peter. *The Revelation of God.* Downers Grove: InterVarsity, 2002.

Johns, Warren Harvey. "Revelation and Creation in the Thought of Bernard L. Ramm and Carl F. H. Henry: The Creation "Days" as a Case Study." Ph.D. diss., Andrews University, 2005.

Johnson, John J. "Hans Frei as Unlikely Apologist for the Historicity of the Resurrection." *Evangelical Quarterly* 76, no. 2 (2004) 131–51.

Johnson, Walter E. "A Critical Analysis of the Nature and Function of Reason in the Theology of Carl F. H. Henry." Ph.D. diss., New Orleans Baptist Theological Seminary, 1989.

Kaiser, Walter C., and Moisés Silva. *An Introduction to Biblical Hermeneutics: The Search for Meaning.* Grand Rapids: Zondervan, 1994.

Karanja, Joseph. "Inerrancy and Sovereignty: A Case Study on Carl F. H. Henry." Ph.D. diss., Andrews University, 1990.

Kis, Miroslav Mirko. "Revelation and Ethics: Dependence, Interdependence, Independence? A Comparative Study of Reinhold Niebuhr and Carl F. H. Henry." Ph.D. diss., McGill University, 1983.

Krentz, Edgar. *The Historical-Critical Method.* London: S.P.C.K., 1975.

Leung, Mavis M. "With What Is Evangelicalism to Penetrate the World? A Study of Carl Henry's Envisioned Evangelicalism." *Trinity Journal* 27, no. 2 (2006) 227–44.

Lindbeck, George. *The Nature of Doctrine: Religion and Theology in a Postliberal Age.* Louisville: WJK, 1984.

MacKinnon, Donald. *The Borderlands of Theology.* Cambridge: Cambridge University Press, 1961.

MacPhee, Donald A. "Carl Henry's Voice Still Speaks." *Fides et Historia* 5, nos. 1–2 (1973) 113–16.

Marsden, George M. *Reforming Fundamentalism: Fuller Seminary and the New Evangelicalism.* Grand Rapids: Eerdmans, 1987.

McCall, Thomas. "Religious Epistemology, Theological Interpretation of Scripture, and Critical Biblical Scholarship: A Theologian's Reflections." In *Do Historical Matters Matter to Faith: A Critical Appraisal of Modern and Postmodern Approaches to Scripture*, edited by James K. Hoffmeier and Dennis R. Magary, 33–53. Wheaton: Crossway, 2012.

McClendon, James, Jr. "Christian Knowledge in the Sunset of Modernity." Unpublished paper delivered at the New Orleans Baptist Theological Seminary. February, 1998.

McGrath, Alister. *A Passion for Truth: The Intellectual Coherence of Evangelicalism.* Downers Grove: InterVarsity, 1996.

Miller, Glenn T. "Baptists and Neo-Evangelical Theology." *Baptist History and Heritage* 35, no. 1 (2000) 20–38.

Mohler, R. Albert, Jr. "Carl F. H. Henry." In *Theologians of the Baptist Tradition*, edited by David S. Dockery and Timothy George, 279–96. Nashville: B & H, 2001.

Mooneyham, W. Stanley, and Carl Ferdinand Howard Henry. "One Race, One Gospel, One Task: Official Reference Volumes: Papers and Reports." Minneapolis: World Wide, 1967.

Nash, Ronald H., ed. *The Philosophy of Gordon H. Clark: A Festscrift.* Philadelphia: Presbyterian and Reformed, 1968.

Newport, John. "The Challenge of Recent Literary Approaches to the Bible." In *Beyond the Impasse?: Scripture, Interpretation, & Theology in Baptist Life*, edited by James B. Robison and David S. Dockery, 64–90. Nashville: Broadman, 1992.

North, Christopher. "History." In *Interpreters Dictionary of the Bible*, vol. 2, edited by George Arthur Buttrick, 607–12. New York: Abingdon, 1962.

Olive, Don H. *Wolfhart Pannenberg.* Waco: Word, 1973.

Olson, Roger. "Back to the Bible (Almost): Why Yale's Postliberal Theologians Deserve an Evangelical Hearing." *Christianity Today*, May 20, 1996. Accessed December 20, 2014. http://www.christianitytoday.com/ct/1996/may20/6t6031.html.

———. *The SCM Press A-Z of Evangelical Theology.* London: SCM, 2005.

Osborne, Grant R. *The Hermeneutical Spiral: A Comprehensive Introduction to Biblical Interpretation.* Downers Grove: InterVarsity, 1991.

Pannenberg, Wolfhart. *Anthropology in Theological Perspective.* Translated by Matthew J. O'Connell. Philadelphia: Westminster, 1985.

———. "An Autobiographical Sketch." In *The Theology of Wolfhart Pannenberg*, edited by Carl Braaten and Philip Clayton, 11–18. Minneapolis: Augsburg, 1988.

———. *Basic Questions in Theology.* Vol. 1. Translated by George H. Kehm. Philadelphia: Fortress, 1970.

———. "Dogmatic Theses on the Doctrine of Revelation." In *Revelation as History*, edited by Wolfhart Pannenberg, 125–55. New York: Macmillan, 1968.

———. "Foreword." In *Basic Questions in Theology.* Vol. 1. Translated by George H. Kehm. Philadelphia: Fortress, 1970.

———. "God's Presence in History." *Christian Century* (March 11, 1981) 260–63.

————. *The Historicity of Nature: Essays on Science & Theology*. Edited by Niels Henrik Gregersen. West Conshohocken: Templeton Foundation, 2008.

————. "Introduction." In *Revelation as History*, edited by Wolfhart Pannenberg, 3–21. New York: Macmillan, 1968.

————. *Jesus—God and Man*. Translated by Lewis L. Wilkins and Duane A. Priebe. Philadelphia: Westminster, 1968.

————. "Response to the Discussion." In *Theology as History*, edited by J. M. Robinson and J. B. Cobb Jr., 221–76. New York, Harper & Row, 1967.

————. "A Response to My American Friends." In *The Theology of Wolfhart Pannenberg*, edited by Carl Braaten and Philip Clayton, 313–36. Minneapolis: Augsburg, 1988.

————. *Theology and the Philosophy of Science*. Philadelphia: Westminster, 1976.

Patterson, Bob E. *Carl F. H. Henry*. Peabody: Hendrickson, 1983.

Patterson, James A. "Cultural Pessimism in Modern Evangelical Thought: Francis Schaeffer, Carl Henry, and Charles Colson." *Journal of the Evangelical Theological Society* 49, no. 4 (2006) 807–20.

Pelikan, Jaroslav. *Credo: Historical and Theological Guide to Creeds and Confessions of Faith in the Christian Tradition*. New Haven: Yale University Press, 2003.

Phillips, Timothy R., and Dennis L. Okholm, eds. *The Nature of Confession: Evangelicals & Postliberals in Conversation*. Downers Grove: InterVarsity, 1996.

Placher, William C. "Hans Frei and the Meaning of Biblical Narrative." *Christian Century* 106, no. 18 (May 24, 1989) 556–59.

————. "Introduction." In *Theology and Narrative: Selected Essays by Hans Frei*, edited by George Hunsinger and William C. Placher, 3–25. New York: Oxford University Press, 1993.

————. "Scripture as Realistic Narrative: Some Preliminary Questions." *Perspectives in Religious Studies* 5 (1978) 32–41.

Plummer, Robert L. *40 Questions About Interpreting the Bible*. Grand Rapids: Kregel, 2010.

Poythress, Vern S. *God Centered Biblical Interpretation*. Phillipsburg: P & R Publishing, 1999.

Provan, Iain. "Knowing and Believing: Faith in the Past." In *"Behind" the Text: History and Biblical Interpretation*, edited by Craig Bartholomew et al., 229–66. Grand Rapids: Zondervan, 2003.

Purdy, Richard. "Carl F. H. Henry." In *Handbook of Evangelical Theologians*, edited by Walter Elwell, 260–75. Grand Rapids: Baker, 1993.

————. "Carl Henry and Contemporary Apologetics: An Assessment of The Rational Apologetic Methodology of Carl F. H. Henry in the Context of the Current Impasse Between Reformed and Evangelical Apologetics." Ph.D. diss., New York University, 1980.

Radmacher, Earl D. "Introduction." In *Hermeneutics, Inerrancy, and the Bible: Papers from the ICBI Summit II*, edited by Earl D. Radmacher and Robert D. Preus, xi–xiii. Grand Rapids: Zondervan, 1984.

Rae, Murray. "Creation and Promise: Toward a Theology of History." In *"Behind" the Text: History and Biblical Interpretation*, edited by Craig Bartholomew et al., 267–302. Grand Rapids: Zondervan, 2003.

Ramm, Bernard L. *After Fundamentalism: The Future of Evangelical Theology*. San Francisco: Harper & Row, 1982.

————. "Is Doctor Henry Right?" *United Evangelical Action* 15 (July 1947) 5–16.

Sailhamer, John H. *Introduction to Old Testament Theology: A Canonical Approach.* Grand Rapids: Zondervan, 1995.

———. *The Pentateuch as Narrative: A Biblical-Theological Commentary.* Grand Rapids: Zondervan, 1992.

Scaer, David P. "Carl F. H. Henry: An Evangelical Tribute to a Theologian." *Concordia Theological Quarterly* 68, no. 2 (2004) 155–56.

Silva, Moisés. "The Place of Historical Reconstruction in New Testament Criticism." In *Hermeneutics, Authority, and Canon,* edited by D. A. Carson and John Woodbridge, 109–33. Eugene: Wipf and Stock, 1986.

Soames, Scott, *The Dawn of Analysis.* Philosophical Analysis in the Twentieth Century. Vol. 1. Princeton: Princeton University Press, 2003.

Springs, Jason. "Between Barth and Wittgenstein: On the Availability of Hans Frei's Later Theology." *Modern Theology* 23, no. 3 (2007) 393–413.

———. "But Did It *Really* Happen? Frei, Henry, and Barth on Historical Reference and Critical Realism." In *Karl Barth and American Evangelicalism,* edited by Bruce L. McCormack and Clifford B. Anderson, 271–99. Grand Rapids: Eerdmans, 2011.

Strachan, Owen Daniel. "Reenchanting the Evangelical Mind: Park Street Church's Harold Ockenga, the Boston Scholars, and the Mid-Century Intellectual Surge." Ph.D. diss., Trinity International University, 2011.

Stuhlmacher, Peter. *Historical Criticism and Theological Interpretation of Scripture: Toward a Hermeneutics of Consent.* Philadelphia: Fortress, 1977.

Thornbury, Gregory. "Carl F. H. Henry: Heir of Reformation Epistemology." *Southern Baptist Journal of Theology* 8, no. 4 (2004) 62–72.

———. *Recovering Classic Evangelicalism. Applying the Wisdom and Vision of Carl F. H. Henry.* Wheaton: Crossway, 2013.

Trueman, Carl R. "Admiring the Sistine Chapel: Reflections on Carl F. H. Henry's God, Revelation and Authority." *Themelios* 25, no. 2 (2000) 48–58.

Tupper, E. Frank. *The Theology of Wolfhart Pannenberg.* Philadelphia: Westminster, 1973.

Vanhoozer, Kevin. "Lost in Interpretation: Truth, Scripture, and Hermeneutics." *Journal of the Evangelical Theological Society* 48, no. 1 (2005) 89–114.

———. "The Semantics of Biblical Literature: Truth and Scripture's Diverse Literary Forms." In *Hermeneutics, Authority, and Canon,* edited by D. A. Carson and John Woodbridge, 53–104. Eugene: Wipf and Stock, 1986.

von Rad, Gerhard. *Old Testament Theology.* New York: Harper, 1962.

Wagner, Travis Mark. "The Revelational Epistemology of Carl F. H. Henry." Ph.D. diss., University of St. Michael's College, 1986.

Waita, Jonathan Mutinda. "Carl F. H. Henry and the Metaphysical Foundations of Epistemology." Ph.D. diss., Dallas Theological Seminary, 2012.

Waltke, Bruce K. "Historical Grammatical Problems." In *Hermeneutics, Inerrancy, and the Bible: Papers from The ICBI Summit II,* edited by Earl D. Radmacher and Robert D. Preus, 71–129. Grand Rapids: Zondervan, 1984.

Warfield, B. B. "The Biblical Idea of Revelation." In *Revelation and Inspiration,* vol. 1, The Works of Benjamin B. Warfield, edited by W. P. Armstrong and E. D. Warfield, 3–36. Grand Rapids, Baker, 1981.

———. "The Idea of Revelation and Theories of Revelation." In *Revelation and Inspiration,* vol. 1, The Works of Benjamin B. Warfield, edited by W. P. Armstrong and E. D. Warfield, 37–50. Grand Rapids, Baker, 1981.

Weeks, David L. "Carl F. H. Henry's Moral Arguments for Evangelical Political Activism." *Journal of Church and State* 40, no. 1 (1998) 83–106.

West, Cornell. "On Frei's *Eclipse of Biblical Narrative*." *Union Seminary Quarterly Review* 37, no. 4 (1983) 299.

White, Michael D. "Word and Spirit in the Theological Method of Carl Henry." Ph.D. diss., Wheaton College, 2012.

Wolterstorff, Nicholas. "Will Narrativity Work as the Lynchpin?." In *Relativism and Religion*. New York: St. Martin's, 1995.

Woodbridge, John D., and D. A. Carson. *Hermeneutics, Authority, and Canon.* Grand Rapids: Academie, 1986.

Wright G. Ernest. *God Who Acts.* London: SCM, 1952.